Soldier of the Queen

Max Hennessy is the pseudonym of John Harris, author of *The Sea Shall Not Have Them* and *Covenant With Death*. Ex-sailor, ex-airman, ex-newspaperman, ex-travel courier, ex-history teacher, he went to sea in the Merchant Navy before the war from his job as a newspaperman. During the war he served with two air forces and two navies. He returned to newspapers as a cartoonist after the war but has been a full-time writer for nearly thirty years. He lives by the sea, but kept up his interest in flying until his late fifties with a private pilot's licence.

Though never a cavalryman, he did a great deal of riding on the rough terrain of the South African veldt. As a young man he met an eye-witness of the Light Brigade's charge at Balaclava, and his father witnessed one of the last great mounted charges – on the Somme in World War I. His grandfather, a horse-breeder, provided horses for the Greek cavalry during the last century, and his son's Virginian wife is connected to the family of Jeb Stuart, the great Confederate cavalry general.

Also available in Arrow by
the same Author (as John Harris)

MAX HENNESSY

Soldier of the Queen

ARROW BOOKS

Arrow Books Limited
3 Fitzroy Square, London W1P 6JD

An imprint of the Hutchinson Publishing Group

London   Melbourne   Sydney   Auckland
Wellington   Johannesburg and agencies
throughout the world

First published by Hamish Hamilton 1980
Arrow edition 1981
© Max Hennessy 1980

Photoset by Redwood Burn Limited
Printed and bound in Great Britain
by The Anchor Press Ltd
Tiptree, Essex

ISBN 0 09 926240 1

Part One

1

Sacred To The Memory
of
Colby William Rollo Goff
1836–1854
Cornet, 19th. Lancers
Only son of Maj-Gen Loftus Yorke Goff
of this Parish
Rest in Peace

He could already see it on his tombstone.

Drawing a deep breath, he tried to compose himself. The officers of the other regiments on either side of him were managing to smoke cigars and eat hard-boiled eggs, as if a battle were something that happened every day of their lives. But, unlike him, they had seen the dead at the Alma, a month before, and even if they'd spent most of that day in a melon field prodding at the fruit with their swords, at least they had some idea what to do.

Colby William Rollo Goff earnestly wished he did.

If nothing else, he felt, the other officers had at least gained enough experience to make sure they had food with them – something that had never crossed the youthful mind of Colby Goff. After all, he thought, it didn't seem illogical to expect your superiors to give you something to eat before you started to die, and as his healthy eighteen-year-old stomach rumbled hollowly, he came to the gloomy conclusion that the one thing war taught you quickly was to allow for the absence of periods set aside in battle for meals.

3

The little knot of horsemen round the divisional general shifted, one of the horses wheeling abruptly as its owner heaved at the reins. The eyes of the riders were turned towards the ridge where the Commander-in-Chief and his staff waited, overlooking the valley.

Sitting with his few lancers, Colby swallowed nervously. Surely, he thought, everybody else must feel as worried as I do. They didn't appear to, however, and since they weren't staring at him, he could only assume he didn't either. He glanced furtively at his trumpeter, Sparks, and his orderly, Trooper Ackroyd. Lances slung, they were staring down the valley with the same blank disinterest they'd have shown if they'd been watching the judging of the saddle-back class in the pig section at a county show. Somewhere behind, a commotion broke out with cries of rage and the thud of hooves on ribs, as kicking and barging swept through the line, and Sergeant-Major Holstead, a small grizzled man with red hair, spurred into action to restore order, quite unruffled by what lay ahead, a hard-bitten old warrior with service in India who was unperturbed by anything except idle soldiers.

Colby wished he felt the same. His heart was thumping wildly, and he felt a desperate urge to empty his bladder. I always felt like this before a game at school, he thought wildly. Can battle be so very different? He drew a deep breath. Yes, by God, it could, he decided. Battles weren't won with just a few black eyes.

The hills about him were curiously silent. Grey-green and forbidding, the heights to the north rose as craggy slopes where he could see men moving. *And* guns, he noted uneasily – big guns, their blunt snouts pointing, it seemed, straight at the last of the Goffs. To his right, the Causeway loomed, high, uneven and apparently empty, but he knew there were enemy soldiers there, because he'd seen them from the other side before crossing to this valley to the north.

He worked his jaw, settling the metal links of the chin strap of his lance cap more comfortably. Wriggling himself more firmly into the saddle, he glanced again at his men.

Most of them, like himself, were from Yorkshire – because that was where the regiment did its recruiting – stoney-faced, stoney-headed men from the little farms, who'd been with horses most of their lives. Colby's orderly, Trooper Ackroyd, edged his horse forward. He was a short, thickset man with a long face as empty as a cow pat. He sat bolt upright in his saddle, the steel butt of his lance in its bucket by his right foot. 'You got everything you'll need, sir?' he asked.

Colby wondered. He'd hardly been in the army long enough to know what he did need and certainly nobody had bothered to teach him. England had been at peace so long and war had seemed so distant, well-trained troops grew sulky under constant repetition and two parades a week had seemed enough. Now, face to face with the enemy, he began to see that a little instruction of some sort might have been invaluable.

At least, he thought, he had the rudiments of sword drill. Always aim at the throat and hold the weapon rock-steady. On the Left Engage, watch what you did with it or you were likely to end up with an earless charger, and when dealing with infantry where you had to lean well over, make damned certain you didn't lose your stirrup or you'd fall out of the saddle onto your head.

He smiled at the orderly. Tyas Ackroyd had been born and brought up on the Home Farm next to the house at Braxby where Colby himself had been born, and they had gone ratting together as boys, swum in the Brack in summer, tormented the village girls, and been chased by gamekeepers off other people's land. His grandfather had ridden with Colby's father in Vandeleur's Brigade at Waterloo, handing over the job of looking after him when he had grown too old to his son, and then to his grandson. Ackroyd men had gone to war with the Goffs for about five generations now and, before Colby had left, the old man had told him gruffly to remember he was a Goff of Braxby and not to let his family down. 'Mind you read the Book,' he had said, 'don't get gambling, and watch out for them war-'orses. They're fiercer than farm animals.'

'Yes, Tyas –' Colby smiled at the old man's grandson – 'My sword's sharp, and I have my mother's picture and the prayer book she gave me in my sabretache. The Lord will watch over me. What have you got?'

Ackroyd gave him a quick grin. 'Rabbit's foot, sir. They say they're right effective.'

As he backed away, a heavy chestnut with a pale mane edged closer. Ambrose la Dell's lance cap, which had never fitted properly as long as Colby had known him, jiggled over his nose with every shift of the horse. When the squadron had landed forty-eight hours before, its commanding captain had gone down with cholera even as he had set foot ashore and, because no other captain or senior lieutenant was prepared to suffer the discomfort of these alien Crimean uplands sooner than necessary, only another cornet could be found to hold Colby's hand. Unfortunately, Brosy was equally wet behind the ears and, with Claude Cosgro, the squadron's only experienced officer, down at the port emitting an indignant wail for help, they had been obliged to pool their knowledge and command the squadron as a committee of two, both hoping to God someone knowledgeable would arrive in time to take over.

Unlike Colby, who was spare and lithe and looked like a stable boy, Brosy was tall and plump, fair while Colby was dark, easy-going and lazy where Colby was quick-tempered and inclined to tear through life like an uncontrolled whirlwind.

He managed a nervous smile. 'Looks as if we'll be in action before long, Coll,' he said.

'Dare say.' Colby was far less frightened of the weapons he was about to face than he was of Colonel Markham, his commanding officer, who would have been livid to the point of apoplexy if he'd allowed a cavalry action to take place without the regiment being represented. In addition to all of this, of course, there were two hundred years of stolid North Country soldiers breathing heavily down his neck, and if he'd let them down, all those other Goffs who lay straight and austere in their stony Yorkshire church-yards, would have set up such a clatter of old bones as they spun in their graves he'd have had to live with it in his ears for the rest of his life.

Aut Primus Aut Nullus. There it was, the regimental title, on a little scroll beneath the eagle on Brosy's lance cap which – typical of Brosy – was worn without its oilskin cover because he'd lost it somewhere en route. *The Best Or Nothing.* If we're the best, Colby thought wildly, then, by God, they *had* got nothing.

Brosy was squinting towards the ridge. 'I saw Billy Russell, of *The Times*, up there when I went to report ourselves,' he said. 'Scribbling away for all he was worth. I expect he's watching what's going on.' His plump placid face creased into a frown. 'What does *he* know about military tactics?' he went on in a bleat of indignation. 'It needs a military man to write about war. Hear that next time that's what the newspapers intend to do, in fact. My cousin owns part of the *Morning Advertiser* and he said they'd pay well.' He paused, then went on again, chattering nervously because he was as worried as Colby. 'That ass, Nolan, was there, too, preaching cavalry fire and slaughter. He's been at it, they say, ever since we got here.' He stared petulantly towards the ridge again. 'Wish the infantry would arrive. I'd hate to go into action without 'em. Why don't someone send a message?'

Colby shifted uneasily. At eighteen he felt devoid of experience, brains, even common sense. Every single man sitting his horse behind him knew more about soldiering than he did. Some had served for seven, twelve or even more years, and some, coming home from India on the outbreak of war, had transferred to the 19th from the 3rd Light Dragoons in case they missed it. One of them, Trooper Vaughan, who had been acting as regimental butcher down by the harbour, galloped up, grinning. He was wearing a white smock streaked with the blood of the cattle he'd been killing and carried nothing but a sabre.

'It coom from t'enemy,' he announced cheerfully, gesturing behind him. 'I picked 'un up down there. Didn't want to miss t'fun.'

Without bothering to salute, he cantered away to find

7

his friends and Colby turned and glanced nervously at his men once more. Their reception in the Light Brigade camp the previous evening could hardly have been called warm and they had not been there an hour before they had been ordered peremptorily down to Balaclava as escort to Sir Colin Campbell, who was commanding the Highlanders guarding the port.

When the first reports of advancing Russians had arrived that morning, however, Colby had announced that, whatever ideas Campbell might have, *he* was determined to fight the coming battle in the ranks of the cavalry, and the grizzled old Scot, probably more experienced in war than any other man in Russia, had given him a grim smile.

'This y'r firrst time in action, boy?' he had asked.

'Yes, sir.'

'Then make sure you use y'r handkerchief to bind y'r sword to y'r hand. Otherwise ye'll lose it. Do ye no' feel the sweat on the palm already?'

His fingers moist on the reins of his horse, Colby shivered violently, aware that for the first time in his life he was about to face someone who was going to try to kill him. Another shiver ran through him. Despite the sun, the morning was chilly and he decided it was going to be a damned uncomfortable winter here on the Russian uplands. It would be a damned sight warmer by far, he thought, at the Markhams' house at Braxby back in Yorkshire, holding Georgina Markham's hand.

The nostalgic thought warmed him. Georgina Markham, the younger of Colonel Markham's two daughters, lived only a few miles from his own home, was pink and white with pale yellow ringlets, and wore blue dresses to set off her charms. He had adored her since he had returned home from school at seventeen and found that the leggy creature who had lived next door and pulled his hair and hit him over the head with her dolls had suddenly developed curves and a luscious bosom that drew his eyes like a magnet whenever she appeared. He'd followed her around like a dog with the desperation of unrequited love, and in his sabretache at that moment, alongside his prayer book and his mother's picture there was a water colour of her, indifferently executed by her older sister, Florentia, which she'd given him offhandedly when he'd announced he was leaving for the East.

Thinking about her now, all he could see in his mind's eye were two white arms, a soft, moist mouth like a ripe cherry and the curve of her breast. A sigh that was more like a shudder ran through his body. Christ, he thought suddenly, I wonder what she looks like with her clothes off!

The thought shook him.

He cleared his throat, embarrassed by his own imagination, and jerked himself back to the present.

Fine time to be thinking of Georgina Markham without clothes, he decided, when any minute he might be lying dead, chopped up by the enemy like a side of raw beef. Decent men didn't think of girls in bed, anyway. Perhaps, however, he wasn't all that decent, because when he'd returned from school, raw-boned enough to have been expelled for tossing a bullying master into the river, there'd been more than one hurried scuffle in the barn with the daughter of a local farmer before he'd set eyes on Georgy Markham's slender whiteness.

He wrenched his thoughts back yet again with a conscious effort. I wish they'd get started, he thought. I wish it were over. I wish the whole bloody war was over so I could go back home, and prance around in front of Georgy, a rough, horse-smelly cavalryman hot from action.

'Hello!' Brosy la Dell was staring towards the ridge again as a galloper hurtled down the last slopes from the Ridge and drew rein alongside the divisional commander. 'Here comes the message from the high altar. That means something will happen. Thank God the Heavy Brigade won't have the day to themselves.'

He glanced behind him. The Heavy Brigade, drawn up like the Light Brigade, waiting for orders, had already crashed into action once that morning in an entirely successful affair which had come off more than anything because of the Russian cavalry's hesitancy.

'It's Nolan,' Colby said. 'I expect that means he'll try to run the affair. He's been telling everybody he knows more about it than the general ever since he came out here.'

Brosy grinned. 'And here comes the infantry at last,' he said. 'It looks as though we'll get moving now.'

He gestured at a column of red-coated men winding down the slopes, the sun glinting on their white belts and accoutrements and catching the tips of their bayonets. Colby wasn't listening. He was watching the group of staff officers, with their plumes and bicorne hats, clustered round Nolan, who was pointing angrily down the slope in front of them.

'The fathead's pointing down the valley,' he said, startled. 'We can't be going that way, surely! There's nothing for us down there!'

But Nolan was still gesturing furiously. At the bottom of the valley a battery of Russian guns was drawn up facing them, backed by a mass of horsemen. On their left on the heights were more troops and guns and, though they couldn't see them, they knew full well there were more on the Causeway.

'It's more than a mile, too!' Brosy's voice became almost falsetto with alarm. 'The man's off his chump!'

There was a stir among the staff officers then Colby heard the colonel of the 8th Hussars, who had just appeared, reprimanding his men for smoking in the presence of the enemy. He glanced round uncertainly. Several men in the little knot of the 19th had clay pipes in their mouths.

'Better get those pipes out,' Brosy said, heaving at his reins. 'Sergeant-Major Holstead!'

'Leave 'em, leave 'em,' Colby snapped. 'They might be dead soon. If it makes dying easier, then for God's sake let 'em smoke.'

'Won't someone complain?'

'I'm in command here!' Colby spoke sharply, suddenly sure of himself. His father had always taught him that the man who ran the circus held the whip.

Brosy stared at him, but he didn't argue and waved Sergeant-Major Holstead away as he cantered up and began to do elaborate things with his sabre in salute.

The staff officers seemed to be arguing even more furiously now. The divisional commander was looking bewildered and Colby saw Nolan point down the valley again.

'He's got it wrong, surely to God,' Brosy said.

Colby didn't answer. His mouth was as dry as if it were filled with ashes and he tried to imagine what it would be like to be dead. Heaven, he thought, with all those angels floating about singing with upraised eyes! It seemed a boring prospect, but the idea of darkness, which was the only alternative, seemed even worse.

Perhaps it would be Brosy who would be killed, he thought, feeling better. Then even that thought troubled him. Brosy and he had been at school together, smoking, drinking, swearing and avoiding work whenever possible. They had spent holidays together, fished together, even joined the regiment together, and, in one of the mad moments of peacetime when Colonel Markham had felt his men needed some knowledge of war, had practiced the rescue of wounded together, so that it had been Brosy Colby had placed 'unconscious' across the saddle of a led horse and allowed to slide off on to his head so that he ended up with a week in bed with concussion.

In his bewilderment and trepidation, his dislike for his missing superior officer increased rapidly. The responsibility he'd been handed was just too much for someone of his age and experience. But Claude Cosgro had never been known as a man of much sensitivity or even sense, any more than his father, while his younger brother, Aubrey, was said to be even worse. The Cosgros seemed to come in bunches of a dozen, with nothing to choose between them.

The low murmur of voices behind him told him that his men were well aware of what lay ahead. Nolan, obviously not intending to miss anything, had taken up a position now in front of the left squadron of the 17th Lancers and the brigadier-general was cantering his horse across the front of his brigade. He looked flushed and excited and, as he passed, Colby lifted his sword in salute.

'My lord,' he said. 'There are only a few of us but I imagine you'll be able to use us.'

Lord Cardigan stared at him with his blue pop eyes: he had a reputation as a womaniser, but his whiskers, Colby noted, were beginning to show grey and he looked old and ill.

'Place yourselves in the middle of the first line,' he said. 'On the right of the 17th and the left of the 13th. Might as well have all the lancers together.'

As he rode off, upright and stiff, more men, seeing action impending, galloped up from their different duties about the field and down at the port. The 19th drew rein alongside the sombre block of the 17th – the Death or Glory boys, they called themselves; the Dogs' Dinners they were known to everybody else from the skull and cross bones on their lance caps. Morris, the officer in command, was still wearing the frock coat of a staff officer, because he had only taken over the night before when the senior officer of the regiment had gone down with cholera.

'With your permission, sir,' Colby said, 'we'll join you.'

Morris turned, frowning. 'We'll be glad of you,' he growled. 'See you keep your line.'

Cardigan had moved forward now to a point two horses' lengths in front of his staff and five lengths in front of the right squadron of the 17th, almost in front of Colby. He looked calmer now than he ever normally looked on parade, stern, soldierly, and upright as a steeple, his long military seat perfect. He wore the full uniform of the 11th Hussars, his old regiment, but his pelisse was not slung like everybody else's — it was worn like a patrol jacket, its front a blaze of gold that accentuated his slim waist.

As the last shouts of the troop officers died away, a strange hush fell over the field. Neither gun nor musket spoke on either side as they settled themselves in their saddles and fidgeted nervously with their equipment, two long lines of horsemen, first the 13th Light Dragoons, then the 17th Lancers with the small knot of the 19th between them, and finally Cardigan's own regiment, the 11th Hussars, known as the Cherrybums from their red trousers. Behind them were the 4th Light Dragoons and the 8th Hussars, and behind them still, the Heavy Brigade, in three lines, with the divisional commander well in front where he could maintain control of both his brigades.

Fishing out his watch, Colby glanced at it. It was eleven-twenty. It seemed a particularly ominous time.

Cardigan's hoarse strong voice came over the shuffle and snort of horses and the clink of bits. 'The brigade will advance! First squadron of the 17th Lancers direct.' He turned his head towards his trumpet-major who jerked at his instrument with an arm decorated with four upside-down stripes under crossed trumpets. Trumpeter Sparks behind Colby began to lick and lap his lips in anticipation.

'Sound the advance!'

The trumpet's notes shrilled sweetly, to be taken up by the squadrons behind. Orders were called, harsh in a curious silence that managed to exist beyond the jingle of equipment, as if everybody was holding his breath. Over it Colby could hear Holstead's rasping voice.

'Git yerself in line, do!' he was snarling at some nervous trooper. 'And sit yer mount proper. I could read the bleeding *Times* between yer legs.'

Colby caught Ackroyd's eye and Ackroyd gave him a re-assuring grin, as his grandfather must have given Colby's father on that muddy June day nearly forty years before in Belgium.

'19th Lancers – !'

Colby's voice seemed to have dried up and, as his command came out as a croak, Cardigan's head jerked round.

'Not yet, damn you!' he snarled. 'Wait for the order!'

Humiliated enough for his fear momentarily to disperse, Colby looked from the corner of his eye at his men. Knowing more about it than he did, they had been slow to respond, and not one lance butt had been jerked from its bucket by the right stirrup. Blushing, facing front again, he

13

saw that Cardigan had wheeled his horse to face the dark mass at the end of the valley. Colby swallowed. He had a stone in his throat and a vacuum in his stomach. He glanced across at Brosy and it was obvious in the quick nervous smile he received that the same thoughts had occurred to Brosy, too.

Feeling he wasn't very far from meeting his Maker, he tried to think noble thoughts. What things, his frantic mind asked, have I left undone that I ought to have done? What have I done, apart from thinking of Georgina Markham, that I ought not to have done? Let me come out of this one alive, he prayed. He had never had a woman and he desperately wanted to live to go home and claim Georgy Markham as his prize.

'Please God,' he murmured. 'Take care of my mother and father, and my sister Harriet. And, while you're at it, please keep an eye on yours truly. There aren't any more Goffs after me.'

2

'Pride, discipline and tradition,' Colby's father had often said, 'are what carry a regiment into battle. And pride, discipline and tradition are what bring it out again.'

Because Colby had never before seen them manifested, he hadn't the foggiest idea what his father had meant and they had remained for him nothing but meaningless abstracts. Now, for the first time in his life, with his heart thumping, his blood thickening and crawling within him, he saw exactly what they stood for.

As he clutched his sabre, a red bandanna twisted round the hilt and round his hand, his mouth felt like sandpaper and his eyes prickled painfully. No man, unless he were an idiot, could advance to what looked very much like certain death without fear twisting his vitals. Yet, as the Walk March sounded, not a man moved from the line, and it was then that it occurred to him that they were held there not through a desire for glory or a wish to get at the enemy, but simply because nobody else had moved and because the regiment had never turned tail in its history and couldn't possibly do so now.

He looked sideways at his men. They sat with lances still at the Carry, the nine-foot bamboo shafts vertical, the red and green pennants fluttering, the burnished barbs flashing in the sunshine. It was impossible to tell what they were thinking because their expressions were blank and they seemed to show no emotion whatsoever. But, because his colonel had not measured up to the moment and his squadron officer was still skulking in Balaclava, they were following him – *him*, Colby William Rollo Goff, the most useless officer in the brigade – simply because he had ordered them to. He felt overcome with pride and remarkably close to tears.

He glanced down at himself. He was thinner than usual, not so well-fed, not so clean as he liked to be and knew he should be. The rifle green of his uniform was stained, the red facings weathered, the gold epaulettes tarnished. His overalls with their double gold stripe were muddy and he could feel a chill round his kidneys where his tunic, following the fashion of military millinery in recent years, failed to cover his middle properly. The campaign hadn't helped, and his Wellington boots were unpolished because nobody had any polish, and the dyed black-cock's plumes in his lance cap had long since been removed from the gold-bullion rosette that normally held them. In a situation where they were overworked and outnumbered, spit and polish took too much time.

As Ackroyd edged into position behind him, Colby's mount snorted as if she sensed something was about to happen. She was shivering with excitement, sidling and fussing, with flickering ears and tail tightly tucked in. She was a lively mare who had been foaled on the Home Farm at Braxby and named Bess after his mother because, his father claimed, 'she had the same sweet temper but was just as bloody stubborn when she wanted to be.' She was the only survivor of the string of three he'd embarked in England, because the transport had caught fire in Malta and his second mount had died with fifty-odd others, while his bât horse had been left behind at Varna in Bulgaria at the other side of the Black Sea to come on afterwards. Her coat was rough and staring and, because something had gone wrong with the Commissariat and the bales of hay were sour and weighted with rubbish, she was so thin her saddle was in danger of sliding round her belly or even over her ears.

As the Brigade moved forward, the lines crossed a patch of ploughed land that disturbed the formation a little, but the silence remained, broken only by the jingling of curb chains and bits, the snorting of horses, and the low grumble of the iron-shod hooves. Despite the depletion of disease and death, the Light Brigade made a brave show, the finest horsemen in Europe, drilled and disciplined to perfection. Even Cardigan made a bold figure, stiff-backed, his sword at the slope, as tall and upright in the saddle as a church.

As the pace quickened, the trumpets shrilled again and the walk became a trot. The brigade looked minute in the wide valley. The silence was intense, and it seemed to Colby that he could hear the laboured breathing of every restive horse, the jingle of every bit, the slap of every scabbard. They had moved about two hundred yards, every man in his place, three lines of horsemen now as the 11th dropped back a little, three lines of nodding heads in a splendid show of force, and it seemed almost as if the Russians weren't going to try to stop them, as if they intended simply to turn tail and bolt as they had before the Heavy Brigade earlier in the morning. But then the men on the slopes on either side came abruptly to life and the riflemen behind every bush and rock flanking their path began to pour a withering fusillade of fire down on them.

Wincing in the leaden sleet, forcing himself to sit upright in the saddle, Colby saw a movement on his right and, turning his head, saw that Nolan, the aide-de-camp, had spurred his horse forward and appeared to be urging them on from their steady controlled pace. His horse, a trooper marked with the number of the 13th, had left the front files and he was galloping forward, waving his sword. He even seemed to be smiling, and deciding that the excitement had gone to his head, it occurred to Colby that Cardigan was not the man to allow this sort of behaviour and that the aide would catch pepper when the thing was over – if any of them lived to see it over!

Morris, of the 17th, who was a friend of Nolan's, was shouting across the heads of his men at the aide, telling him to return to his place. 'That won't do,' he was calling. 'We've a long way to go!'

The aide didn't look back. Then, as he began to move up in line with the brigade commander, the guns on the

17

heights opened fire and a shell whirred over Colby's head with a rushing sound to explode with a crash and envelope Nolan with flame and black smoke. As the smoke cleared and the flying clods of earth stopped rolling, Colby saw that the aide's body had twisted in a spasm of agony in the saddle, his bridle arm and knees curling together to clutch convulsively at his torn chest so that his horse wheeled and swerved out of line, almost colliding with one of the 13th advancing just behind. Then it began to bolt rearwards, the gold lace and blue cloth of the rider's uniform burned and scorched round the gaping wound, his face blackened by the smoke. His sword gone but his arm still held high in the air, he was already swaying in the saddle, an unearthly shriek coming from his throat as his lungs collapsed, then he disappeared through the ranks of the 13th to fall from the saddle and sprawl in the grass, his dark hair stirred by the breeze.

The incident was a dramatic and horrifying start to the attack and even seemed to contain a kind of awful justice. But it was also unsettling and frightening, especially as every one of the Russian guns and every man ranged on three sides of the advancing horsemen was now pouring in a murderous storm of fire, filling the shallow bowl of the long valley with flame, smoke, flying clods of earth and puffs of dust that were slashed through by red-hot splinters of metal.

Colby's breath seemed to stick in his throat and his heart was thundering in his chest. The order 'Draw swords' was greeted with a cheer as the blades came up and the lances shifted to the Guard. Cardigan, riding in front, didn't seem to hear, still staring down the valley, his back straight, his seat as unbending as ever as he rode into the increasing smoke.

A few paces behind him, Colby was struggling to hold his mare to the pace Cardigan was setting. But she was worried by the noise and almost out of control, and having already once been reprimanded, he was terrified of what Cardigan would say if he found Colby Goff charging up alongside him like the field approaching the first fence at a point-to-point. As the thoughts raced through his brain like frightened mice, he heard Ackroyd just behind him swearing in a steady monotone like a litany, one oath, it seemed, to every stride of the horse.

'Shut up, Tyas,' Colby snapped, taking out his anxiety on the orderly. 'And make sure you keep your dressing.'

Battery after battery and rank after rank of riflemen were pouring in shot, shell and bullets now at point-blank range. A man cried out and vanished from the saddle, then a horse crashed to the ground, its rider rolling over and over like a ball. The pace remained steady, but then a shell brought down a whole knot of horsemen in a cloud of dust and smoke, from the centre of which a sabre spun upwards end-over-end and a dragoon's shako bounced away until it was trodden down by a flying hoof, and the speed began to increase.

'Get up close to your 'orse,' Sergeant-Major Holstead yelled to a fallen trooper, and Colby saw the running man dive for the shelter of a dead animal.

Cardigan showed no alarm. 'Steady there, Morris,' he called towards the 17th, then, glancing to his left, he saw Colby looking scared not far from his elbow.

'Steady there, boy,' he warned in a voice that for once wasn't full of irascibility. 'Watch your dressing.'

For most of the campaign, it had been Colby's view that his brigadier had no more skill than the average corporal but, at that moment, he would have followed him anywhere, because he seemed unafraid and understanding, and knew exactly what he was doing, his deep sonorous voice coming again and again. 'Steady, 17th! Steady 19th! Close up and keep your dressing!'

Through the inferno of smoke from the bursting shells, Colby saw the battery at the end of the valley glare red with the flame from a dozen mouths then vanish in the whirl of smoke as the shells cut down more men and horses like a sickle through grass. As the smoke cleared, he became aware of a new phenomenon. The line was extending to clear the fallen animals, then closing again to the shouts of NCOs and officers – 'Close in! Close in to the centre!' –

opening and shutting like a huge concertina.

It seemed to Colby as if they'd been riding down the valley for hours. The bonds of discipline still held, however, and only the terrified horses forced the pace.

There was a curious exhilaration, too, beneath the fear. The thunder of hooves, the yells, the crashing of explosions was like a dreadful nightmare that would end eventually to leave him shaking and sweating with terror, but at that moment, also as if in a nightmare, he was being swept along on a high pitch of excitement.

The inner squadron of the 17th had broken into a canter now. The 19th's rear rank followed suit and, as the pace quickened, some of the stronger pullers pushed to the front. Forced to quicken his own pace to keep ahead, Colby spurred the mare to keep his distance, but as he drew level with Cardigan, an arm shot out and waved him back irritably.

'Get back, boy, blast you,' Cardigan snarled. 'Don't ride in front of your brigade commander!'

But it was impossible to hold the horses now and one after another they were breaking into a headlong gallop, and even Cardigan was forced to let his charger have its head to avoid being ridden down.

'Come on, Nineteenth,' Ackroyd was yelling, 'Don't let the Dog's Dinners get in front!'

Spurs had gone home, lances were levelled and swords had come to the Right Engage. There was a yell and Colby saw the butcher, Vaughan, on his left, clutch at his thigh as he was hit by a musket ball, then the whole leg below the knee vanished in a hideous splash of crimson as his shin was pulverised, and he screamed and rolled from the saddle, the bloody smock flapping over his head as he fell. Riderless horses, drilled to hold their place in the line, were closing in on Colby now, mad with fear, their eyeballs protruding, the blood from their wounds smeared along their necks and flanks. A bay charger belonging to the 17th barged against him, almost unseating him and smudging a red stain across his overalls. Whacking at it with the flat of his sword, he drove it away, only to find another on the other side, blowing a crimson froth from its nostrils across him.

A shell swept away three men to his right, then round shot and grape from the flank began to mow down whole groups. His leg was painful, he noticed, and, glancing down, he saw he'd been hit in the thigh. He was just wondering how bad it was when another musket ball knicked his arm. For a moment he wondered if he should fall out but he was terrified of being ridden down by the second line.

'I think I'm wounded, Brosy,' he yelled across to la Dell. 'What should I do?'

'If you can stay on your horse, you'd better stay in the line,' Brosy yelled back. 'There are Cossacks behind waiting to nobble stragglers.'

Gritting his teeth, Colby tried to look back to find out where the Cossacks were, but it was impossible to see anything through the smoke except the head-on view of the second line and he hoped they looked as terrifying to the Russians as they did to him.

Sergeant Holstead had just bored up alongside him when his head exploded in a splash of red hair, flesh, blood, brains and bone as a round shot carried it away. But the headless body remained in the saddle, the lance still couched under its arm, a grisly figure leading the advance until it rolled slowly over and dropped out of sight.

It wasn't courage that kept them going now. It was chiefly the desire to get beyond the batteries, but, in front, Cardigan was still riding forward as though totally unconcerned.

'Come on, sir,' Ackroyd yelled at Colby. 'It's time you had your sword at the Engage. We're almost at the guns!'

In a daze, Colby swept the sabre up and held it out alongside the mare's head, hand turned down slightly so that the thumblay along the line of the blade. Infantry on either side of the battery began to pour in a heavy cross-fire and he felt his foot jump as he was hit again. I must be like a bloody sieve, he thought wildly, but he could still feel no real pain, though Bess was utterly blown after the long gallop and was limping with a wound in her leg.

The lancer on his right had his bridle arm shot away and fragments of flesh spattered Colby's face and chest, then a shell burst overhead and he saw Ackroyd go down. Oh, Christ, he thought miserably, he'd have to answer for that! If the Ackroyd men had gone to war with the Goffs for generations they'd also always managed to come home with them, too, and his father would want to know why he hadn't seen to it that this one had.

His sword was in the air. He seemed to be acting from impulses outside his body and brain. 'Steady, steady! Close in!' He realised he had been shouting the words ever since the forward movement had begun and his voice had become cracked and strained.

Just at that moment, the Russian battery in front fired again and he felt the heat and heard the whirr as a shell passed him. Then he was on top of the battery, and, wrenching at Bess's head, he chose a space between two of the guns and charged into it.

That last salvo had brought down most of the remnants of the first line, so that only isolated groups of men passed into the battery. Bess gave a tremendous leap into the air, but in the smoke Colby had no idea what she cleared, then horsemen were swirling about him, silhouetted against grey wraiths of smoke, and he tried to remember what little he'd been told about attacking infantry.

'Let's have none of your cissy prodding.' The words of the sergeant-major instructor of fencing rang in his ears. 'Make it a good jab and transfix the bastard!'

As he lunged with all his strength, the Russian in front of him fell away, blood welling from his mouth, but, as Colby returned his sword to the slope, he almost removed Bess's ear, and he decided that, since she always indicated with them what she intended to do, he'd be at a considerable disadvantage if he left her without them. A second Russian jabbed at him with a sponge staff and he slashed with all his strength so that the staff leapt into the air, one of the Russian's hands still grasping it. As the gunner staggered

22

back, staring at the stump of his wrist, a dragoon officer swept down on him and caught him across the neck with a swipe that almost severed his head, to leave Colby with a mouth full of bile.

Suddenly alone except for Trumpeter Sparks, he saw a sergeant of the 17th sweep by and yelled at him to rally on him before he realised the sergeant was as dead as a stone, still in the saddle, his eyes fixed and staring. A dismounted Russian, like Colby thinking him alive, took a swing at him with his sword, but missed and laid open the horse's breast instead. As the animal came to an abrupt stop, its legs trembling, its eyes rolling with terror and pain, the dead sergeant toppled from the saddle and flopped in a heap at the startled Russian's feet, seconds before he was skewered himself. The lance which drove through him into the wheel of the gun bent like a bow and snapped off, leaving half its length still protruding from the Russian's chest. The other half shot from the hand of the man who was holding it and lifted upwards in an uneven arc, while its owner yelled with fury and dragged at his sword as he was surrounded by a cloud of Cossacks. For a second, as he wrestled with his excited mare, Colby stared, shocked at the savagery, then he came to life and, charging from behind with Sparks, flailed about him with his sword until the Cossacks bolted into the smoke.

The battery was full of horsemen now, the Russian gunners diving under their guns or running for their lives. One of the 17th was on his knees beside a dying dismounted officer. 'Don't ride us down, sir!' he was yelling. 'Don't ride us down!' Bullets seemed to be plucking at Colby's clothing from all sides and Bess had almost come to a standstill now, blowing hard. Three Cossacks appeared, pale ugly men with flat caps, and a lance point caught Colby's belt, almost wrenching him from the saddle. As the blade appeared under his arm, tearing at his skin, he saw it had a little barb on the end covered with a tuft of hair.

Swinging wildly, he sent the Cossack head over heels across the tail of his horse, and rode on, dragging the lance behind him, still caught in his belt. For a while, he struggled to free himself of it but in the end he had to undo the belt and let the lot go. As he did so, another Cossack appeared through the smoke, but Sparks came thundering past him and his lance took the Russian in the throat.

'Thank you, Sparks.'

'You're welcome, sir.'

Just ahead, a small group of light dragoons were fighting, and one of the aides hurtled past, pointing at them. 'Rally!' he was yelling. 'Rally on Lord Cardigan!'

Colby, who couldn't see Cardigan anywhere, was beginning to grow angry, and when a Cossack came at him, he went for him bull-headed, but his sword bounced off the Russian's thick coat as if it had no edge at all and, without bothering to recover it, he smashed the Russian in the face with the hilt. As he reeled aside, a British lance thumped into his back and he rolled over his mount's head and crashed to the ground.

What was left of the first line had dissolved into tiny groups of shouting men by this time, and as they tried to sort themselves out, the second line arrived. One of them collided with one of the 17th, so that both chargers went down with kicking legs, and the unhorsed men stumbled past Colby, trying to dodge the frantic animals screaming with shattered jaws and torn flanks as they galloped through the smoke.

A light dragoon, trapped by one leg under his fallen horse, yelled at Colby, and he dismounted hurriedly to drag him free while Sparks kept guard. Retaining a good grip on his sword, as a couple of Russians bore down on them, he swept the lances aside with his left hand and thrust upwards. Something hit him on the head and for a moment he was sure he was dead.

He came to, to find himself being pushed into the saddle by the man he had rescued. His head was ringing and blood was running down his face from somewhere above his eyes. He had lost his lance cap and the dragoon was thrusting a peaked forage cap at him. It had gold lace on it and looked as if it belonged to a staff officer.

'That's not mine,' he said.

'Better shove it on all the same, sir,' the dragoon said. 'It'll protect your 'ead.'

Jamming it well down over his ears, Colby swung the horse round, and as a riderless charger appeared, he snatched at the bridle and held it until the dragoon could leap aboard.

Further down the valley, drawn up in lines, was a mass of Russian horsemen, but Colby had long since lost touch with the rest of the brigade, and even Sparks, the last mounted survivor of his small detachment, had vanished now.

'We can't charge that lot,' he yelled. 'I think we'll be safer in the smoke.'

As they re-entered the battery, he found himself among a mixed group of hussars round a gun attached to a limber. The gun team were in a confused tangle of leathers, their eyes bulging with fear, the off-rear animal lashing out with its hind legs at anything that came near. An officer of the 4th was rallying his men with his sword in the air and, catching up with them as they swung up the valley, Colby jammed his spurs into his jaded mount. A cloud of Russian lancers was across his path and, knowing he was no swordsman, he flayed the air with his sabre and the Russians gave way. Driving hard at an officer in a pale blue uniform, his sword went in to the hilt, and as the Russian fell he was almost dragged from the saddle. Bent over, fighting to free the weapon, he was dazed by a blow from a slashing sabre which hit the heavy gold acorn in the centre of the staff officer's forage cap he was wearing and split it in two.

A 17th lancer was alongside him now fighting with the fury of desperation, whirling his nine-foot weapon in a circular motion to parry the blows aimed at him. As they burst clear, a Russian sword seared Colby's back, almost dragging him from the saddle, but they were heading back up the slope now as hard as they could get their mounts to stagger. The air stank of saltpetre and the turf was pitted and torn by shellfire and littered with broken swords, abandoned lances, busbies, shakoes and lance caps. Horses beat and kicked at the ground in their death agonies, and men stumbled and ran through the smoke to safety. Across Colby's path a man sprawled, biting at the turf in his agony, and an officer, his chest a mass of bloody lace, crawled on white-gloved hands, his sabretache twisted between his legs.

'Sir! Mr Goff, sir!'

Swinging in the saddle, terrified of a lance thumping into his shoulder blades, Colby drew rein. Ackroyd was stumbling up the slope, his overalls drenched with blood from a wound in his thigh. 'Thank God you're all right, Tyas,' Colby said. 'My father would give me stick if I lost you!'

Ackroyd managed a weak grin as Colby shoved him into the saddle. 'What about you, sir?'

'Never mind me. Get up there to our lines.'

With Ackroyd looking as if he were about to swing from the saddle again, Colby slapped at Bess's rump. The terrified mare cantered for a few yards before slowing to an exhausted trot that carried Ackroyd to safety, and it was only when he looked round that it occurred to Colby that Cossacks were moving among the wounded just behind him, spearing anybody who moved.

A horse wearing Russian accoutrements galloped past him, its head up, its eyes wild, and as he snatched at the reins and brought it to a standstill the jerk almost swung him off his feet. Trying to fight down his panic, he moved to the horse's head talking to it softly and wondering insanely if it understood English. As he swung into the saddle the Russian guns were still sending cannon balls bouncing across the valley to tear great scars in the turf where they hit, and he was just congratulating himself on his escape when he saw one of them coming towards him, visible every inch of the way.

It hit the Russian horse on the head, smashing it to bloody pulp and spinning the animal round to fling it to the ground with a clatter of harness. Sprawling alongside it, wanting to cry out in rage and horror, Colby scrambled to his feet, his neck muscles straining, his eyes staring. But nothing came out beyond a silent shriek of agony deep down inside himself, then the air burst into his lungs and seemed to tear him in two. A shell exploded near him and he felt pebbles and rock splinters hitting him. Blood spurted from his hand and pinprick cuts on his face dribbled red to his chin. Dazed, deafened and stupefied, he recovered his senses just in time to see a group of Cossacks bearing down on him. But he had almost reached safety now, and all save one of them turned away. The last man's lance caught his collar and he felt the blade tear at his neck. Writhing on the ground, in desperation he flung a handful of grit in the Russian's face, half-blinding him, then jumping up and gripping his leg, yanked him from the saddle with a crash.

The Russian was on his knees at once, yelling for mercy, but in a fury of fear Colby slashed at him, and his face seemed to split into a red mask, the eyes out of alignment and staring at the sky as he fell back. Sickened, Colby stumbled after the Russian's horse but it was frightened and remained just out of reach. As he turned again up the slope, he passed a hussar removing the saddle and bridle from his dead charger.

'I'll get a new mount,' he said, 'but never another saddle.'

As he spoke, he was hit in the chest by a musket ball and staggered back, his eyes startled. Sitting down heavily, he slowly sagged backwards, dead, the saddle still in his arms and, picking it up, aware of safety not far away, Colby held it over his head and started to run. Horses passed him, and from the shouts he could tell they were ridden by Russians. Twice he felt thumps on the leather over his head that he took to be sword blows and once something tore at his sleeve and the flesh beneath. Then he was alone, stumbling among other stumbling men and weaving horses. An English voice called out to him and, tossing the saddle aside, he found himself staring at a huge dappled horse and between its ears the face of one of the Scots Greys who was helping a wounded lancer to dismount. Close by, a light dragoon, hit in the head, was lying across the neck of his

27

horse which was being led to safety by an infantry officer. Other exhausted, bleeding men were staggering in, cheered and greeted by handshakes as they arrived. A charger with a man on its back hobbled by, its broken hind leg swinging agonisedly, its eyes bulging with pain and terror, and a sailor from one of the naval batteries, wearing a dragoon's brass helmet, grabbed it, pulled the man off its back and shot the horse with a farrier's pistol.

'We had that bloody battery!' someone was yelling furiously. 'We had it! It was ours! Where was the infantry support?'

Colby had no idea where his men were, but then he saw Ackroyd sitting on a hummock, his eyes closed and white as a sheet. He still held on to the exhausted Bess's reins and the mare's head was drooping over his bowed figure.

'You all right?'

Ackroyd shook his head without opening his eyes. 'I think I'm dying.'

Colby's temper flared. 'Don't talk bloody rubbish, Tyas!' he snapped. 'Look to your front. Your eyes are wallowing about like eggs in a frying pan! And what's all this nonsense about dying? It's an offence to die after you've been rescued. Get better at once!'

After all the shouting he'd done, his voice whirred away almost to nothing like a broken watch spring, but it was enough to bring Ackroyd to his feet, despite his torn leg, his eyes wide open, his face shocked and startled. That, Colby thought grimly as he moved on, ought to shift any remaining self-pity. Self-pity was what you died of.

He saw his troop officer, Claude Cosgro, approaching him. He looked plump and clean, as if he'd put his visit to Balaclava to good effect.

'Good God!' The smooth round face registered shock. 'It's young Goff, ain't it?'

A surgeon grabbed Colby's arm. 'You all right, my boy?' he asked.

He dragged a mirror from his pocket and held it up so that Colby found himself staring into a pair of shocked eyes in a red-masked face. Blood was streaming across it from

28

two separate wounds above his hair line and there was more blood about his throat from the gash in his neck and the pinprick wounds in his cheeks. The surgeon, who was stout and middle-aged, was moving round him, counting. 'Eleven, twelve, thirteen – my God, boy, you must be the most wounded man on the field! Are you sure you're all right?'

To his surprise, he was. As the surgeon wrenched off the forage cap, they found the sword stroke had removed the acorn but the badge and the peak had taken the force of the blow.

Farriers' pistols were putting crippled horses out of their misery and soldiers' wives were appearing, to take care of wounded and dying men. All round them, officers were arguing about the cause of the disaster. Some blamed it on Cardigan and some on his brother-in-law, the divisional commander. It didn't require much sense to realise that the blame didn't lie there at all. Everybody had seen Nolan point down the valley.

The surgeon was still sponging Colby's face as Brosy la Dell appeared. Inevitably, he had lost the ill-fitting lance cap and in one dirty paw he held a beef sandwich he'd begged from one of the staff.

'Fancy a bite, Coll?' he asked. 'I could eat a dead horse, I'm so hungry.'

The brigade was lined up, a curiously shrunken brigade, first the 17th, four men of the 19th, only one of them mounted, then the 13th Light Dragoons. Behind them a man of the 4th was standing by his dying charger, cursing steadily, watched by his friends. As the rolls were taken, names were answered from huddled heaps surrounded by surgeons or soldiers' wives. The 19th didn't take long because there appeared to be only six unwounded men.

Morris of the 17th was carried past, his face a mask of blood, muttering 'God have mercy on my soul' in his agony, then Cardigan appeared, his tunic undone, a rent in his overalls. Reining in, he faced the remnants of his brigade. 'It was a mad-brained trick, men,' he burst out. 'But it was nothing to do with me!'

There was a thin cheer. 'We'll go again, my lord,' someone yelled.

Colby lifted his head indignantly. If any bloody idiot suggested *him* going again, he decided, he was prepared to stand up in front of the Commander-in-Chief if necessary and tell him he wanted his head examining.

As the surgeon finished cleaning his face, he looked down at himself. His uniform was blackened, scorched, and torn in a dozen places. Nearby, a woman was kneeling over her dead husband. Further along, another was crouched over her man, trying to persuade him to drink from a water bottle. Come darkness, they'd be down the valley bringing in the bodies of others, washing them, wrapping them in their blankets or cloaks and preparing to put them in the cold hard graves where the best of the women would place flowers for a while before taking up with another man.

War, Colby thought, seemed to be a bit different from the way it had looked at home. In books and newspapers, it had always seemed a little more noble. 'Laying down your life for your country', he realised, was merely a phrase invented by writers, and the truth was different. You didn't lay down your life at all. You probably had it blown out of you by a shell, or leaked out drop by drop through half a dozen crimson holes, like some of the men about him. Then it occurred to him that if he were going to make the pursuit of arms his profession, it was more than likely that at some time or other he might be faced with this sort of shambles again, and that it might therefore be a good idea to bone up a bit on cavalry tactics and the use of the sabre.

Finally another thought struck him: By God, he thought, I wonder if they'll send me home! I'm wounded; they might!

In a sudden resurgence of enthusiasm brought on by good health and the resilience of youth, his spirits rose. This time, he thought, even Georgy Markham ought to be unable to resist him. Men who'd faced death could make demands and, when they did, sentimental girls often gave way. She was always going on about how proud she was of

30

a cousin of her's in the Navy who'd been lost in the Arctic with Franklin's expedition a few years before. Perhaps this little lot would give her someone else to admire: Colby William Rollo Goff, for instance.

3

'The charge at Balaclava,' Colby lied airily, 'was nothing. The winter that followed and the heat of India during the Mutiny were far worse.'

Georgina Markham's big blue eyes stared at him, round with admiration. Since, on the onset of bad weather, her father had taken a grave dislike to the Crimea and bolted for home and retirement, she knew little or nothing about either campaign.

'It was a disgrace,' she said. 'Sending you all out there to put down those dreadful Sepoys, after you'd gone through so much!'

Colby shrugged. 'Experienced troops,' he explained lightly. 'Needed us. Whole of India was ablaze.'

He looked down at Georgina as she walked alongside him through the lush afternoon meadows from the Markhams' house. In return she gave him an enthusiastic glance, which, like the weather, was warmer than he had ever expected to see.

'I looked forward so much to your return,' she said.

He didn't reply, because he wasn't so damned sure about that. The few months he'd spent at home before going to India had hardly been a great success. Though she'd grown more luscious while he'd been in the Crimea, she had kept herself utterly beyond his reach and only once, at the marriage of her sister, Florentia, to a captain in the Diehards, had he succeeded in getting his hand round one half of that splendid bosom. Florentia's had been a wild sort of wedding, with a lot of tipsy young officers and girls trying to be daring, and he'd managed to get her into the rose garden for a mere fingertip touch of soft flesh before she'd escaped to the safety of the buffet, leaving him full of fury and mounting frustration. From then on there had been nothing but the warm womanly smell of her, the whiff of the perfume she'd started to use, and glimpses of those magnificent plump white breasts in the low-cut gowns she wore at hunt balls and soirées, always blue like her notepaper and the ribbons with which she wrapped gifts.

The period had been one of sheer agony for him, with Mrs Markham or one of the elderly aunts the family supported always within earshot. Whenever they nodded off to sleep he had immediately stepped up his assault, only to find that the eighteen-year-old Georgy appeared to have ten pairs of hands, all engaged in fending him off. He'd been allowed to say goodbye to her alone before leaving for India – but with her mother listening outside the door – and she'd told him not to be so ardent, and that the sort of thing he was urging could only be permitted between married couples. She had melted sufficiently nevertheless to say she would keep herself for him, his prize and his booty when he returned from this new campaign, though he had always had a suspicion that she hadn't meant quite the same as he had.

He glanced again at her. His sister Harriet, who was older than he was and claimed to have more sense, had never liked Georgy and, with years and experience, he was beginning to see why. By now there were other women with whom to compare her and, far from being the match in looks for Caroline Matchett, who lived at Hounslow and, when she wasn't in a fit of depression and trying to drown it with brandy, was an actress of no mean repute, she wasn't even on the same mental level. While, for sheer entertainment value, she was totally outclassed by a French dancer whom he had met in Paris – now, thanks to the reliability of trains and paddlewheel steamships, within easy reach of London – who, though of somewhat dubious ability on the stage, possessed an unparalleled virtuosity in the bedroom.

She was wearing a white dress and carrying a parasol against the heat. Thank God, he thought, she wasn't wearing one of those bloody silly crinolines that had become all the fashion. In one of those things, a man couldn't get within a yard of a girl and, given half a chance, he intended to. Though Georgy's mind was not to be recommended, her shape hadn't changed.

As it happened, Georgy's brain was as full of ideas as Colby's and the walk had been her suggestion. Normally she hated walking, but she had begun to notice Colby's growing indifference. There was an aggressive maleness about him these days, she had realised, and an air of ancient wisdom, and, assailed by thoughts she knew were not part of the make-up of a pure young girl, she was aware that he had become a hard soldier, used to grabbing what he wanted.

'I was always in such an impatience for your letters,' she said.

He didn't answer and she gave him a soft dewy look. 'You have such a descriptive turn of phrase, Colby. Most men's letters are so dull and I'm such a silly with them myself. Yours make everything clear.'

His thoughts busy, he didn't answer. What he had taken in the past for unrequited love, he decided, was really nothing but honest-to-God lust, because she appeared to have the brains of a newt and when they'd ridden together he'd noticed disgustedly that she was frightened of her mount and flopped about in the saddle as if she were bone-less. Into the bargain, until his return, she'd been carrying on a heavy flirtation with Claude Cosgro, and any girl who could feel affection for a Cosgro, he felt, must surely have a fatal flaw in her somewhere.

'What a wonderful thing it was you did,' she was saying. 'Mr Tennyson's poem made us all realise'

'Nothing much,' he said offhandedly. 'Just first over the line in the mile-and-a-half at the Balaclava meeting. Known now as Cardigan's Bloodhounds. Every man in the regiment, whether he was there or not, thinks himself better for it.'

She drew a deep breath. 'You looked so strong and soldierly when you came home, Colby.'

His eyebrows rose. 'I was rotten with malaria.'

'When must you return to the regiment?'

Colby grinned. 'If I have my way,' he said, 'not for a long time. That ass, Cosgro, takes six months off regularly.'

Her lips tightened because she suspected he was taking a dig at her, but she pressed on. 'Your medals look so spendid. Especially the one they gave you for Balaclava. It was terribly brave of you to save that man's life.'

'"That man,"' Colby said coldly, 'was Tyas Ackroyd from Braxby and having Russians shooting at me wasn't half so frightening as the thought of what my father would have said if I'd let him be killed.'

'But you put your own safety at risk by giving up your horse.'

Colby grunted. 'Didn't make much damn difference,' he said. 'The Commissariat, the Russian winter and that fool, Raglan, and his staff killed her off in the end.'

'I'm sure they did their best.'

Colby sniffed. Criticising the staff always seemed to be regarded as something lacking in good taste if not even bordering on the sacrilegious. 'Unfortunately,' he said, 'it was about as good as a snot-nosed drummer boy could produce without trying. Raglan's tendency to avoid giving orders made him about as effective on a battlefield as a regimental mascot, and eighteen thousand casualties, of which less than two thousand died in battle and most of the rest of neglect, seem to indicate he was also a bit boneheaded.'

She noticed he grew more brusque and forceful on the subject of the army, and brought the conversation back to where she could cope with it.

'They say you got your medal from the Queen herself.'

'That's right. Special parade. Hyde Park.'

He had stood rigid in the sunshine as the small plump figure had walked between the lines and, as he had looked down on the homely shape of his monarch, the thought

35

that had been in his mind, he remembered, had not been one of pride or awe, but simply that she'd have made a damn good Goff.

Georgina's eyes were on him again. He had changed a lot in the years he had been away, broader across the shoulders and leaner in the body with the puppy fat gone. He was not tall but he was slim-hipped, fierce-eyed in a dark Spanish way, and strong-faced with an assured manner that made her suddenly doubt her ability to handle him.

'The malaria,' she said,' has left you thin.'

'And yellow as a bloody Chinee!'

His replies, devoid of the flattery she was used to, left her at a loss. She wracked her brains and, for something to say, tried to remember what she'd read in *The Times* that morning. 'This war that has started in America,' she came out with. 'It's a terrible thing, don't you think? Men are always wanting to fight.'

'You could hardly expect 'em to behave like middle-aged spinsters.'

'But *civil* war! Like fighting your own brother! Like Cain killing Abel!'

Still chattering, she led him between the trees. The weather had gone mad and the day was a scorcher, full of the sound of bees. Finding a stream and a grassy bank covered with poppies, celandines and daisies, she sat demurely alongside him, spreading her skirt and taking off her shawl.

'It's so hot,' she explained. 'You won't think I'm fast if I unbutton my dress a little at the throat, will you?'

Colby was all for unbuttoning the neck of her dress if it gave him a glimpse of that glorious bosom of hers. She was lying back in the grass now, smiling up at him. Her hair had come loose and lay in a blond cloud about her face. By God, he thought, startled, she wants me to kiss her!

He tried it, gently, warily, and to his surprise, after a preliminary flutter, her arms came up and swept round his neck. He'd been right, he decided, it wasn't love he felt, just plain ordinary lust, and he could feel his loins stirring.

36

He touched her breast and was surprised again when one of the dozens of hands she'd always seemed to sprout on previous occasions didn't come up and push it firmly away.

Hello, he thought, what's this? She wants to indulge in a little fun and games, by God! After the constant parading of her virtue, it was a new idea that required some taking in, but her mouth was moving under his, her lips parted with passion.

'Colby,' she breathed. 'Do you love me?'

Encouraged by the fact that she hadn't stopped him unfastening the last one, he was busy unfastening another button, and he left the question unanswered.

'You are so naughty to do that,' she whispered. 'And I expect you think I'm terrible to permit it.'

He was about to protest that if she persisted in lying about in this tantalising fashion, she had to expect a certain amount of sauce, when she sighed. 'Why must men spoil everything with passion?'

That magnificent bosom of hers was rising and falling swiftly now and he was kissing the hollow between her breasts. Her hand was on his, not restraining but with convulsively clutching fingers, and he could feel her swift breathing on his cheek.

'Oh, Colby,' she murmured. 'We are so wicked. May God forgive us for what we are about to do.'

He lifted his head, startled. He'd just been enjoying a roll in the grass, like any other hot-blooded young man, and he'd imagined she'd been enjoying it, too, like any other hot-blooded young woman. But she seemed to be expecting more!

'Tell me what I must do,' she breathed. 'I know so little about these things.'

With a married sister? He didn't believe her.

She was melting in his arms, her eyes half-closed, her lips apart, her face flushed and pink. Her dress had ridden up so that he could see what seemed to be yards of plump leg encased in white stocking. He could even see the red garters with which she held them in place, tied neatly just above her knees. Her bodice was open to the waist now, with all the ribbons that secured her underslip unfastened, and he realised she wasn't wearing stays.

By God, he thought, she'd come prepared! She'd planned it all!

Her breasts, white and pink-tipped, were soft beneath his hand. There were pale blue veins in the marble whiteness of them and, over the sound of the stream and the hum of the bees, she was making little passionate mewing noises in his ear. Far from fending him off now, she was even helping him, her breath coming in swift little pants, and he seemed to be knee-deep in discarded linen.

'No one will disturb us here,' she whispered. 'Take me, Colby, take me!'

She had thrown aside all the coy pretence. For a second his senses shouted 'No', then a flame of desire shot through him that threatened to scorch his soul, and a towering wave thundered over him as his arms closed round her.

Staring at Georgy's letter which he held open inside the *Morning Post*, Colby was hardly aware of the headlines beyond it.

She had always been in the habit of sending him notes and usually they were gushing, but now there was a new tartness in her words that he'd never noticed before, a new firmness that allowed no leeway and no room for manoeuvre or excuse. '*The wedding could easily be held before the autumn, as you well know,*' she wrote. '*Certainly, too long must not elapse. No one must ever know how wicked we have been and you cannot possibly turn from the girl you have wronged.*'

He stared at the prim round writing, his eyes blank and defeated. She had been talking and writing about marriage for days now, making no bones about what was in her mind and, with Colby always stubbornly dodging the issue, here she was again, with another bloody note, sharper in tone and finally putting the ultimatum squarely on the mat before him.

Wronged! Considering it had been her idea, she was stretching it a bit.

'You all right, boy?'

As his father spoke, Colby jumped and hastily stuffed the letter away. Major-General Goff was old now but he was as straight as a ramrod, even when he was seated. It had been his grandfather, Joshua Pellew Goff, who had raised the 19th in 1760 after Eyre Coote had smashed the French at the Battle of Wandewash. Returning home with the despatches, he had been granted two thousand acres in Yorkshire, the sum of five hundred pounds and the charter to raise a regiment of light dragoons.

The room was dark and contained prints of officers in ceremonial dress; pictures and statuettes of horses; mounted spurs; a sabre; and a rake, poker and shovel made out of French cavalry swords collected on the field of Waterloo, which were often used to demonstrate weapon drill. The old man studied his son.

'Look worried,' he observed. 'How do you feel these days? Quite recovered? No problems? No colic, strangles or thrush?' Having rattled off a string of questions to which he clearly expected no replies, the general shifted in his chair and shook the folds out of his *Times*. 'Better get your hair cut next time you go to see the doctor, by the way,' he added. 'It's almost down to your hocks.'

Settling himself more comfortably, he absorbed himself in his reading again, satisfied his son was on the mend. Colby watched him overtly across the top of his own paper, black despair in his mind. No, Father, he thought gloomily, no problems! Not one! Only Georgina Markham trying to rush me into marriage!

Her surrender had been complete but there had been little in it of the grand passion he had expected. She had been unresisting and had seemed no prize at all, letting him work his will on her without apparently joining in, laying in the grass, her clothes undone, her breasts out of her bodice like superb fruits, and wearing the same triumphant expression Joan of Arc must have worn as she went to her death.

She had spent what had seemed hours titivating herself afterwards, and he had to go backwards and forwards to the stream to fetch water in his hat to cool her flushed face before she would even make an attempt to move. He was still recovering from the shock of disappointment. After all those years of waiting, planning and scheming, he had expected crashing cymbals and there hadn't been even the tiniest tinkling bell.

He had been more than glad to leave and had snapped at Ackroyd who had been waiting at the front door of the Markham house with the horses, spinning a yarn to Annie Oldham, one of the housemaids. For a few days he had felt uncertain and ill-tempered. There had even been an honest feeling of guilt because he'd been brought up to be decent and reasonably moral, and writers had it that what had happened to Georgina was a fate worse than death. That she hadn't suffered overmuch, however, had soon become clear and as time had elapsed it had appeared that he hadn't put her in the family way either. The only fly in the ointment was her growing possessiveness. Instead of him chasing Georgina, it was now the other way round.

He frowned. Dammit, if a girl came at you with her under-garments at the slope, what could a man do but oblige? A cavalryman was supposed to have an eye for opportunity.

He was still surprised that anyone as devoted to over-heated rooms as Georgy should want a horse-smelly type like himself, but she had clearly had it all planned and he realised now it had all been part of a campaign. He looked again at the letter she had sent, opening it furtively once more inside the newspaper. Her words seemed to burn in his brain. Marriage meant 'love, honour and obey' and 'till death do us part', and at twenty-five, with the whole world before him, it seemed a dreadful prospect.

He supposed he would have to marry some time. His father would begin to imagine there was something odd about him if he didn't, and the old man was a stickler for the line continuing because there had been Goffs at Braxby probably since Adam. But Georgy! The idea of lying alongside that flaccid white body every night, while she expected him to do his duty as a husband, listening to her conversation, drinking her everlasting cups of tea – a flat-footed dismounted drink if ever there were one – seemed like a distant view of Hell.

Yet he couldn't see any way out of it. If he tried to back off, she'd have her father round like a shot, demanding, accusing, talking of the honour of the regiment. And his own father, stiff with pride and rigid with integrity, would back him up. The prospect was terrifying.

He became aware of his father speaking again. 'Following this business in America, boy?'

He hurriedly got his thoughts into line and dressed by the right. A quick glance at the paper put him in order, because *The Times* and the *Morning Post* were full of the war in the States. And a damn funny affair it was, too! Civil war was strange enough in any event, but this one seemed to be conducted in a manner based on a cross between the viciousness of a blood feud and the class consciousness of a vicarage tea party. While men were killing each other between the two capitals, in New York vacant stores had been opened as recruiting booths, and pullers-in from the social register or the nearest political office had appeared on the sidewalks to encourage enlistment – on the understanding, of course, that when the regiment was raised, they would be its officers. Everybody had wanted to be in the war. And still did. Even Brosy la Dell.

'My cousin's with the *Morning Advertiser*,' he had written the previous day from Dover where he was energetically pursuing the daughter of a naval captain,' and I suggested that, since Billy Russell of *The Times* seems to be making a botch of things over there, they might be glad to have me go over to write it all up for them. He replied that they could certainly do with *someone*, as the chap they sent out last year has just got himself shot by accident, but that, since I couldn't even write a bill for a load of coal, I'm not the man they want.'

Brosy's letter showed all his old undimmed cheerfulness. Like Colby he had advanced in rank not by purchase but by the simple process of stepping into dead men's shoes, and also like Colby, seemed to have the same skill at survival.

Colby was aware of his father still waiting for his answer. 'Yes, Father,' he said. 'I've been following it. Who do you think'll win?'

'South.' The old man had no doubt. 'The South's got the cavalry. They were the horse-owners, and horse-owners are good horse-masters. I can't imagine horse-masters coming from New York where they only use horses to pull carriages, can you?'

'All the same, Father, they haven't yet got Kentucky and Missouri to secede, Arkansas and Tennessee are now in Northern hands, and they're already beginning to encircle the South.' Colby gestured with his paper and, as he did so, the thing hit him like a blow in the face. Good God, he thought, it's the answer to everything!

'How long do you think it'll go on, Father?' he asked.

'Two or three more years.'

Colby was sitting bolt-upright now, his brain racing. In two or three years Georgina would surely have decided it wasn't worth waiting and turned to someone else. 'That's what I felt, Father,' he said cheerfully. 'And here I am excused duty until I'm recovered. Where better for my health than Virginia, where they're fighting? Warm, dry and no malaria. Good place to get over an illness. I could write for the newspapers. Everybody's at it these days.'

The general thought for a moment. 'How about your career?' he asked.

Colby beamed. 'Won't suffer, Father. Could even open the way to a staff appointment. I think I'll take the train to London tomorrow and go and see the *Morning Advertiser*.'

4

'Lying in the shadow underneath the trees,
    Goodness, how delicious, eating goober peas!'

Riding slowly down the dusty Maryland road, one leg
cocked over the horn of his saddle, Colby sang softly to
himself. Just behind, with a mule in tow carrying their
luggage, Ackroyd looked up.

'What's goober peas?' he asked.

'Dunno.' Colby smiled. 'Just a song I heard. Eggs laid
by a goober bird, or something, I dare say.'

Ackroyd nodded and, as he lapsed into a satisfied
silence, Colby went on singing, well content with the way
things had turned out.

It had not taken him long to get the measure of the
Morning Advertiser. They were very much uncommitted and
anxious to avoid personal views of the war because Russell
of *The Times* had got himself into trouble with a speech at a
St Patrick's day dinner that had not only been repudiated
by his editor but had also made things difficult for himself
in the States.

'Avoid opinions,' Colby had been told. 'Avoid anything
controversial.'

'What do you want?' he had asked cheerfully. 'Sermons
or recipes? Or shall I send you a hymn?'

They had landed in New York where, as befitted a man
holding the Queen's commission, Colby had stayed in the
best hotel he could find. It had a perpendicular railway
called an elevator going through each storey and was full of
politicians and salesmen masquerading as soldiers. But,

where he had expected to see an embattled city, there had seemed instead to be more of an emotional fervour than a desire to get to the front. The women dressed their children in outlandish costumes as soldiers, the politicians were still playing at politics, and the negroes, despite the avowed declaration that they were equal, were feared and hated, something that showed very plainly when riots broke out over the introduction of conscription and most of the victims proved to be black.

The real contact with the war started at Washington. With its cobblestones and iron wheels, its hoop skirts, livery stables, taverns and high stoops, Washington was more Southern than Northern in character and its charm had been enhanced by the gentle widow of a Northern cavalry colonel who had taken a fancy to Colby and allowed him to use her home as his own.

In the last weeks, however, the war seemed to have changed. The Northern army had been moulded only slowly after many humiliations at the hands of a much smaller, worse-supplied force, and seemed even now to be composed of volunteers, conscripts and bounty jumpers whose quality varied from splendid to awful. The business men and politicians who had been the original officers and leaders had disappeared, however, and there was now a dangerously aggressive mood in the air, so that the sort of officer who abandoned his regiment when the weather was bad had gone.

And since the great battle at Gettysburg in Pennsylvania that summer, it was becoming clear that the power of the Confederacy, once so virile and strong, was at last in decline. Its losses had been enormous and while the North's had also, the North could accept them, and people who before had gone about their business dourly, feeling that whatever they did the South did better, were now holding their heads up as though they could at last see the light at the end of a long dark tunnel. The North was scenting victory and was pushing hard to win it. Things were being tightened up. The gentlemanliness was disappearing from the war and paroles to captives were no longer permitted, because the one thing the South needed was men.

'There's a smell of victory in the air,' Colby said out loud.

Dozing in the saddle in the late autumn sunshine, Ackroyd lifted his head. He obviously hadn't the same sense of smell, though, bought out of the army to accompany Colby as his general factotum, he had shown a remarkable ability for getting away the news letters Colby wrote, able to find a telegraph that was working when no one else could and managing to by-pass delays to get the reports to New York. It had been Ackroyd who had discovered they could use ordinary mails, with the occasional expedient of the mail steamer at Boston or New York, and Ackroyd who learned that certain items could be speeded up by use of the telegraph to Nova Scotia, from where, if their arrival coincided with the departure of a fast steamer, they took only seven days to London instead of fourteen.

Colby went back to his thoughts.

His sympathies were mixed. He liked the forthright attitude of the Northern soldiers he had met but, because the South was less hostile to Britain and had been so successful against the odds, there was the romantic aura about the Confederates of a lost cause.

More than anything else he had noticed the changed methods. Precision weapons and long-range artillery had ended the old habit of advancing in close order, and it looked as though this would be the pattern for the future. And while, once, an army a long way from its base was finished when it had lost ten thousand men, here in America they had discovered armies could be reinforced by rail and stay in the field. Soldiers had become moles and the movement of cavalry was as strange to Colby as it was mysterious. Its use was not for shattering infantry but for marauding expeditions, cutting railways, destroying crops, capturing waggons; as far as a pitched battle was concerned, it didn't seem to be of much use at all because it was invariably employed as mounted infantry, never using the sabre and only utilising its horses to get at speed from one part of the field to another. His father, Colby decided, would have been horrified.

Magruderville was typical of the small towns of Maryland. One or the other of the two armies had recently passed through it and it was a ruin of blackened chimneys and fire-scarred walls.

As they moved down the mainstreet, a hound with a voice like a trumpet came out from under a porch, yelled at them for a moment or two then slunk back, and a few children stared at them from doorways. The hotel had been shattered, the lounge a ruin, the mirrors starred by bullets, the stuffing ripped from the chairs. A torn portrait of Abraham Lincoln taken from a magazine and tacked to a wall had been punctured by a dozen revolver shots.

The owner's wife was a large woman with red hair and a bosom like a frigate under full sail. 'Sure,' she said in reply to Colby's question. 'We can give you a room.'

The landlord, gestured with the whisky jar he held. 'Good, light and plumb airy,' he grinned. 'Window got knocked out.'

Colby was staring round him. 'What happened?'

'Them goddam Rebs. Came through here raidin' and burnin', toot-tootlin' on their bugles and stealin' everythin' they could lay their hands on. We ain't had time to get things straight yet.'

Maryland and South Pennsylvania had been scoured clean as Lee had swept up to Gettysburg and they were scared sick in case he came again. The whole area had been cleared of shoes by the barefooted men – even women's and children's shoes had been snatched up for their families back home – and there had been uproar all along the Mason-Dixon line, with burned townships, fresh graveyards, ruined farms and shattered homes.

The landlord gestured at his wife. 'Flora there wrapped the Stars and Stripes across her front and stood on the porch to show 'em what she thought of 'em. But one of them there Texicans saw her and yelled out 'Lady, take care! We're good at storming breastworks when the Yankee colours is on 'em! She took 'em off right quick and went inside.'

Grinning at his wife's blushes, he studied Colby's clothes. 'You English?' he asked.

'Yes.'

'Your goddam Queen better not recognise them Rebs! What you payin' with?'

'Yankee money.'

The proprietor grinned again. 'Better'n Confederate notes,' he said. 'Ain't much to eat, but we druv the chickens and shoats into the woods. We could do fried pig-meat or chicken.'

Colby shrugged. 'Shan't complain,' he said. 'Two of us.'

'Only one bed. And you take your spurs off before you lie down. Got any arms?'

'Just a couple of Colts for our own protection.'

'Don't wear 'em around. Guy gets at the whisky he likes to shoot the chandeliers down. Stables round the back. Advise you not to stay in Magruderville. There's somethin' brewin' up.'

'What sort of something?'

The landlord shrugged. 'Battle, I guess,' he said. 'A big one. The army's just passed through.'

'Which army? Yours or theirs?'

'Depends where your sympathies lie. Northern, matter o' fact. They say the hills is full of Rebs.'

Ackroyd brought the saddlebags upstairs. He accepted the cigar Colby offered and, pulling the coverlet of the bed down, indicated the grubby sheets.

''E said the Northern army just passed through. I think they all slept in this 'ere bed.' He grinned. 'Considering 'ow big this bloody country is, sir, it's thoughtful of 'em to fight their battle so 'andy.'

Colby put his feet up on the bed, and sat back while Ackroyd produced a flask and poured them both a drink. Leaning back against the soiled pillow, he fished out the last letters from home that he'd received via Washington. One of them was from his sister, Harriet, to say that Georgina Markham had at last got married – to Claude Cosgro. Harriet seemed pleased. For some reason she seemed fond of her younger brother and had never liked Georgina; while for Claude Cosgro, who had once tried his tricks with Harriet and got her fist in his eye for his trouble, she had a sheer active dislike. She seemed to think they were well suited and Colby wondered if the union had been the result of another big seduction scene. Judging by the participants, it seemed likely, one way or the other. At least, he decided, it ought to be safe enough now to go home.

The only other worthwhile item of news was that Brosy la Dell was also now in the States. He had returned to the regiment but had taken six months leave and written to Washington to say *he* was going to have a look at the war, too – from the South, getting through the blockade via Mexico.

Because it was Saturday, there were a lot of soldiers in the town, staging a get-together in the lounge of the hotel with fiddlers, hard cider, whisky and girls. They made enough noise to wake the dead but, since they might well be among the dead themselves before long, Colby had a feeling they probably deserved it. Among them was a pale-faced young man in a blue suit that had a military cut to it but was not a uniform.

'Von Hartmann,' he introduced himself. 'Hans-Viktor von Hartmann. 19th Prussian Lancers.'

'Colby Goff. 19th (Prince Leopold's Own) Lancers.'

Von Hartmann smiled. 'We have much in common, I think. Almost we are brothers.' He spoke excellent English with only a slight accent.

'You with the Northern troops?' Colby asked.

'No.'

'Newspaper?'

Von Hartmann's lips tightened. 'Hardly the profession for an officer. I am a military observer from the Prussian Government. I'm here to find out all I can about American methods.'

The noise was growing louder round the bar so they took their drinks and sat outside on the stoop where they could talk.

'We take a different view of the army in my country,' the

Prussian said. 'Ours is a martial capital, and war belongs to the province of social life. We believe in studying other people's methods. It's such a help if you have to fight them. Do you do the same?'

'We have rather more chance of first-hand experience. In Egypt, Africa and India.'

Von Hartmann stiffened. '*We* are a young army,' he said. 'But we have already beaten the Danes.'

'Beating the Danes is nothing to boast about,' Colby observed dryly.

'No, of course not.' There was a hint of resentment at Colby's words. 'But it establishes a principle. "*In Gottes Namen drauf*!" That was what Von Wrangel said at Duppel: In the name of God, forward! That's our policy. We don't look back. Only forward to the next conflict. There will be greater battles than Duppel. Against Austria perhaps. We are determined that the leadership of the German peoples shall not rest solely in the hands of the men in Vienna. With Austria out of the running, we shall then organise a Federation of North German States, and it will be controlled by Prussia.'

'And then?'

Von Hartmann shrugged. 'Perhaps France,' he said. 'Few nations have had so bad a neighbour as Germany has had in France. They have invaded our country fourteen times in a hundred and fifty years. Who do you think will win the war here?'

'The North.'

'Exactly,' The stiff smile appeared as the Prussian approved of Colby's view. 'They have made it technical and that is what *we* believe in. We too, are perfecting the railway machine. With the railways and the telegraph, a commander-in-chief can handle vast numbers of men and move his troops by mathematical calculations, not guesswork. Everything that can be done before a battle should be done, and this of course, reduces the question of luck. Our general staff has a plan in the case of a war with Austria or even a war with France.'

'What about a war with England?' Colby asked.

Von Hartmann's eyes flickered. 'I shouldn't be surprised,' he said.

The Northern soldiers were still in the lounge of the hotel when they arrived downstairs the following morning. Sprawled in chairs and corners and on and under the billiard table, most of them seemed incredibly young and Colby wondered if he'd looked that young, too, when he'd had his own first taste of war.

Setting off just as daylight arrived, they passed a group of small wooden houses clustered round a church as though afraid of what the day would bring. Then, with the long ranges of the mountains shouldering their way southwest, they crossed a river by a wooden-roofed bridge, the horses' hooves thumping hollowly on the planking, and began to come on acres of picket lines occupied by blue-clad men, and slopes dark with mules and horses, vast stacks of fodder, heaped ammunition and kegs of powder. What seemed fields-full of spare wheels for guns and limbers were laid out in rows according to size, and artillery parks were set up in squares, with spare caissons and cannon lined up like hansoms outside a station.

'Battle coming all right, sir,' Ackroyd observed. 'They're loading ammunition, not rations.'

Like everyone else except the civilians well behind the lines, the soldiers were sick of the war and when the military band that was playing started on 'Home Sweet Home' there was a derisive cheer. From the cavalry camp there was a lot of whinnying and a squadron of blue-coated men was making the ground tremble as it moved off. The high sweet notes of trumpets shrilled and the guidons cracked in the wind as the horsemen formed into column. It made Colby feel homesick.

Infantrymen were also on the move, some of them munching hardtack and cold beans as they waited for orders by fires where coffee was brewing at the sides of the road. Escorting cavalry had broken out nosebags but stood ready to snatch them away in the event of an alarm, while other men carried buckets of water from the river, slung on poles cut from the woods. Here and there a deserted regimental camp stood with tents flapping.

There was an air of excitement everywhere. It was obvious everybody was expecting a battle and they seemed to be expecting to win it, too. The armies had passed through this stretch of country before and there wasn't a house left standing. Even the birds seemed to be wary, flocks of crows flying from one patch of woodland to another, cawing loudly as they went. There was no foraging and no looting because the farms were heaps of ashes.

The colonel of a regiment of Maine infantry looked up as they were ushered into his tent. He was staring at a map spread on a camp bed, frowning deeply and making notes in the margin. He was young and tired-looking but he showed no surprise as Colby announced himself. The Americans were growing used by this time to the interest shown by Europeans in their war. Half the British army had contrived to cross the Atlantic to have a look.

The colonel was far from happy with the disposition of his men. He was a lawyer by profession and, with his lawyer's instinct, he clearly wasn't prepared to take things at their face value.

'I got some problems, you see, Captain,' he said. 'This war's brought some queer types over here. We'd got some queer types of our own, mind: generals who make political speeches and politicians who make battle plans. But this guy they've put in command here's different. He's a Frenchman. Name of Cluseret. Gustave-Paul Cluseret. Know him?'

Colby shook his head and the colonel went on. 'Sonofabitch's nothing but a common soldier of fortune. Commissioned at St Cyr but got himself involved in the revolution in Paris in 1848. Said he was wounded in the Crimea and promoted captain with the Legion of Honour. Maybe he did. I don't know.' He was obviously worried by his disloyalty but clearly had little time for his commanding officer. 'I guess, as a captain in the British army, you've maybe got more experience than me.'

'Well,' Colby agreed, 'it takes longer to get to be a

colonel.'

'Yeah. Sure. Well, I was a lieutenant when this war started and I'm still only just beginning to find my way about.' The colonel offered a long black cigar and lit one himself. 'I asked around in Washington. I have friends there practising law and they'd heard of him. The goddam man was cashiered. In Algeria, for stealing stores. Well, that's none of my business, but it seems when the war started he got himself a job as an aide to some political general and now we've got him shoved on to us.'

The colonel sighed. 'I'm sure worried. I even heard the guy fought for the other side originally. Maybe their politicians aren't so goddam interfering as ours and he could get nothing out of 'em and came north to try his luck.' He shrugged. 'You go talk to him. I guess he'll see you. He likes newspapermen.'

As they moved westwards again, a last troop of horsemen thudded past in the dust trying to catch up the infantry. They moved swiftly, their equipment jingling, different from European soldiers, horsemen without grace, a squadron of light cavalry in active operation against the enemy, troops without the polish of peacetime or any of the glitter of the parade ground. They wore blue blouses with brass buttons, trousers with yellow stripes and heavy spurred boots. Carbines sat in leather buckets on their saddles and blue metal Colt revolvers hung from rings, while their sabres were carried under their left legs where they didn't slap against the leathers.

Cluseret's headquarters had a Gallic air about them. A glee club was singing somewhere in the darkness and they could hear a violin going. Cluseret himself was tall with a pale skin, black hair and beard, and he possessed the sort of coarsely-handsome face that must have made him a favourite with women. He spoke English with a racy style, chewing all the time at a cheroot held in the corner of his mouth, and willingly discussed his plans for the coming action. Two of his aides, both Frenchmen with moustaches, imperials, wide-skirted coats and the pegtop trousers the French favoured, brought out a map and spread it on a table made of planks and barrels. 'We are 'ere,' Cluseret said, pointing. 'Tomorrow we will move west. Their left, which outflanks our right, will then be 'anging in the air, while we get round their rear.'

There was a chilly lack of appeal about him that repelled Colby, and his plans were lazy and indifferent, while there was a clear carelessness in the way he was moving his troops, because by this time, his cavalry must have been ten miles away, and his brigade was strung out with great gaps in it that could be hit anywhere by the enemy.

'Suppose they move first?' Colby suggested. 'Wouldn't that enable them to leave *your* left hanging in the air?'

'Pooh!' Cluseret snapped his fingers. 'These Americans know nothing of war! They know nothing of anything, in fact. Their wine is tart. Their food consists only of fried meat. Their bread is dreadful. And their music is the sort a peasant from the Ardennes makes on a Saturday night at the café. They are totally devoid of taste.' He gestured contemptuously. 'They will never move to my right. The 'ills are in the way and they 'ave been too-tooing on their bugles for two days over on the left. In any case, it is a matter of indifference to me 'oo wins this ridiculous war. All I want from it are my naturalisation papers.'

It was a cynical attitude, and with the Southern army diminishing, it seemed to Colby that Cluseret was overlooking the fact that the Southerners had nothing to lose by taking risks.

As evening approached, the crows disappeared and a curious lull seemed to fall across the land. In the distance, they could hear the high-pitched wail of an engine as a train brought up more men. There had been a little skirmishing during the day among the outposts and the ambulances were taking away the few wounded, while the surgeons commandeered the sutlers' canteens, laying out their instruments and cleaning the counters, so that when the battle started they could do their operations and amputations there.

The camp settled for the evening, and tents began to glow from the lanterns inside. The glee club was singing again in the darkness – 'Was My Brother In The Battle?' and 'When This Cruel War is Over' – then suddenly the song changed for 'Rock of Ages' and, looking at his watch, Colby saw that midnight had arrived. It was now Sunday and the Americans were strict with their religion.

He could hear a constant chorus of nightbirds. Near his feet Ackroyd dozed in his blanket, his back against a log. The singing started again, softly, coming through the trees which stood out starkly black against the distant firelight, and he was just about to light a cigar when somewhere among the trees higher up the slopes he heard a faint shout and a clatter. No one seemed to notice and the hymn-singing went on near the fires. He nudged the dozing Ackroyd with his foot.

'Tyas! Get up!'

Ackroyd had just pushed aside the blanket and was climbing to his feet when the woods came alive with the crash of firing.

'Great Christ in the Mountains!' The voice came from near the officers' tent. 'It's the Rebs!'

Dragging Ackroyd with him, Colby plunged into the undergrowth just as horsemen came roaring down the slope from the trees. Lights were knocked over hurriedly and bullets started flying in every direction. Shouts were going up on all sides now and the whole area seemed to be shaken by the pounding of hooves as a swarm of ragged riders, difficult to see in the darkness, exploded across the camp. A tent went down and a fire was kicked to sparks and flying embers as a horseman crashed across it.

The colonel of the Maine regiment appeared out of the darkness. He was riding a horse in front of a small group of blue-coated soldiers who were firing raggedly at the flitting shadows. But they were silhouetted by the fires and as a solid volley crashed into them from the trees, the colonel fell to the ground and the few men still on their feet bolted.

An officer in a grey coat with a yellow sash wheeled his mount and, slipping from the saddle, bent over the sprawled figure.

'That's not him,' he said.

Alongside him a trooper, gaunt, hairy and barefooted, was dragging the boots and socks from the colonel's feet. Stuffing them under his arm, he let the naked foot flop back to the ground and held up the boots, grinning gleefully. The colonel was clearly dead and his worries would bother him no more.

Carbines were still snapping among the trees and yells of delight came as food and whisky were unearthed. The Federals had vanished into the woods down the slope and were keeping up a smart rattling fire, but it all seemed to be going too high. Flames were leaping into the air, and an ammunition waggon exploded in a crimson flower, sending showers of sparks and rocket-like trails in every direction, to scatter the grey-coated soldiers. The blast bowled Colby over and, as he scrambled to his knees, he saw a running fight going on. Giving Ackroyd a shove, they half-fell into a clump of mountain laurel, and raising their heads, they saw Cluseret's French aides trying to make a dash for safety. One of them succeeded and vanished into the shadows, but a shot brought down the second so that he fell on his face, his body skidding inertly across the ground until it was stopped by a shrub.

The officer with the yellow sash was just about to dismount again when Cluseret himself appeared, wearing only a shirt and trousers. The young officer hauled his horse around.

'Cluseret!' he yelled. 'You two-timing sonofabitch!'

As he spurred forward, Cluseret's arm lifted. His revolver jerked, and the young officer dropped the sword and rolled over the tail of his horse. His eyes flickering from side to side, Cluseret plunged into the clump of laurel alongside Colby just as the Confederates swarmed round them.

'You bastards was supposed to be attackin' the other end of the line,' a captured Federal corporal was yelling disgustedly.

'That's why we attacked this end,' one of the Confederates said. 'Who's your commandin' officer?'

The man he addressed jerked a hand. 'That's him, lying

55

there. You bastards shot him.'

'Not *him*,' the Confederate snapped. 'The general. Who's the general?'

'Cluseret? He's a Frenchman.'

'The treacherous dog was fightin' for us until he went north with our goddam plans. How the hell did you think you whipped us at Pegler's Mill. It warn't skill, I can tell you!'

The camp was clearing rapidly and the Confederates were moving out already, stumbling under their loot. Two or three waggons lurched away and a man on a horse went past dragging at the halters of half a dozen led animals.

As the last of them vanished among the trees, the camp became still. A rifle popped occasionally and there was shouting among the trees, then suddenly it was silent except for the movement of shadows and the crackle of flames.

Rising to his feet, Colby glanced round. Cluseret was still hugging the ground among the laurels, and Colby stared at him, unimpressed.

'Let's see if we can find our nags,' he said to Ackroyd. 'Perhaps they've escaped.'

As they stepped from the clump of bushes, there was the click of a weapon being cocked behind them, and a quiet voice spoke.

'If you two gentlemen would kindly step into the light of the fires, we'll see to it that you're not left behind by your friends.'

As they turned – slowly, because the Americans were always quick on the trigger – they found themselves staring into the muzzles of half a dozen Colt revolvers held by a troop of Confederate horsemen among the trees. They were led by a young officer who looked no more than a boy.

'Your name Cluseret?' he demanded.

Colby's glance flickered to the bushes where he could see the grey material of Cluseret's shirt just out of the sight of the horsemen.

'Goff,' he said. 'Representing the *Morning Advertiser*.'

The Colt jerked at Ackroyd. 'His name?'

'Ackroyd. Tyas Ackroyd. He's my assistant. And friend.'

The revolver moved again to indicate the body of the French aide sprawled by the tree.

'Who's that?'

'Haven't the foggiest.'

'You seen this guy Cluseret?'

Colby shrugged. Cluseret hadn't appealed to him much, either as an individual or as a soldier, but these men would more than likely lynch him if they found him.

'Heard he left on the train,' he said.

'Did he, by God?' The officer glanced at the riders with him. 'Seems we missed him. You got proof of your identity?'

'I have letters,' Colby said. 'They're in my baggage. Over there.'

'They'll have to stay there. We haven't got time. You'd better come along, anyway. If you're tellin' the truth, we can send you back under a flag of truce. If you're not, you're due for Andersonville or Belle Isle. Come to that – ' the young officer grinned ' – why not see what the war looks like from our side for a change? The Bluebellies have all the famous newspaper names. Tell your man to get up behind the sergeant. You get up behind me. And no tricks. I reckon Beauty Stuart might like to see you.'

5

It was the sound of music coming through the trees that indicated they had arrived. The young officer turned his
head.

'That'll be the General's band,' he said. 'They pluck a
good string. The General's a great guy for music.'

They were moving between a long avenue of oaks, and
there were lights in the distance, and fires illuminating the
front of a tall pillared house with high windows.

'The Burtle House,' the young officer said. 'Kinfolk of
mine. I'm Micah Burtle Love.' He was riding now with his
head twisted round, talking to Colby over his shoulder.
'You been with those Bluebellies long?'

'On and off, about a year.'

'You'll enjoy seein' the war from our side.' Love seemed
to have accepted Colby's identification quite happily. 'We
aren't right fond of Europeans round here, mind. We had
several. Guy called Fremantle. One called St Leger Gren-
fell. What you think of that St Leger? He said he'd done a
bit of fighting here and there but nary a one of us took to
him much. He had side-whiskers long as your arm and
went about lookin' like he didn't like our smell. Soon after
Gettysburg we got set upon by Buford near Madison Court
House, and he bolted back to headquarters to say we'd all
been captured. But we'd all got away safe and he hasn't
showed his face in camp since. Then we had this Cluseret.'
Love's face darkened. 'That sonofabitch deserted and the
Bluebellies ambushed us at Pegler's Mill.'

As they drew nearer to the house, Colby saw its beauty
was marred by damage. Shutters were missing. Trees had

been chopped down and fences torn up, and there were windows broken on the ground floor.

'Grierson's lot came by,' Love said laconically.

The cavalry horses were not tethered in neat lines in the British fashion but all over the place, to fences, rails, trees, some even left to graze where they felt like. Coffee and frying meat scented the air. There were a few women and girls about the steps under the great verandah of the house and Love gestured towards them.

'The womenfolk sure are findin' the war a terrible business,' he said. 'Can't get any feathers or furbelows and all the time their menfolk are away fightin'.'

As he drew rein by the steps, several officers strolled towards him, their faces interested. Colby noticed that their uniforms were patched and threadbare, but they had a great deal of style about them with their long boots, curly-brimmed hats and huge sabres.

'Who you got there, Micah?' one of them asked.

Love grinned. 'Says he's British. Mebbe the General'll want to talk to him. Where is he?'

'Inside. Eatin'. Guess maybe he's finished now. The music's goin'.'

Accompanied by Ackroyd, Colby followed Love into the house. The girls on the verandah gave him a curious look as he passed and he noticed that their clothes, like the officers', though clean and neat, looked threadbare. The sentry standing by the steps was barefoot.

'We'll get some more boots soon,' Love told him. 'Soon's we kill some more Yankees.' He laughed at Colby. 'Better encouragement than final victory, footwear.'

The interior of the house also showed that damage had been done to it. Slashed furniture had been neatly repaired and half the chandeliers seemed to be missing. In a dining room where the furniture should have been of oak, the table, chairs and sideboard were of crude pine and looked as if they had been brought from the kitchen to replace what had been stolen or destroyed. The few candles that burned were in bottles.

Near the head of the table was a group of men and

59

women listening to a banjo. Alongside the player a skeletal, white-haired black man rattled a set of bones in time to the music. From among them a squarely-built soldier with a high forehead, deep-set eyes and a huge cinnamon-coloured beard rose to his feet. Like most of his officers, he wore a neat uniform, with the addition of a yellow sash and a general's stars.

'Who have you there, Micah?' he asked.

Love shrugged. 'Says he's a British soldier, General. Got a fancy name long as your arm.'

The other man frowned. 'We're not over-fond of Britishers with fancy names,' he said slowly. 'What might it be?'

'Colby William Rollo Goff,' Colby said. 'Watching the war for the *Morning Advertiser*.'

'Not fighting in it?'

'It's not my war, sir.'

'He was writing it up for the other side, General,' Love said. 'We picked him up near Magruderville. We did a mighty good job there but we didn't find Cluseret.'

The general considered for a moment. 'We've had Vizetelly of *The London Illustrated News* and Colonel Garnet Wolseley,' he said. 'Good soldier that. Do you know him?'

'Yes, sir.' It wasn't hard to recall Wolseley. He was only small, with one eye and a limp, but there was something powerful about his personality. 'I met him in Washington. I heard he bribed a Federal officer with a cigar and a fisherman with a boat with a sovereign to carry him across Potomac.'

The general smiled. 'Slipped into the States from Canada, I believe. What do you say to joining us and writing up our side for a change?'

'All the same to me, sir,' Colby said cheerfully. 'The *Morning Advertiser* might even be pleased.'

The general put out his hand. 'Stuart,' he said. 'James Ewell Brown Stuart, major-general; Confederate Southern Army. You must forgive me if I don't join you in a drink but I've been a lifelong teetotaller.'

Someone pushed a punch into Colby's hand and the

banjo player struck up again. One of the men began to sing 'Lorena' and two more joined him in a shaky trio.

One of the girls approached Colby. 'We're havin' a ball here soon, Mr Goff. The General likes dancin' and it sure enough looks as though the army will be movin' north again soon. So we thought it might be a good idea. Everybody helps. I hope you-all will stay. I'm Hannah-May Burtle. My brother's with General Lee.'

She had a pale pretty face and a bosom that reminded Colby of Georgina, and she delivered her chatter in a breathless rush. None of it seemed very interesting or important but, he thought, her features and her shape were all right and he decided if he got to go to the ball she talked about, he'd make a point of seeking her out.

Two days later, dressed in a blue serge coat and trousers and with an oilcloth cape against the rain, Colby rode out with Love's regiment of Stuart's cavalry towards the Rappahannock, where Union troops had been seen. He was armed with nothing but the Colt revolver he carried for self-protection, but Ackroyd had added a sword.

'If I'm going near a battle,' he said, 'I want a weapon in me fist.'

There was a cheerful air as they left camp with the men singing as they went.

'If you want to see the Devil ... have a good time –
                    Jine the cavalry.'

The song was light-hearted and there was an air of gaiety about the files as they thudded down the road. But to Colby there was an air of desperation, too. Issue clothing was in rags and half of them wore trousers and hats stripped from dead Northerners. Most of the horses were captured mounts and most were gaunt. Colby's was a rawboned mare and Ackroyd straddled a minute animal so swamped by its heavy saddle, only its ears and tail appeared to show.

It was a mixed command. After three years of war, the old district regiments had been split up and there were

61

even Germans from Bavaria, Baden and Wurtemburg who sympathised with the South, and French mill-workers from Roswell in Georgia. Like the waggons, the guns that jolted and rolled at the tail of the column all bore the letters 'US' to show they had been captured from the Northern army.

They were short of everything, even officers. Instead of being commanded by a full colonel, the regiment was run by Love who hadn't long been promoted from major, and instead of three majors there was only one. The squadrons – or companies as they were called, because they were used to fighting as infantry – were run by captains or lieutenants and instead of the eighty-odd officers there were only fifty, most of them mere boys. Love's sole major was a short grizzled man with the accent of a backwoods farmer whose uniform was wrinkled and covered with dust.

'Ed Farley,' he introduced himself. 'I ain't no soldier. I just learned to shoot straight, that's all.'

'Don't you take any notice of him,' Love grinned. 'Ed's a dab hand.' He jerked a hand to where one of the captains was riding on the flank with a troop of men, a long, lean figure whose heels seemed almost to trail on the ground. 'We're luckier than most. We've got some know-how in this regiment. That's Jabez Jenkins. He was a builder who gave it up to become a horse-doctor. He isn't so good with a gun but he sure knows what to do with horses and bridges.' He gestured towards the guns bouncing behind their limbers. 'We've also got Sigsbee who was with Pelham until he was killed. Pelham was the best artillerist in the South.'

As darkness came, clouds crowded across the thin moon and the rain came down. Within an hour, under the dozens of hooves, the dusty road became a quagmire, the waggons sinking up to their axles, the horses up to their hocks, and, huddled under his oilcloth cape, Colby noticed it was growing colder. But the men around him didn't complain and even tried to be cheerful, though there was a kind of numb heroism about them, too, a dumb sense of fatalism because they were as aware as the Northerners that the tide had started to run against them.

The following morning they moved on again, heading northwest. Love was in the lead with Colby alongside him. He had studied history at Charlottesville University before joining the army and had gained his experience on the frontier against Indians.

'It was the silence was the worst,' he said. 'You'd be waitin' with your heart thumpin' and your breath caught in your throat, then suddenly they'd be all round you, whoopin' and shootin' and cuttin' and stabbin' and wantin' to rearrange your hair and insides. You sure needed strong nerves.'

He was silent for a while then he turned in the saddle. 'I guess things have changed some since then. This war's not only different, it gets more different every day. Once we could stampede the Bluebellies at will. Now they've found their courage and it gets harder. You ever see anythin' of their cavalry?

'I met Custer in Washington.'

The thin-featured, sharp-nosed Northerner had been ambitious and full of confidence, a curious mixture of disciplinarian and insubordinate subordinate. Colby hadn't liked him much but it had stuck out a mile he was a cavalryman to his fingertips.

Love was nodding. 'Sure is a good soldier,' he said. 'How about Sheridan?'

'I met him too. Typical Irishman. Willing to fight anyone – even his own side. He's transformed their horsemen. And he's got a lot of good men like Custer round him.'

A bleak expression crossed Love's face and he began to talk, almost as if his worries were crowding in on him and he needed to tell them to someone and had chosen Colby because what he had to say might be considered defeatist by his friends. 'We whipped 'em in the spring at Chancellorsville,' he said. 'And when their cavalry tried to get into Georgia we wiped 'em up and captured the lot.' He sighed. 'Things have changed since Gettysburg, though, and we're fast runnin' out of horses. With the blockade we can't get any more, while they can import as many as they want.

We're losing 'em all the time, from disease and lack of forage. The men aren't much better. There's scurvy in Lee's army and they've just reduced the rations again. I reckon we're the longest, leanest soldiers in the world.'

He was silent for a while. 'The way they run things is crazy,' he went on after a while. 'Richmond's supposed to provide feed, shoes and smithying and pays us forty cents a day for our horses, and their value if they're killed. But if they're lost any other goddam way – captured or worn out or break a leg – we have to find another ourselves or transfer to the infantry. It takes away half our strength, because there's always a horde of men away tryin' to find a new horse. I once saw one of our farriers leadin' a string of limpin' nags with greased heel, and slung over the saddles were the hooves of more dead ones. They'd cut 'em off for the sake of the shoes. That's no way to fight a war.'

As he became silent again, a horseman appeared in the distance. Immediately, Love's hand went up and the column scattered into the trees on either side of the road. Colby's horse, which had a habit of neighing at every mount she met, lifted her head and he hit her quickly about the ears with his gauntlet to stop her.

Love watched the approaching rider from the undergrowth. 'In a darned hurry,' he observed.

The approaching horseman was almost on top of them when he swung his mount out. 'Halt!' he roared.

The rider turned out to be a boy, pink-cheeked, excited and ragged. 'Colonel,' he said, 'the Yankees –!'

'What about the Yankees, boy?' Love's eyes narrowed as he leaned forward from the saddle.

'Five miles away, sir! At Parks Bridge! It's Sheridan. I saw him myself. Custer's with him. I saw his yellow hair.'

'Go on, boy! Go on!'

'They're searching for the army, Colonel.'

'Whose army?'

'Our army, sir! Your army! My army! The Army of Northern Virginia! They're heading south-west, sir, towards Charlottesville.'

'Are they, by God?' Love swung his horse round. 'Then

it's our job to warn the general and get between 'em to hold 'em off.'

'Colonel –' the boy's voice cracked and rose to an excited squeak '– that's not all!'

'There's more?'

'Yes, sir. There sure is! They've left their waggons behind 'em alongside the railroad at Marble Stop. There's trains there and only a small guard.'

Love leaned over and grasped the boy's coat. 'How do I know you're not lyin' to get us ambushed?'

'Sir, I wouldn't lie! I lost my Daddy at Chancellorsville and two of my brothers with General Pickett at Gettysburg. I'm all that's left.'

Love released him. 'I think you're tellin' the truth, boy.' He gestured to one of his soldiers. 'Find him food and drink, Henry, and water his horse! Curtis, take six men and ride back at the gallop to the General and tell him what the boy says. He'll want to move across to cover the army.' He swung round and slapped at Farley with his gloves, raising a puff of dust. 'Ed, split the command down the centre! Tell Jabez to take one half to watch Custer. We'll take the other half and drop on the waggon train.'

They found the waggon train alongside the railway track at Marble Stop, just as the boy had warned. The vedettes came tearing back, pointing and grinning.

'They're still unloadin', Colonel,' one of them chirruped. 'They ain't even got outposts in place.'

Love's raised arm swept forward and the whole column, its bouncing guns cutting deep grooves in the turf, cantered forward. Reaching a belt of trees, the pace slowed and they began to pick their way through. At the far side, Farley was waiting.

'Right in front, Micah,' he said. 'An' a nice slope down, to give us weight.'

They were at the top of a meadow that ran downwards to the railway track without any impediment of fences, ditches or brushwood. A cold sun was shining on the twin rails running north-west from Richmond to the curve of a hill in the distance, where they disappeared between the trees. A huddle of wooden sheds and a line of poles indicated a telegraph, and two trains of freight and flat cars were watering their engines from a high tank. In the fields alongside there seemed to be hundreds of tents, waggons, horses and men.

'Jesus Christ in the Mountains!' Love was staring through his glass. 'Sheridan must have brought 'em down for a drive on Richmond, and as usual that hothead Custer was in such a goddam hurry, he's moved off without 'em.'

'It's perfect cavalry country,' Colby observed.

'Sure is. And they've laid it wide open for us.' Love grinned. 'Custer's reputation,' he pointed out. 'He reckons it's enough to keep away marauders. We'll show him he's wrong. It isn't often the Lord God gives us a chance like this these days.'

He rode back to his command, waving his arm. 'Column into line,' he called and the column broke up into companies which moved away among the trees, swinging to face the slope in front until there was a grey line of horsemen waiting just out of sight on the reverse slope of the hill, silent except for the soft snorting of the animals and the jingling of bits. There was a low hiss as sabres were drawn.

'Shove those things away,' Love said contemptuously. 'We aren't going to fight with carving knives. Draw your pistols.'

He reached into a saddle holster and thrust an enormous revolver at Colby. 'It's a LeMatt,' he said. 'Nine chambers and an over-and-under barrel. Fires .52 bullets and a charge of buckshot.'

'I'm not fighting your damned war,' Colby said hotly.

'Maybe you're afraid of bangs,' Love grinned. 'That guy, Fremantle, who came over – he'd never seen a shot fired in action in his life.'

Colby frowned. 'Perhaps he hadn't,' he said. 'But *I* have.'

'Where?'

'Light Brigade, Balaclava, for one.'

Love's eyebrows almost disappeared under his hairline.

66

'You were in *that*?' he said.

'And a few more.'

'Then what in tarnation are we waitin' for?' Raising his sword, Love let out a shrill yelp and kicked his horse direct from a standstill to a gallop. Colby was caught by surprise as the rest of the horsemen hurtled past him, yelling shrilly, and poured down the slope.

He looked at Ackroyd and shrugged. 'Seems we're going to war, Tyas,' he said and kicked at his horse's flanks.

Love's yell had set the blue-coated soldiers swarming about like ants in a disturbed nest. As the horsemen approached there was a movement away from the rails and, in a moment, the Federals were streaming towards the woods at the far side of the valley, led by a colonel.

'Political,' someone yelled delightedly. 'See him go!'

No more than a few shots were fired, then the Confederates were pouring over the rails and swinging round the freight cars in grey eddies like water from a broken dam. The engineer of one of the diamond-stacked locomotives attempted to get his engine moving and a jet of steam shot into the air with a shower of sparks, cinders and clinker, but a sergeant rode alongside and pushed his gun into the engineer's face, and the steam hissed out.

There was no fighting. The Federals had all disappeared, and when Colby arrived, Love, his hat gone, was swinging his horse in circles, from spraying out in all directions, looking for someone to kill.

'Sutlers,' he said furiously. 'Goddam supply troops! Not worth shootin'!'

Already the whole camp was ablaze, hundreds of tents burning together. The freight cars were on fire too, now, with the buildings, all going up in one vast conflagration. A trooper started to swarm up one of the telegraph posts and was called down again by a young officer with a shrill voice.

'Come down, George, you darned fool!' he yelled. 'There's an easier way than that!'

He gestured and one of the troopers ran towards the hut

where they heard him smashing the equipment. Then another man found an axe, and the poles came crashing down across the burning freight cars.

The smoke was lifting into the sky in a brown rolling column and the din was tremendous as excited men yelped with glee or fired off their pistols into the air. Then the yells changed to laughter as a load of champagne was found, and corks began to pop until Love dashed among the yelling men, swinging his fists.

'Cut that out,' he roared. 'Any man who gets drunk gets left behind!'

But there was no stopping them where the fruit and vegetables were concerned, or among the canned meat, oysters, lobsters, cases of beer, barrels of sugar, and eggs packed in salt, all in danger of being roasted. There was clothing, too, and the siding was converted in a moment into a vast dressing room as yelling, laughing men supplied themselves with overcoats, blue trousers, woollen socks and boots, dragging them on, one on top of another, so that there would be spares not only for themselves but also for their friends.

A man with a beard and long hair was hopping about one-legged, trying to heave a pair of trousers over the grey rags he already wore. An officer was smashing kegs of spirit and soldiers on their knees were trying to lap it up, indifferent to the whacks delivered across their backs by the flat of the officer's sword. More ragged men were swallowing pickled oysters and potted lobster, others were hacking at an enormous cheese or emptying bottles of wine, while still more were snatching up blankets and even lowering and rolling tents to carry them away. Yelling like madmen, the officers were trying to preserve order and a whole flood of captured horses was being driven up the slopes to the trees, ridden bareback by ragged riders leading their own mounts.

As the ammunition and powder went up in a colossal explosion, they all ducked and ran, clinging to rearing, frightened, white-eyed horses. Planks, wheels and timbers soared into the air with pieces of metal, sacks and boxes of food, to come thudding down in a shower. By a miracle nobody was hurt.

Love, his face blackened by smoke, grinned at Colby. 'You-all sure found somethin' here to write about!' he yelled.

Many of the Federal soldiers who had bolted for the woods had tossed down their weapons and Love's men were picking them up in armfuls. Baggage, waggons, newly-slaughtered and dressed sides of beef lay around in confusion, and Love's men were rounding up blue-coated soldiers in dozens. Then scattered shooting started from the woods but Sigsbee had brought his guns round the trees at the gallop and, swinging round, the iron-shod wheels carving the turf into the great black swathes, they came into line. Men jumped off at the run and within a moment one of them banged out in a puff of white smoke. As it rolled back, bouncing on its wheels, they saw the shell strike the trees, bringing two of them down. Two more guns were brought into action and they could see the Federals moving about in the undergrowth searching for shelter. Then a rider burst from the wood and started westwards, low over his horse's neck.

'Gone to tell Custer,' Love commented to Farley as he watched with narrowed eyes. 'We'd better call the boys off, Ed.'

Gathering the troopers into column, they trotted back up the slope and round the edge of the woods, every man with coats, trousers and boots strung across his saddle, rifles and pistols festooning his figure, and bottles, tins and sacks of food hanging from his belt. Behind them, mounted on captured horses or waggon mules, were the prisoners, sometimes riding two to a mount, and behind them again, driven by troopers whose mounts trotted on lead reins in rear three dozen waggons loaded with equipment, clothing and food. 'Reckon we'd better go find Jabez now,' Love said. 'Before Custer finds him for us.'

They found Jenkins sitting on a hill near Parks Bridge staring into the distance. It was bitterly cold now and there had been a few flurries of snow, so that he was wrapped in a blanket as he gazed through his telescope. He was a lugubrious-looking man with a dreadful scar, gained at Chancellorsville, stretching down the side of his face.

'Custer ain't givin' up none,' he said. 'He's still heading for Charlottesville. But Curtis came back to say the general was moving between him and Lee. There's one other thing.' He gestured into the distance. 'He's sent one regiment back towards Marble Stop.' Jenkins grinned, his thin face crinkling under its fuzz of beard. 'It's right there in front, Colonel, all on its ownsome, looking for a fight.'

Love grinned. 'Maybe we'd better give 'em one,' he said. 'That Custer's goin' to split his force just once too often.'

Leaving the guns to catch up, Love drove his men as fast as they could ride and came up with the Federal horsemen at noon the following day. Scouting ahead, Jenkins had found a position in the trees across their path and Love sent one of his squadrons to the right under Farley to watch the flank.

They waited in silence as the first file of blue-coated men breasted the hill where they had halted. As they paused on the summit, they seemed to suspect something was wrong, then they began to move warily forward again.

'Classic ambush,' Love observed calmly. 'Get out your little notebook, Coll. *These* aren't lines of supply troops, and we'll show you how we deal with 'em.'

The Union soldiers still seemed uncertain and Jenkins was rocking back and forth in his saddle as if trying to urge them on. 'We got 'em,' he breathed. 'Come on, Bluebellies. A bit further. Just a bit further.'

As he spoke, however, a shot brought their heads round and Colby saw a Union vedette go tearing along the fringe of the trees towards the column, pointing back to where Love's men waited.

'Goddam!' Love snapped. 'Where did he come from?'

'The sonofabitch saw us!' Jenkins wailed as the Federals immediately began to open out into line, and an officer came tearing up the slope to place himself in front.

'Guess this is it,' Love said, and the Confederates moved out of the trees at a trot across the long slope towards the waiting Union troops.

The Federal cavalry had halted again, as if uncertain what they were facing, and for a while there was a lot of manoeuvring and waiting. Then the column of Union soldiers came over the summit of the hill in line of battle, drawing slowly nearer until they were within four hundred yards of the Confederates. The officer in front waved his sword to order a charge and it looked for a moment as if the whole line was going to crash into the Confederate ranks. But Colby noticed that a number of the blue-coated horsemen were reining in and he knew immediately what it meant. The untrained Russian cavalry at Balaclava had shown the same hesitation when faced by the Heavies, and the British, leaping at once to a charge as their forward momentum stopped, had routed twice their own number. These men in front of him were inexperienced and as uneager to advance as the Russians.

'Now,' he said to Love. 'Now!'

Love gave him a fleeting grin and a nod, then turned to order a charge. As he did so, there was a crackle of firing from the blue line and he was flung back, his spine bending over the crown of the saddle. Two more saddles were also emptied and as Love recovered his balance and huddled, bent double over his horse's neck, Colby heard him groan.

'Jesus Christ and all His pink angels,' he moaned. 'The bastards have hit me!'

His face had gone grey and he was already swaying. As a sergeant appeared alongside and held him upright, he lifted his head, slowly as if it weighed a ton, and held out his sword to Colby.

'You rode at Balaclava?' he whispered.

'Yes, I did.'

'Then go to it. Show the boys how to do it.'

Colby gazed at him for a moment then he took the sword and spurred to the front of the line. Federal pistols were still crackling away and two more men rolled from the saddle and a horse went down with a crash. Ackroyd had joined him, no longer mounted on his ridiculous little horse but on one of the splendid Union chargers captured at Marble Stop. He, too had seen the opportunity that had been presented and was settling himself in the saddle and reaching for the sabre he had acquired.

As the Union firing died, Colby sensed that the blue-coated men had all discharged their weapons in the surprise of seeing the Confederates and, now feverishly trying to reload, were virtually defenceless.

'Sabres!' he roared. 'While they're hesitating!'

It was against all the rules of the game as played on this side of the Atlantic but he sensed he was right. Then, as he set off up the slope followed by Ackroyd, it occurred to him that, since he wasn't a Confederate officer, he might be heading for the enemy alone. But, glancing round, he saw that the grey line was following him, not exactly with the precision of a line of highly-drilled British cavalry, but well enough. Here and there it ballooned as the men watched their front rather than their neighbours, and in parts where men had better mounts it had even edged in front of him so that he could see the bobbing rumps and floating tails and the clods of turf kicked up by iron-shod hooves. A wild yell broke out and he could see several of the men, caught by the elation of the charge, swinging their swords.

'Points,' he screamed. 'Give points!'

A Union battery had appeared over the crown of the hill and was trying to swing into line. The guns had already been unhitched and the teams were being trotted back down the slope as the two lines came together. Colby was several lengths ahead of his nearest men, with Ackroyd just on his quarter, and seeing the screaming horsemen coming towards them, the Bluecoats had started to edge backwards so that the shock of the collision sent the whole line recoiling on itself. Horses reared and fell as they were barged backwards and several went down, their riders flung under the flashing hooves.

Colby found himself facing the officer who had taken command. He was a big man with a black beard, but he hadn't the slightest idea how to use a sabre. As he slashed,

Colby parried and, as he thrust under his guard, the officer vanished over the tail of his horse. There had been no time for Colby to bind the sword knot of the weapon round his hand and it was wrenched from his hand. As he swung away, reaching for his pistol, he saw the grey line surge among the Federals, fighting hand-to-hand in a din of clashing sabres, the rattle of small arms, frenzied curses and appeals for mercy. A sergeant on a bay horse broke from the mêlée and headed for Colby, swinging a rifle by its barrel. Grabbing for Love's LeMatt, Colby cocked it with his thumb. The kick as he pulled the trigger almost knocked him off his horse but the sergeant's face disappeared in a bubbling mask of red, and he crashed past, both the reins and the rifle dropped, to claw at his face. As he brushed by, spraying Colby with blood, a thin high shriek came from the hole where his mouth had been.

'Christ, sir,' Ackroyd said, appearing alongside. 'What the 'ell was in that thing?'

The blue line was beginning to fray now as the outside riders drew back, and finally the whole lot began to turn their horses and swing away, the Confederates in pursuit. There was a pell-mell rush, and Colby saw a second smaller column of blue-coated riders coming up the slope to the rescue.

But then, from the corner of his eye, he saw Farley's squadron coming across the field flat out, crouching over the necks of their horses, the animals at a stretch gallop, manes and tails flying. There was a distinct crash as they smashed into the side of the fresh squadron. Horses and men went down, bowled over by the impetus of the charge and Colby found himself with Ackroyd and several others swirling round the battery. Gunners jabbed at him with sponge staffs and one of the guns actually fired. Men went down as the shell tore through the crowded riders, then a sword smashed down on the head of the gunner and he rolled between the wheels, screaming, blood pouring through his fingers as they clutched at his scalp.

There was no longer any leadership on either side. Farley's men were boring in from the flank, mingling with the rest of the grey-coated riders, then abruptly, the Federals broke and fell back, the Confederates still locked with them in a confused battle.

'Rally,' Colby roared. 'Rally on me!'

He swung his horse in circles, his pistol high in the air. At first he thought the wild Confederate horsemen hadn't enough discipline to obey, but gradually the fighting died and they swung away in ones and twos and groups to line up behind him. The Federal cavalry were streaming away through the woods now, followed by infantry who paused from time to time to fire a volley.

Farley appeared, grinning, his face dripping sweat despite the cold. 'Guess we'd better vamoose, son,' he said. 'Before that Custer finds out. That sure was a neat bit o' work.'

As the smoke slowly drifted away, the field was littered with blue-clad figures, one or two of them trying to crawl to safety on hands and knees. A sergeant appeared alongside Colby carrying two guidons.

'Thought these here would look right nice in your boudoir, sir,' he said, saluting.

'You don't salute me,' Colby said. 'I'm not your officer.'

The sergeant grinned. 'Sure looked like you was, sir,' he said. 'That's the first time I ever seen anybody win a battle with cutlery.'

6

'According to Micah Love, Mr Goff, you distinguished yourself near Parks Bridge.'

With Love safely established in bed, Colby, still haggard with weariness, his clothes daubed with mud, waited as Stuart rolled up the map he had been studying. With generations of horsemen behind him, Love's sortie had been meat and drink to him.

With Custer's remaining half-column quartering the countryside for the men who had destroyed his supplies, it had been Colby who had got the regiment on the road again. The river had been high when they had regained it and, with the horses exhausted and the weary riders' heads hanging almost to the pommels as they dozed in the saddles, there had been a danger that they would be trapped, until Colby, riding up and down the bank, found the abutments of an old bridge. Jenkins' skill as a builder had been clear as he had dragged down a deserted barn and used the ancient timbers to reconstruct it, and, as Colby and Sigsbee's guns had waited with the rearguard, the waggons had trundled across. Smoke was already curling from the timbers as the last man reached safety and, as they had turned their horses at the top of the far bank to watch the flames, they had seen the first of Custer's troopers galloping down to the river.

Stuart was still studying Colby speculatively. 'You have a cavalryman's eye, I think,' he said. 'Why not join us? We could do with good men. I could find you a place on my staff and arrange with Richmond to grant you a major's rank.'

Colby shook his head. 'I was only helping, sir. The

Morning Advertiser might object if they found their correspondent getting too involved.'

Stuart sighed. 'I have to accept your decision,' he said. 'Under the circumstances, you'd better ride to Neese Ford. Colonel Love has relations there who'll probably wish to be with him until he's recovered.'

The road south was rutted by waggons and caissons, and occasionally they came across wrecks with shattered wheels and the whitened skeletons of mules and horses. Virginia creeper had already half-covered them, its flaming colours fading. In a hollow in the trees they passed a wrecked gun and, in a clearing in a cornfield, the grave of a group of Northern soldiers killed in a raid south during the summer. There were no names, just regimental buttons tied to the crude crosses and the single message – 'Nine Northern Soldiers. Rest in God.'

The wild pawpaws had been opened by the frost and the rhododendrons and mountain laurel were busy with feeding quail. Behind, mountains like gigantic waggons marched southwards into infinity.

Neese Ford rested in a valley below the curve of a hill, and a river ran in the shadows where withered frosty grass lay among the dead remains of the summer's flowers. On top of the slope was a farm building that had been built of clapboard as if it had originated in Kent. It was painted white with dark green shutters, and hanging over it were leafless oaks. Beyond it, the winter fields were white with rime.

Colby stared about him. Ackroyd and the two troopers who had accompanied them were tethering their mounts to the rail and hitching at their trousers.

'Give 'em a shout,' Colby said.

'Anybody to home?' One of the troopers threw back his head and yelled.

There was no sound.

'Guess they've gone to Richmond, or mebbe Atlanta or Charleston,' the trooper said. 'It's a mite safer down there.'

The house appeared to be empty, though everything was in order, the antimacassars neat on the chairs, the family photographs in rows on a sideboard. Then Colby saw a glass of tea with the steam still curling above it.

'Somebody's home,' he said. 'Give 'em another yell.'

The silence after the trooper's shout seemed deeper than before and Colby frowned. There were no cattle or horses in the fields, no negro workers, and no indication of life. Yet the house didn't look neglected, despite the peeling paint. Suddenly wary of marauders, he laid his hand on the gigantic LeMatt revolver Love had given him. Then, in the silence, he heard a shot, and, dashing round the house, saw one of the troopers just pushing his carbine back into its saddle bucket. Twenty yards away a turkey lay kicking in the roadway, a few feathers still floating down.

'Came out as cool as you please,' the trooper said. 'Thought at first it was a Yankee.'

He picked up the turkey and, using his knife to bare the tendons of a leg, threaded the other through it and hung the bird over the pommel of his saddle.

The shot had brought no reaction from the house and, finally convinced nobody was at home, Colby was standing near the closed doors of the stable when he heard a faint clink inside. Swinging round, he put his eye to a crack in the door. Inside he could see a big chestnut horse. As he began to open the door, a female voice stopped him.

'You-all! Hold hard!' The voice was firm, strong and unhesitating. 'You're not havin' my horse! It's the last we've got and we need it!'

'Look –!'

'I've got an axe in my hand,' the voice came again. 'You just open those doors and I'll sink it in your head. I mean it. I aim to keep this horse.'

'For God's sake –' Colby's voice rose' – who wants to steal your damned horse, Ma'am? I've come from General Stuart with a message for you.'

There was a long silence, then he heard chains being moved and a bolt being pushed back. Slowly the door opened and through the gap a girl emerged.

'Who're you?' she asked.

'I'm from the cavalry.'

'I can tell that – from the smell of the horses! Whose cavalry?'

'General Stuart's. I've been sent to find you.'

For a moment she didn't speak. She was very young, tiny with a heart-shaped face and enormous slanting violet eyes under a fringe of dark hair. Her mouth was too wide, though it curved upwards at the ends as though she enjoyed laughter, and her body was slender to the point of skinniness, lacking the rich curves of Hannah-May Burtle, her wrists so thin they looked brittle, though he noticed that she held the restive horse without trouble.

Though her appearance was undramatic, her face a curious mixture, as though it had been put together haphazardly, her straight back and her wary expression indicated a firm will, a strong mind and a no-nonsense attitude to handsome strangers appearing on her land. Wondering what Georgina would have done if she'd been faced with a Northern cavalryman, Colby decided she'd probably have had a fit of the vapours and got herself raped for her trouble.

Small as she was, the girl was staring at him hostilely. 'How do I know you're not Yankees?' she asked.

'Do I sound like a Yankee? I'm English.'

'Then why're you wearing blue?'

'It's not a uniform.'

'Your men are wearing blue pants.'

'Taken from Yankee cavalrymen, Ma'am. Two days ago. At Marble Stop. We gave 'em a bloody nose.'

'You a Southern officer?' She wasn't intending to relax without good reason.

'No, Ma'am,' Colby said. 'I'm not.'

'Then what were you doing at Marble Stop with Southern soldiers?'

'Mere accident, Ma'am. I'm supposed to be a correspondent for the *Morning Advertiser* in London.'

The blaze went out of her eyes and she dropped her gaze

and blushed. 'Everybody wants to steal our horses,' she said. 'We've only got one left to pull the buggy. I'm Augusta Burtle Dabney.'

'Handsome name, Miss Augusta.'

'Big,' she agreed. 'Important. Maybe because I'm so small. Most people call me Gussie.'

'Colby Goff, Miss Gussie.'

She gave a sudden grin that changed her whole face, melting the stern expression and setting her mouth in a long curve.

'Guess I'd better call Ma,' she said. 'She's upstairs hiding with her head under a pillow.' She was about to turn away when she stopped again, frowning. 'You said you'd got a message from General Stuart,' she went on. 'Has something happened?'

'Yes, Miss Gussie. I don't bring the best of news. Your cousin, Micah Love, was hurt at Parks Bridge and the General thought you might like to come to his bedside.'

For a second she gaped at him then the violet eyes blazed again. 'Land's sakes!' she said. 'Why didn't you say so? Here, get this animal into the buggy while I go get Ma.'

They left within the hour, Mrs Dabney, a plump, pink-faced woman who clearly hadn't her daughter's straight-forward courage huddled in rugs alongside Ackroyd, who was driving the carriage. The troopers rode as vanguard, and Colby trotted behind with the girl, who sat astride Ackroyd's horse, her skirts carefully draped to cover her legs. Despite its size, she had it well under control.

'Born in the saddle,' she pointed out calmly. 'Did a few laps before breakfast every mornin' on Pa's back. 'We all ride 'cept Ma, who came from Atlanta and only saw a horse when it was between shafts.' She ran her hand over the pommel of the saddle. 'Ought to be a side saddle, by rights. Pa'd have fits if he saw me like this.'

Colby eyed her curiously. 'Don't all that horse-sweaty leather come a bit hard on your – er –'

'My unmentionables?' She gave him a quick smile and lifted the edge of her skirt. Underneath it, he saw a pair of boots and cord trousers. 'Belonged to my brother Marston. He was a bit younger then. They fit me fine.'

'There was talk of a ball. You'll find 'em a bit warm for dancing, won't you?'

She flashed him another smile. 'I got other unmentionables,' she said. 'With frills and lace and all on 'em. Packed in the trunk. I also got a hoop skirt. Still has the white roses of 1860 on it. It was my cousin Louie's. She married a boy from Memphis and gave it to me when she went down there to live. It's right handsome, but it looked better on her, I guess. I haven't the shape.'

'Where's your brother now?'

Her face tightened. 'He was killed at Gettysburg. I've got another with a Philadelphia regiment.'

'A Northerner?'

'It's not all that odd,' she retorted sharply. 'You ask General Stuart. His wife's father's a Northern general and her brother's fightin' for the South.'

'Where do *your* sympathies lie?'

Her eyes flashed. 'With the boys who do the fighting,' she said quickly. 'Of both sides. It's a politicians' war.'

'I suspect they *all* are.'

'And the South's going to lose it, I think.'

It was the first cold logical appraisal of the situation he'd heard from anyone and it startled him, coming from a girl.

'You think so?'

'Don't you?'

There was no point in beating about the bush. She seemed strong-minded enough to look harsh facts in the face.

'Yes, Miss Gussie, I do.'

She seemed satisfied that he had agreed with her. 'I think all we can do now is go on fightin' until we can finally give up with honour.' She managed a wry smile. 'Maybe it's the best thing, anyway, because peace will be awful.'

She seemed so small and slight, and at the same time so realistic and courageous, he found he was concerned. 'What'll happen to you?'

She shrugged. 'I guess we'll be all right. Pa has business

80

interests in Washington. They're bein' looked after. That's how my brother, Fitz, came to join the Northerners. Marston stayed in the south. He was here when it started and he and Micah Love were friends.'

'It's a strange position.'

She gave him her quick grin. 'It couldn't be more neutral, though, could it? I expect it'll be all right whoever wins. My father knows Abe Lincoln. Either way, we shan't sit and weep. Ma might, but not Pa and me. We're not that kind. If we win, that's fine. If God should decide it goes the other way, I for one shan't walk about with my heart on my sleeve cryin' for the old days.' She paused. 'Last year it was easier. I guess we're beginnin' to see it different now.'

The skies were heavy as they stopped at an inn along the road. The place was in a state of disrepair and run entirely by a worn-looking woman whose husband was with Lee. There was little to offer but bacon, coffee and potatoes.

'It's like this all over the state now,' Mrs Dabney said sorrowfully. 'They tell me there are women and children and old folk who never taste anythin' but boiled oats and corn meal mess.'

'Even the Yankees have to bring their own provisions when they come south,' Augusta went on. 'It's better in Atlanta, of course, but even *they've* not got much to laugh about, with all the luxuries stopped by the blockade and all the boys with the army.'

It was still bitterly cold when they went outside again and the sky seemed full of crows that moved from one clump of trees to another, cawing dismally, like a flock of evil omens. Augusta watched them with her huge slanting eyes, her thick dark eyebrows drawn together in a frown.

'There's nothing to fear from the Yankees down here,' Colby said.

'It isn't the Yankee troops I'm thinkin' of,' she said. 'It's the end of the war.' She watched the crows for a little longer. 'It was excitin' at first,' she said slowly. 'Even to me. There were even times when I wished I could be with the armies and Ma once slapped me when I said I ought to go and work in the hospitals. But you got swept along.

Everythin' was so wonderful. There was victory after victory and everybody said the Yankees were cowards.' She stopped again. 'I guess they weren't really. Then when General Lee took the army north last year we were all wild with excitement and began to say the Yankees would know what it was like to have the war fought over *their* country-side. We wanted to see Pennsylvania a sheet of flame. I guess *I* did anyway, and we all said with one more victory the war would be over.'

Colby listened quietly. In her words was a nation's agony.

'But then in July all the news stopped.' Her voice had grown quieter. 'It was slow in comin' because it had to come a long way. And when nothin' arrived we began to dread what had happened. It was not knowin' was the worst. While we waited, we heard that Vicksburg had fallen and the Confederacy was cut in two. That was bad enough, but just then we hardly noticed. I was in Rich-mond at the time visitin' with my kinfolk and everybody knew somethin' dreadful had happened. People waited in groups and stood on porches in the sun, tryin' to say no news was good news when they knew it wasn't anythin' of the kind. Then we started gettin' rumours that a big battle at Gettysburg had been lost.' She sat in the saddle stiff and straight, her face blank, as though reliving a nightmare. 'People began to wait at the railroad where the telegraph was, but nothin' came so everybody went to the newspaper office. They brought out casualty lists. My brother's name was in them. I didn't think I'd ever get over it.'

Abruptly she relaxed and managed a twisted smile. 'But, I have, Mr Goff. I have. Most times, anyway.'

Her cheeks grew a little pink, as if she'd talked too much, and she looked hard at the crows again. Then she turned to Colby. 'You-all have learned a lot about me, Mr Goff,' she said. 'What about you? Why are you in America writin' for the papers?'

'Because I'm a soldier, Miss Gussie.'

'*Why?*'

'Because my father was. And he was because *his* father

82

was, and his grandfather, and his great-grandfather. I think we were soldiers when Boadicea fought off the Romans. We're too stupid to be parsons or go into business, but too honest to be politicians. It only leaves the army. My father was at Waterloo. My great-grandfather raised the regiment I'm in. It's a good regiment. Nineteenth of the Line. Only cavalry regiment in the British army to wear green.'

'Why?'

He gazed at her, wondering if she were pulling his leg. 'Has to,' he said. 'Always has.'

She seemed puzzled that it should matter so much and he was equally puzzled that she couldn't see that it did matter.

She was staring at him coolly. 'If you're a soldier, sir,' she said, 'how come you're able to be here writin'. Shouldn't you be back in England guardin' your Queen?'

He smiled at her naïvety. 'I think she's got enough people at home for that,' he said. 'I was on sick leave. I had malaria.'

'We have it further south. Do you have it in England?'

'I was in India at the time. The Sepoy Mutiny.'

'Murderin' black men, I suppose?'

'At least, Miss Gussie,' Colby said gently, 'we only killed 'em. We didn't make 'em slaves.'

The shaft went home. 'We never had slaves,' she said quickly. 'At least, not many. Why did they send you to India?'

'Not *me* in particular. My regiment. It was experience. We'd just come from the fighting in Russia. The Crimea. I expect you've heard of it.'

'I've read Mr Tennyson's poem. It's a fine piece. "*Into the Valley of Death rode the Six Hundred –*"'

'Not impressed myself,' Colby said. 'There were nearly seven hundred of us for a start and *we* never called it the Valley of Death. *That* was the Worontzov Ravine, which was a route from the camps to the trenches, and you couldn't have squeezed a couple of horses down there abreast, let alone ten squadrons.'

She was staring at him with shining eyes. '*You* were with the Light Brigade?' she said. 'How is it you weren't killed?'

'A few of us managed not to be.'

'What a hero Lord Cardigan was!'

Colby's eyebrows rose. 'I doubt if he'd be considered fit to command a corporal's picket in your army.'

'But he was so brave.'

'Bravery don't always go hand in hand with virtue. Ask Tyas there. He's brave enough and he's even been known to swear.'

'Was *he* there, too?'

Ackroyd puffed out his chest. 'That I was, Miss. Right in the front line be'ind the captain. 'E saved me life. Stuck me on 'is 'orse when I'd been wounded.'

'And they sent *you* to India to fight those horrible black murderers after all that?' She was staring at him with shining eyes now. 'Were you with Cousin Micah at Parks Bridge?'

'Couldn't avoid it. He gave me a shove and there I was, right in the middle; we were hoping we might get Custer, but he was somewhere else and we had to be satisfied with one of his colonels!'

She looked shyly at him. 'As a matter of fact, Mr Goff, not only are we related to General Stuart through my mother's side, but we're also related by marriage on the Burtle side to Custer.'

Colby's eyebrows rose. 'You certainly do manage to hedge your bets,' he said.

7

When Colby brought Gussie Dabney and her mother to his room, Micah Love was looking pale and thin, but he managed a faint smile.

'My old flame, Gussie Dabney,' he murmured.

'She was never your old flame, Micah Love,' Mrs Dabney said quickly. 'Your new flame either.'

'She used to throw her dolls at me,' Love whispered. 'That's supposed to be a sign of true affection.'

Augusta gave Colby a quick glance and blushed. 'Well, it wasn't with me,' she said. 'All the same, we're glad to be here to help.'

Love grinned weakly and indicated Colby. 'You'll know by this time all about this handsome devil here, I suppose.'

She became stiff and prim. 'Mr Goff and I have talked.'

'Stuart's throwin' a dance,' Love said. 'It won't be much because his banjoist, Sweeney, died during the winter – I heard it was smallpox – but it'll bring a little good cheer. You goin' to let Gussie go, Mrs Dabney?'

Mrs Dabney was already fluttering round the room, seeking linen and bowls for hot water.

'I guess I'll have to,' she said. 'But it'll be hard for everybody to find somethin' to wear. Everythin's torn up long since for bandages. They say you can even tell a Yankee spy these days because he's the only person wearin' new clothes.'

'Better down round Texas,' Love murmured. 'The people round the coast always got the pick of the blockade runner's cargoes. Texans were always different, though. They had difficulty raisin' infantry regiments down there because nobody in Texas walks, and they had to raise mounted regiments then dismount 'em. Y'all goin' to the dance, Gussie?'

Standing by the bed, small and embarrassed at the teasing, Augusta became severely practical. 'My duty's to look after you.'

'Your duty's to enjoy yourself, Gussie Dabney. You know Stuart. He likes music and company and if I died tomorrow, you'd have wasted a good evenin's entertainment. So go to it. If you want to see a good time, jine the cavalry. Doubtless, Mr Goff will lend you his arm.'

It had been in Colby's mind to seek out Hannah-May Burtle, who was a lot less scrawny and a great deal less prickly, but it was difficult to say so and Love smiled.

'That's settled then,' he said. 'All I ask is that you come and see me from time to time and bring me a glass of punch. It would be nice to get drunk. At least I'd sleep without pain.'

As Augusta bustled off to join her mother, Love laid his hand on Colby's sleeve. 'See she gets a good time,' he murmured. 'It might be the last she'll get for a long while. It might be the last any of us'll get. The General's had word that Sheridan's about to make a move towards Richmond and the whole shebang'll be movin' off to get across his route tomorrow.'

When Colby went downstairs, there was a strange air of gaiety and grimness about the house. The Burtle family were busy putting up decorations and hanging regimental flags on the stairs and over the doors, and neighbours kept arriving with precious candles and sweetmeats.

There was a lot of noise and chatter but behind it there was an atmosphere of tension and the men wore smiles that disappeared the minute they were alone. Further news had come in. Two Federal corps were moving down the cold roads from Culpeper towards Madison Court House; Custer, with fifteen hundred well-mounted men, was in Charlottesville at last; and Stuart was intending to head there the following morning. Maps were spread on tables in quiet rooms and waggons were being discreetly loaded behind the house. There was a great deal of pretence, as if nobody knew what was going on, but Colby saw Hannah-May Burtle with tears in her eyes as she gathered a group of girls round her at the grand piano in the library.

A group of musicians with banjoes and fiddles were settling themselves in the big living room where the carpet had been removed. Despite the cold outside, the room was warm from a blazing fire and aglow with the light of dozens of borrowed candles. As they waited for the music to start, several young officers, one of them a twenty-one-year-old colonel with a wooden leg, clustered round the girls at the piano, their voices thin and reedy over the buzz of conversation in the hall.

The song was clapped and Colby turned to find Augusta Dabney alongside him, the top of her dark head somewhere at the level of his shoulder. She wore a white dress festooned with fading roses, and over her shoulders had draped a yellow scarf of silk. The paleness of the colour set off her olive complexion and dark hair and the mysterious violet eyes. Pity she wasn't a bit less scrawny, he thought, because there was something about her that was curiously disturbing.

She caught his eye on her and lifted the edge of her dress so that he saw the frills round her ankles. 'Not whipcord this time, Mr Goff,' she said, giving him a smile that was intimate and warm and indicated that they already shared secrets. 'They'll sing again,' she observed coolly, glancing at the piano. 'Though they shouldn't. Cousin Burtle always sings off-key, and the tenor's flat.'

He gazed at her, impressed by her forthrightness, and she beamed up at him, confident and sure of herself. 'It'll rain before the night's out, Mr Goff,' she announced. 'I heard thunder, too. While I was dressin'. Considerin' the time of the year, I think the Lord's got it in for us.'

The singing came to its unsteady end and, as the group at the piano split up, Colby heard the steady patter of rain outside. Almost immediately there was a clap of thunder and several of the girls started wailing, putting their hands to their ears and clinging to the arms of the officers. A flash of lightning lit the trees outside with a purple glow and the girls screamed as the thunderclap which followed shook the house.

As the storm struck, the young men made protective noises. They seemed to have come out of the past, their talk, their clothes and their manners reminding Colby strangely of his father. They had arrived in their best, carefully-preserved uniforms wearing cloaks and riding rangy horses; plumed, bearded, proud, and looking as if they were about to set off for Waterloo. It was the same heady atmosphere his father must have felt that night in Brussels at the Duchess of Richmond's ball fifty years ago, before the two great armies clashed on the hillside at Hougoumont.

There was another clap of thunder and more wails.

'It's done for show, Mr Goff.' The cool appraising voice came from alongside. 'To show what tender flowers they are. They're not frightened and neither am I, but if I couldn't get attention without screaming at thunder, then I guess I'd give up and go home.'

He glanced at her, amused. She was only about five feet two in her stockinged feet and was built like a sprite, but there was a stout-heartedness about her that suggested she was in terror of being overlooked and was determined not to be.

Stuart was all smiles and full of gallantry, calming nerves, pretending that nothing was amiss, quietly speaking to the Burtle girls when their expression slipped. The dance started as the storm drifted away among the hills, beginning with charades and a tableau in which the officers took part. As the orchestra struck up the tune, 'Hail, The Conquering Hero Comes', Stuart stepped forward in full uniform, grey tunic, plumed hat, long thigh boots, scarlet-lined cloak, yellow sash and heavy sabre. With a hiss, the long blade was unsheathed. Stuart clearly enjoyed the acting and his eyes were alight as he moved forward and stood with folded arms, his head down, his eyes on the floor in a posture of humility and defiance, while a voice offstage intoned a verse:

> 'To arms, to arms, ye brave!
> The avenging sword unsheath!
> March on, march on, all hearts resolved
> On Victory or Death!'

'Bravo! Bravo!' Shouts interspersed the clapping and Augusta was radiant with enthusiasm.

'No wonder the General's called "Beauty",' she said excitedly. 'He *is* beautiful.' She looked at Colby and realised that his face had unexpected sharp planes and angles that excited her. It was a fine face, she realised, a sensitive, strong face, clean and narrow as the blade of a new axe, the gentleness and strength hidden beneath a frosty British exterior. '*You* are beautiful, too, Mr Goff,' she went on in a sudden rush of confidence. 'There are beautiful women, among whom I never number myself, and there are beautiful men. The General is one. And so are you.'

Colby was startled at the enthusiasm. 'I've shaved,' he smiled. 'That's why. When there's anything requiring valour, whether it's fighting, courting or dancing, I always shave. Young women like it that way and all men are hounds at heart.'

She gave him a bright-eyed glance and grinned. 'It's their most excitin' quality, Mr Goff.'

He grinned back at her. There was something enormously appealing about her forthrightness. She was warm-hearted and generous, had little time for sentiment and, with a strong streak of practicality, believed in standing up for herself, so that he imagined the whole structure of her family rested on her small shoulders. As the music started, he held out his arm.

'May I have this dance, Miss Gussie?'

She smiled and placed her hand on his wrist. 'You bet,' she said.

She was as light as a feather. She danced well and managed to avoid getting her feet trodden on.

'I'm no dancer,' Colby said.

89

'So I notice.'

'But it's easier with you.'

'That's because I'm clever, Mr Goff. With two brothers, I learned to keep from under the feet of a man. There are moves in the North, I'm told, by women who feel that females should be more emancipated. Land's sakes, any girl with a bit of intelligence can wind a man round her little finger!'

'Can you?'

'Not just yet. But I'm practisin' a lot. I shall always remain myself, though, and people who don't like it can go to hell and pump thunder. Don't you prefer honesty?'

He had to admit he did.

She stared up at him, her eyes shining. 'I think I'm in love with you, Mr Goff.'

'Already?'

'It need not take long.'

He held her a little more tightly round the waist and she seemed to enjoy it. Then she looked up and grinned in that straight-forward honest way of hers so that he decided there was more to her than met the eye. There seemed no point in beating about the bush any longer.

'Shall we take a walk?' he suggested.

There was a conservatory at the back of the house, filled with plants, and he manoeuvred her among them.

'Are you goin' to kiss me, Mr Goff?' she asked.

Dammit, he thought, she was two lengths ahead of him already. 'That was my intention,' he said.

'Then you'd better get on with it, before someone comes.'

There was no coyness and no false modesty, and she was as aware as he was that she possessed some quality that other girls didn't have.

As she held up her small face, he had to stoop. As he kissed her, she sighed and he put his arms round her. This time the kiss was more than mere admiration and she returned it with interest. Then, as his arms tightened, she gave him a little push.

'I ought to warn you, Mr Goff. I'm only fifteen.'

He released her as if she'd been red-hot. 'Fifteen!'

'Does it surprise you?'

'Yes, by God, it does!' he said. 'I thought you were eighteen, at least.'

For a while they stood staring at each other, Colby confused, Augusta clearly enjoying his discomfiture, then he seized her arm disgustedly and yanked her round in the direction of the dancing.

'There's no need to pull my arm out, Mr Goff! And there's no need to go so fast. I can't keep up with you.'

As they reached the dancing, someone on the stoop shouted and they heard the thud of hooves over the music. The notes died away at once in a vague ripple of disquietude. It was hard to put a finger on it, but a shiver of fear and mingled dread seemed to move behind the patriotic bravado everybody showed, as if they suspected the shadows were drawing nearer.

'There's going to be fightin',' Augusta said bluntly, in a way that made her seem gauche and unfeeling. She seemed aware of it and hastened to put it right.

'I know what's comin' after tomorrow,' she said quietly. 'I've seen it before. And I've seen the tears and I know what's happenin'. Micah told me when I last went upstairs.'

She shuddered uncontrollably in a spasm of shivering that was part shock, part fear and part pride. There was a heavy weight of anxiety in her breast but she made an effort not to show it. 'We've lived with it a long time now, Mr Goff,' she said staunchly. She glanced at the young colonel with the wooden leg who had appeared with Hannah-May Burtle. 'Soon the whole of the South will be full of men without arms and legs. Are you intendin' to go on fightin' for us?'

Colby frowned. He was becoming too involved with this damned chit of a girl. 'No,' he snapped.

'Our country would be grateful, sir.'

He turned to face her. 'Would *you* come to the help of my country?'

She ignored the question. '*I* would be grateful, too,' she

said quietly. 'It might help us salvage a little honour. We haven't much else left. Will you ride with the cavalry tomorrow?'

'I expect so – in some capacity.'

She pulled him to one side and spoke softly. 'I'd like to give you a present, Mr Goff. Somethin' to take with you. Nothin' much. Just a keepsake. Will you accept it?'

He was beginning to grow worried. This persistent child was harrying him when he didn't wish to be harried. He'd come to America to dodge one ardent female and had no wish to be involved with another, especially at an age when she'd barely given up bibs and tuckers.

Standing in the cold air, their breath heavy on the frosty night, they saw Stuart talking earnestly with a young officer who had just arrived. His horse stood by the steps, its head down, trembling and smeared with lather.

'Sheridan's on the move,' Colby heard.

There was a quiet discussion then Stuart turned to his staff. 'Get the men mounted and the waggons and guns on their way,' he said as he strode into the house.

As Colby watched, the area in front of the house began to boil with men. Officers ran down the steps, buckling on their belts and weapons without stopping to look back, the girls, still in their finery, standing under the tall pillars, their eyes moist, waving and trying to catch their attention.

Colby saw Ackroyd approaching. Augusta had disappeared, and it seemed a good idea to bolt while he could.

'Get the nags, Tyas,' he said. 'There's something brewing and I think we ought to be there to see it.'

As Ackroyd vanished, he turned and headed for the stairs. Augusta was by the dining room door comforting one of the Burtle girls, who was in tears, and she flashed Colby a glance as he passed that encouraged him to move faster.

Two spots of feverish pink in his cheeks, Love was lying back in bed while his orderly moved about the room packing his belongings. 'Hello, old man,' he said as Colby appeared. 'They're movin' me to Neese Ford. This place could well be behind the enemy lines in a week's time, so I might as well move while I can do it without hurryin'.' He paused and looked gravely at Colby. 'Go with my boys, Coll,' he said. 'Ed Farley's a good soldier but he's a bit headlong and needs the reins at times. He'll not let you down and I guess he thinks a lot of you. He said so. You don't have to do any fightin'. You can write all you want. Just advise him some when he needs it.'

Colby was just about to turn away without committing himself when Love called him to the bed. Turning back the coverlet, he indicated a sabre which lay alongside him in its scabbard. It was a handsome weapon with a yellow sword knot.

'You'll need a sword,' he said with a faint smile. 'Sign of authority. All good officers carry a sword, even if they don't know how to use it. It's the one they presented to me after Chancellorsville. I'd be honoured if you'd wear it.'

Farley was waiting on the verandah when Colby appeared. He was strapped and buckled in all his accoutrements. 'Micah said you'd be comin' with us, Captain,' he said.

Colby said nothing and he went on earnestly. 'I don't read and write so good and I ain't no soldier really.'

'I think you're a pretty able one,' Colby pointed out.

Farley managed almost to blush under his grizzled beard. 'Not me, Captain. I'm just a farmer who can ride a hoss. I've learned a bit since 'Sixty-one, of course – who ain't? – but I'm still an amachoor. It was Micah looked after things. I just did what he told me. When he said "Go", I went; when he said "Git", I got. I could do with some help.'

Colby slapped his shoulder. The dust rose in a cloud. 'I'll be right behind you, Ed.'

Horsemen were thudding off between the trees in ones, twos and groups to the road where waggons and guns were on the move. A column of infantry went past, marching in a different way from the Northern troops, not even in step, in huge strides, carrying long rifles, their faces lean under their shabby-brimmed hats. Their expressions were grave, as if they knew that final defeat could not be far away, and he wondered what was going through their minds.

The music had started again but this time it was the sentimental 'I'm Leaving Thee In Sorrow, Annie' and the women stood in disconsolate groups, some in shawls, some still only in their evening dresses, waving and weeping. It reminded Colby once again of his father's description of Brussels on the eve of Waterloo. The coming battle might not be quite such a holocaust but the agony could go on longer as the South sagged to defeat.

He hitched at his belt and clipped on the sabre Love had given him. Ackroyd handed him the great LeMatt which he stuffed into his saddle hoster, and the Colt revolver which he pushed into his belt.

An unexpected feeling of irritation caused him to heave his horse's girth so tight the animal snorted in protest, and he was just about to mount when he saw Augusta hurrying towards him through the crowding animals and men. She was using her small shoulders to push her way through and he saw her slap heartily at a horse's rump and skip neatly out of its way as it let go with a cow kick. She fetched up in front of him, shivering in the night air, the yellow silk scarf in her hand, her small face peaked and thin with worry. Her very smallness softened the annoyance he felt.

'You'll catch your death of cold,' he said gently.

She gave him a quick, twisted smile that told him volumes about her agonies of apprehension. 'The cold doesn't worry me, Mr Goff,' she said. 'When you're young, you can stand anythin'.' The smile widened, shaky and game, to mock him. 'It's when you're growin' old, like you, it begins to worry.'

She paused and went on quietly. 'We shall be leavin' with Micah,' she said. 'Ma insists we refugee south.' She stared at him unblinkingly, feeling bereft. For the first time in her life she'd been treated like an adult; she found it tremendously moving and couldn't bear the thought of parting.

Abruptly, awkwardly, with the gracelessness of youth,

she thrust the yellow scarf at him. 'I'd like you to wear this, Mr Goff. Every soldier needs a sash.'

She looked so young he hadn't the heart to say no. Silently, he unfastened his belt and allowed her to tie it round his waist and arrange the ends so that they hung by his left thigh. Then he solemnly buckled the belt over it.

She stepped back and admired the effect, then, as she reached up to her hair, he realised she had stuck a feather into the neatly brushed strands. 'It isn't exactly a plume,' she said. 'Matter of fact, it's out of our old gobbler's tail. Wear it for me.'

Still without speaking, he took it from her and, working it under the leather thong round the crown of his hat, jammed it in place. Putting the hat back on his head, he watched her studying it.

'Doesn't really look much, after all,' she said critically. 'But there's a lot ridin' on it, Mr Goff.'

He bowed and was about to take her hand to say goodbye when she drew a deep breath. 'I've got one more thing.'

He smiled gravely. It was too solemn a moment for her, to make a joke of it.

'It's a St Christopher medallion,' she said. 'Catholics wear 'em. I'm not a Catholic but this one's special. It's got a strand of my hair in a locket behind.'

She thrust the locket at him in that awkward rangy way that was strangely moving. Taking his hat off, he slipped the chain over his head and pushed the locket inside his shirt.

'Next to my heart,' he said.

There was an awkward silence and he was just about to mount when she laid a hand on his arm. She appeared to want to say something and he bent to listen. As he did so, she kissed his cheek.

Her lips moved as they touched his flesh, cold and soft and tremulous. He stared at her, startled, then hurriedly swung into the saddle, waved abruptly, and, pulling his horse's head round, set off down the road between the trees. His ears were burning. Her voice had been so quiet she had seemed almost to be speaking to herself. He wasn't even sure, in fact, that he'd been intended to hear what she'd said. But he had. Every word of it.

'One of these days, Mr Goff,' she had murmured, 'I shall marry you.'

8

Freezing rain started before they had been long on the road, and by the time they reached Charlottesville, they found that Custer had vanished northwards again. Turning east and finding that only one of the Northern regiments had slipped past, they set pickets and settled down to wait for the rest.

The rain pelted down all night and Colby came to life in the early hours of the morning to hear shouts and shots coming from the distance. Scrambling from the muddy shelter under the bole of an overhanging tree where he had spent the night, he was stamping and beating his hands together to revive the circulation when a horseman thundered into camp, the horse's hooves splashing him with muddy yellow water.

'Custer's got past,' he was yelling. 'Custer's got past!'

The northern column had found the half-starved, ill-equipped Southern pickets in a pitiable state after the freezing night and, superbly mounted, had easily brushed them aside and were now heading for their base. Clad in an oilskin cape, the water dripping off his hat, Stuart was already conferring with his staff and trying to look at a map in the drenching rain and poor light.

'Colonel Hackett also says to tell you, General,' the messenger was saying, 'that he's heard that almost four thousand Yankee horsemen crossed the Rapidan at Ely's Ford and are almost at Beaver Dam Station. We saw their fires.'

'They must be almost into Richmond,' Stuart said. 'Still, Wade Hampton ought to be able to contain them.

Mount the men.'

There was a rush and bustle in the darkness, the whinny-ing of horses and the clattering of hooves as troopers, stupid with cold and sleep, began to move off. Jogging, slouch-backed, through the bitter weather, two days later they heard that the Yankee raid had been turned back with heavy losses in men, horses and equipment, but it was an indication of what the future held.

Waiting with Farley and Jenkins, sharing their discom-forts and occasionally writing what he could for Ackroyd to file away until it could be sent to London, Colby watched the north with tired eyes. It was important for the South to guard Richmond, but the Northern armies seemed set now on a policy of attrition from which only they could gain. With the armies locked together, the remorseless killing could only be of advantage to them, and their policy seemed to be to force Lee to fight, draining his armies of men, animals and equipment which could never be replaced. What was worse, as they were pushed south, Lee was running out of elbow room. The intrusion of the sea on the right precluded any serious movement in that direction and, as the Northern armies moved to the west to get behind them, they were constantly pushed backwards.

Rations were short, horses were short, ammunition was short; and no more came from the South. What they needed they had to find for themselves because the South's economy was beginning to crumble. There was no mail and no word from home. The only news that arrived came through men who had been on furlough or to find a horse, or were rejoining after being wounded. To Colby's sur-prise, one of them brought a letter for him. Unable to imagine who it came from, he was surprised to find it came from Augusta Dabney. It was short, unsentimental and brisk, and was studded with capitals, underlinings and ex-clamation marks.

'Dear Mr Goff,' it said. 'I have never felt so profoundly your presence in spirit as I did today!! Though I could not see you in the flesh, I felt you were near! I realise that when I beseeched you to help our CAUSE I never considered that you might possibly be <u>hurt!!</u> Looking after my cousin Micah's <u>injuries</u> has made me realise how SELFISH I was!! It isn't *your* war and I am so <u>ashamed!!</u> There is much illness here at the moment – typhoid as well as scurvy and fever – all caused by this CRUEL WAR!! Yesterday the enemy shelled Glenby. Several houses were <u>burned</u> and people were <u>hurt!!</u> You must always feel that when you are not <u>fighting</u>, you are welcome to visit our home. It is not MUCH, but we <u>can</u> offer you hospitality. Cousin Micah sends his regards, which accompany the respects of your <u>good</u> friend, Augusta B. Dabney.'

It was full of ink spots and mistakes, but there was a headlong enthusiasm about it that made him want to laugh. He could just imagine her sitting at her desk, her wide mouth twisting with the effort of writing, a frown between her brows, her small figure hunched over the paper.

Spring came imperceptibly and they moved into a hot dry May that made the flowers sag on their stalks. The Northern troops had got into Georgia again. Their last attempt had been repulsed at Chickamauga but this time they seemed determined to sweep across it. It was unravaged, a vast granary, machine shop and storehouse supporting enormous hospitals and most of the South's cotton and woollen trade. At Atlanta, the junction of four railroads quartered the Confederacy.

As the Northerners pushed on, the piecemeal attacks of the past stopped. From now on, it seemed, it was to be one concerted drive on every front, to bring the Confederates to battle in every possible area at once to wear down their armies so that their old habit of rushing men from one front to another could no longer be indulged in. Scouts brought news that the Army of the Potomac was on the move again, slipping away from their camp fires in thousands. Lee was already on the march to meet them.

Colby was lounging in the grass when orders came, and immediately the whole camp came to life, with men grabbing up their belongings and reaching for their horses. Earth was kicked over the fires and cursing men who were in the middle of preparing a meal, crammed half-cooked meat into their mouths.

As they hurried towards Orange Turnpike, the country changed, and as the road descended into a valley, they found themselves in gloomy second-growth forest stretching for fifteen miles.

'The Wilderness,' Jenkins said. 'That's what this place is known as. And I guess the Children of Israel musta felt the same as I do, because I don't like it.'

Dense timber filled irregular ravines and low hills in dark patches that looked full of ghosts, and it was difficult to make out the direction of the Northern advance. Columns of lean ragged hairy men with no outward detail of military show came past. Their uniforms were every shade of grey and brown and their canteens, knapsacks, sabres and revolvers all seemed to be stamped 'US'. They seemed incredibly dirty and many carried nothing but a rolled piece of carpet for a blanket. But they were bronzed and muscular, with bright hard eyes that saw no future for themselves or their country but still saw enough faith to go on fighting.

Colby spent most of the day moving about after Farley in heavy timber and thick undergrowth, but there was no sign of the Federals, though the woods were echoing with the sound of musketry and bullets were hissing about and thumping into the boles of trees. Then they heard the artillery start and knew that the armies had met. Love's regiment was dismounted and the horses were taken to the rear.

They were all tired and falling asleep as they waited. Shells began to land among them but Sigsbee brought up two rifled guns and began to reply in a steady banging from a field of dry broom sedge about two feet high. As Northern shells set the field on fire, they had to retire, shrapnel still crashing among them, the thud of shells, balls and fragments filling the air. Farley hung on all day but the following day Northern assaults drove back the troops on their left, and they had to retire themselves.

'This ain't cavalry fighting,' Ackroyd complained bitterly as they moved back to the horses. 'Walking about on your hinds.'

There was another brush with the Yankees in the afternoon but Love's regiment wasn't involved, though the roar of musketry filled their ears until nightfall. The smoke lay thick and dense over the field so that it was impossible to see more than fifty yards in front, and the sun looked like a red ball of fire through the grey haze. By this time the brushwood and timber were ablaze and fires crackled all round them. A few men began to look over their shoulders, less worried by the enemy than by the flames.

The air was filled with noise, from the roar of the conflagration and the crackle of musketry to the wails of wounded caught by the flames. As the fighting died away with dark, the woods were still ablaze, dead trees on fire from top to bottom.

They slept where they fell to the ground and, waking the following morning, Colby was aware of silence, Ackroyd was sitting up nearby.

'It's finished,' he said.

'Perhaps it just hasn't started again yet,' Colby pointed out.

As Ackroyd began to prepare coffee, a messenger came clattering through the woods to Farley. 'They're on the move,' he shouted. 'We have to cover Spotsylvania Court House! Fitz Lee's men were ordered to stop 'em, but they didn't manage it. You're to strike camp!'

'We ain't got no camp,' Farley snorted.

'Well, whatever! You're to join Fitz Lee.'

'How about breakfast?'

'*Now*, the General said!'

As Farley's men fell back slowly, Colby could see the Federals moving forward in the distance as if on parade, their brass buttons and bayonets glistening in the sun, their striped banners floating in the breeze. It seemed that the Union troops had slipped past the Confederates, but eventually they came on Fitz Lee's men, dismounted and holding positions along a line of woods.

'Dismount!' Farley yelled and, as the horses were taken

to the rear, they moved forward to fling themselves down.

The place where they had halted was not very imposing, a mere huddle of houses, a church, a store and a scattering of outbuildings in the middle of a level plain surrounded by low hills. It was full of cavalry and the smell of horses dominated. In the heat the air was filled with dust kicked up by wheels, iron-shod hooves and hobnailed boots. A few women in slatted sunbonnets and faded calico dresses watched in agony as they prepared to give battle round their homes. Already the litter of the army was filling the streets, putrefying and bringing flies. In every corner cavalrymen were asleep, their arms through the reins of their mounts.

Outside the town, the country was wild and barren and chiefly covered in scrub oak barely fifteen feet high but so thickly tangled it was difficult to push through it. It was difficult country to move in and well chosen for defence.

Fitz Lee, a fleshy-faced young man with a mop of dark hair and full beard, put them in the picture quickly. 'The General says we don't give way,' he announced. 'He's herding 'em towards us. Casualties are heavy but I gather the main army's already behind and starting to dig in. Lee's across Grant's path again.'

As he spoke, there was a yell and he went cantering off to another part of the line. The Federals had broken out of the wood and as Sigsbee's guns roared to life, the charge broke up into scattered groups which retreated a little way, reformed and started again, only to suffer the same fate. Once again the Federals fell back over the brow of the slope so that the guns were firing only at a skirmishing line, the shells hissing over like steam engines.

'Here they come again!' Farley yelled.

As the Federals ran forward, the guns continued to bark until the last moment, then were limbered up and moved to the rear. As they did so, one of the drivers was hit and fell, and Farley jumped into the saddle to drive the piece from the field. There was a cheer for him as he appeared, but the bullets were still flying like sleet and, as the guns clattered past, Colby saw his face change and he reeled in the saddle.

With the gun swinging round to come into action again, Colby ran forward and caught him as he fell.

Propped with his back against a tree, Farley sat with his legs splayed, blood dribbling from his nostrils. As Colby bent over him, he lifted his head and a burst of red blossomed from his nose like a huge crimson flower and rushed down his mouth and chin. As the blood flowed over his uniform he began to splutter and choke, drowning in a red river. Frantically Colby tried to open his jacket to find the wound, the blood flowing over them both, slippery and sticky.

'For God's sake –!' Farley coughed, spraying blood everywhere. 'Help me – I –!' Then he gave a wheezing noise and flopped back, and the hand that was grasping Colby's relaxed and dropped down by Colby's foot.

As he was carried to the rear, the cavalrymen pulled back again, fighting from hill to hill, fence to fence, tree to tree. By now there were large numbers of Confederates about and unexpectedly the air was filled with bird song. As the sun came up, the temperature rose and they moved back again, winding down to a stream and up a long hill towards a bank surmounted by a rail fence and woods. Then, as the Federals charged once more, they were swept by a volley of firing from men they thought had vanished, and fell back again. As the battle flared, the cavalry retreated yet again, all that were left of four thousand-odd who had forced the Northerners to take more than a day to advance a mere seven or eight miles. Occasionally they saw Stuart moving about behind the line, and once Lee on a grey charger.

More and more Federals appeared, but the firing died down with darkness and as the battle drew to a close, Colby, his face blackened with smoke, looked at Ackroyd who stared back at him indignantly.

'I thought I was coming over 'ere to send off messages to the *Morning Advertiser*,' he complained. 'Not to keep the bloomin' Confederacy on its feet.'

In front of them the slopes were slippery with blood. The dead were piled three feet high, the wounded struggling to pull themselves from under those who lay on top.

Jabez Jenkins appeared, his long face lugubrious. 'Heard Ed Farley was hit,' he said.

'Yes.' Colby gestured to the rear. 'I'd like to go back and see how he is now things are quiet. Can you hold it?'

The town was filled with wounded, packed everywhere among the hop vines and honeysuckle, lying on white sanded paths, stretched under magnolia, wisteria or snowball bushes for shelter. The men who had been hit early in the day had already been attended to and sent away in jolting waggons, but by now, there were hundreds more, laid out on counters in the store and filling the houses and gardens, the blankets on which they lay saturated with blood. There were men who had been kicked by horses, with broken faces and smashed limbs, men with head wounds caused by Federal canister, and bodies torn by bullets, or raw from sabre cuts. Men shot in the stomach dragged themselves in as the surgeons worked at tables hastily erected in the street, their saws crunching through bone, cutting, stitching, probing, leaving the bandaging to orderlies and the women from the houses around. The chloroform had long since run out and the screaming men were being held down by brawny soldiers. Sperm oil for cauterising was bubbling over fires and the smell of seared flesh filled the nostrils, while the flames on sweating faces and beards and the agonised cries of the hurt created a picture of Hell.

Colby found one of the doctors trying to draw breath away from the reek of disinfectant, festering wounds and frightened malfunctioning bodies that blotted out the smell of grass and flowers. On a wooden building that looked like a stable was a sign 'EMBALMING – FREE FROM ODOR OF INFECTION'.

The doctor was taking great gulping breaths of air. Nearby was a pile of arms and legs, at the top of which a stiff finger pointed steadily at him. The grass was stiff with blood and the one or two women who moved about had the edges of their dresses stained red.

At that moment the night birds started calling, almost as

if their chorus had been started by some hidden conductor, and in the next field, a preacher in a black coat began to intone over an open hole in the ground: 'Oh, God of love, Lord God of hosts, allow the battle to pass from our valley and halt the hand of those who slay . . .'

The doctor sighed, shook his head as Colby spoke, and drew deeply on his cigar. 'I don't recall the name,' he said. 'But I'm so goddam tired I guess I misremember everything. Ask the sergeant.'

The sergeant couldn't remember either, but an orderly appeared with a list. 'Yes, sir,' he said. 'I got his name on this here paper. Captain Edwin Soames Farley.'

'Where is he?' Colby asked.

'He ain't, sir.' The orderly shook his head. 'He's in the field there with the preacher.'

When Colby returned to Jenkins, they could hear desperate calls and cries from the wounded still in the woods and fields drowning the owls and the maddening call of the whippoorwills. A ploughed field in front of where they stood was strewn with horses and men and the area behind the line was a trampled wreck; the dead lay among the bushes where they had been dragged during the fighting, still staring up at the sky, the startled expression they had first shown already giving way to a stretched grimace that showed their teeth.

Jenkins sighed as Colby told him about Farley. 'I guess it's up to you now, son,' he said. 'I ain't no soldier, that's for sure, and the boys sure as hell know *you* are. They'll send someone along eventualy but it sure enough won't be just yet.'

He was right and at dawn the next morning as the guard emptied their rifles in case the charges were damp Colby was summoned to headquarters. Stuart looked grim. 'I know it's none of your business,' he said. 'But I beg you to look after Love's people for a while. It's not your war, but we've been badly hurt and I know they'll follow you.'

Perhaps it was the despairing look he'd seen on Jenkins' face that swayed Colby. It was against all common sense, he knew, but he remembered the doctor and the dressing station, and, curiously, Augusta Dabney's small peaked face. He nodded and Stuart managed a smile.

'The Confederacy will be grateful, Mr Goff,' he said. 'And now you'd better be getting back to your command. We've heard Grant has sent Sheridan to raid south. He's going to cut the roads through Gordonsville, Charlottesville and Lynchburg, and the high road to Richmond. Scouts say there are around fifteen thousand troopers with artillery and waggons and they stretch over thriteen miles of highway. And this time they're taking their time as if they're not afraid.'

They came up with the Federals at a place called Mitchell's Shop where they could see a whole army of blue-clad horsemen streaming away, squadron after squadron of them, regiment after regiment, in a solid mass, the sun catching stirrup irons, sabres and an occasional fluttering flag. The Confederates had been thrown back with heavy losses and were depressed at their inability to make any impression on the mass of men in front. Stuart's presence put heart into them and there were cheers.

'No, no, my friends,' he said, beating the dust from his gloves against his saddle bow. 'We'll save our hallooing until we're out of the woods.'

He had news that at Beaver Dam Station Custer's men had put Lee's supplies to the flames, filling the air with the odour of burning bacon. Meat, bread, flour, sugar, meal, molasses, liquor, medical stores, arms and tents had all gone up in one vast pyre, then the tracks had been torn up for ten miles with the destruction of trains, locomotives, telegraphs, culverts and bridges. With nothing in their path, the Southern cavalry rushed on through the humid May heat to reach Beaver Dam just as Custer pulled out, and, with the road blocked by felled trees, they were forced on to a parallel route to reach Hanover Junction where they learned that Sheridan was no more than twenty miles from Richmond.

Appearing alongside Colby with Fitz Lee, Stuart was in a thoughtful mood. His long black boots were mud-spattered but he looked as if he were dressed for a ball with his yellow sash and plume and a rose in his buttonhole.

'Sir –' Fitz Lee's words came wearily ' – we can't take much more punishment.'

'A little longer, Fitz,' Stuart said. 'A little longer. The Lord God of Hosts is on our side.'

As Lee moved away, he turned to Colby, his eyes curiously sombre. 'I've just said goodbye to my wife, Mr Goff,' he said. 'I never expected to live through the war, though, and if we're beaten I'm not sure I want to.'

They drove on a few miles more before they were allowed to halt, and they were asleep in their saddles almost at once. As Colby moved back among Love's men, one of the troopers swayed and crashed to the ground at his feet. As he sat up, blinking, wondering what had happened, Colby turned to Jenkins.

'Dismount 'em,' he said. 'Keeping 'em in the saddle does no good to man nor beast.'

They managed only an hour or two, then a message came to move on again, and Colby went among the sleeping men, kicking them to wakefulness. Gradually he got them mounted and stumbling off towards the south again. Stuart appeared once more, gaunt with weariness.

'How far are we from Richmond?' he asked.

'Six miles, General.'

'We must let 'em know in Richmond, that we've reached Yellow Tavern but that none of the enemy has passed.'

As he vanished, Colby caught sight of a familiar figure on horseback, sitting under the trees.

'Von Hartmann,' he said. 'How the devil did you get here?'

'Via the blockade.' The Prussian smiled. 'I slipped into Richmond. I think the Confederacy is finished, don't you?'

Colby said nothing and, in his precise manner, Von Hartmann went on. 'I have seen the mistakes of both sides,' he said. 'It will be as well in case we ever have to fight them.'

'How the hell can Prussia fight America?' Colby's voice was sharp with weariness. 'The Atlantic Ocean lies between!'

'One never knows,' von Hartmann said seriously. 'Are you still reporting the war?'

'I seem to be fighting it at the moment. And it looks very much as if it's going to start here shortly, so I'd advise you to clear off, because I don't want to be responsible for you.'

Von Hartmann smiled and turned his horse away. 'I shall head south into Mexico,' he said. 'The French are trying to set up a puppet monarchy there. It might be instructive to watch them at it.'

As he waved and vanished, Colby looked round. Nearby was an abandoned inn, the paintless ghost of a previous era. The country was gently rolling with green fields, cultivated farms and gardens and there was a stream nearby where thirsty horses were already drinking. As the sun got up and the day grew warmer, they could hear firing to the north. As they waited in the sunshine, men and horses wearied by the headlong ride, a few small fires were built and the men moved around the abandoned tavern looking for the best of the scanty cover. Ackroyd produced coffee and as they drank he looked at Colby.

'We goin' to win this one, sir?' he asked.

Colby shrugged. 'Not with two understrength brigades, Tyas.'

The troops were ranged in a right angle to the north of the inn, with skirmishers in gulleys and among the trees. Artillery was on the left of the line and, behind, black servants and orderlies held the horses which snatched eagerly at the sparse grass, switching their tails at the first flies of the summer.

As the Federals appeared, they split into two columns, one pushing south to Richmond. Stuart was close by as they watched a line of mounted men appear, sitting his horse near a group of aspen trees lining the road. As the bullets started, the pickets bolted for shelter, and Stuart and his staff moved forward, Stuart with one leg over the saddle writing a despatch.

The Federal horsemen were edging forward, and there

was a yell as they broke into a gallop. Stopped by the volley of musketry, the charge degenerated into hand-to-hand fighting.

'Go in there, Mr Goff, and help!'

Stuart was gesturing forward and Colby turned to Love's men. 'Mount!'

As the horses were brought up, they swung to the saddle, and, moving into a gallop in a few strides, they smashed into the Northern troopers, who turned and bolted before they could get properly among them. Scattered shooting emptied a few saddles as they rode back. Stuart met them as they came.

'I think that will do nicely,' he said. His face was unsmiling and grave as he watched them pass. 'Custer's over there,' he said. 'I've seen his yellow hair through my glass. We must watch ourselves today.'

As they reformed, there was a yell and Colby turned in the saddle to see an infantry regiment running towards them. There was no need to issue orders. The horses were cantered away to the rear in bunches, while their riders flung themselves down and started firing. The artillery was hammering away with shell and canister. In front of the battery the road ran over a fenced bridge where only three or four men could pass at a time. The Bluecoat cavalry crashed towards it in columns of squadrons, trumpeters blaring away behind. They lost heavily as they thundered across and several horses crashed down. As they cleared it they opened into line and began to gallop. Sheer force of numbers carried them through the battery, firing and slashing at the gunners.

They were swarming thickly in the woods now and during a lull Ackroyd came up to Colby. 'There's a rumour that the buggers are in our rear,' he said.

'Stuart doesn't seem too worried,' Colby said.

'I am,' Ackroyd said flatly, 'This isn't no place for a British soldier who wants to go 'ome and get married.'

Another wave of skirmishers had spilled from the woods now and a mounted brigade was hurtling towards them at full gallop.

'Don't stop to count them, boys,' Stuart shouted. 'Shoot them!'

The Northerners were using sabres and, as they reached the heavy fence where the Southerners were established, they tried to reach over and slash at them, but they were soon piled up in heaps of dead and struggling wounded. Stuart came riding back alone. He was whistling as he took up a position behind the firing line.

'Give it to 'em, boys,' he was calling. 'Hold 'em there, Mr Goff!'

He emptied his big silver-chased revolver at the Federals and men on horses began to canter slowly away from the firing, dismounted men stumbling after them among the riderless chargers.

'Steady, men, steady!' Stuart was still shouting orders when one of the dismounted horsemen turned and fired on the run and Colby saw him press a hand to his side. As he bent forward in the saddle, his hat fell off.

'General –' one of the Southern soldiers turned and ran to him '– are you hit?'

'Yes.' Stuart's voice came in a thick, strained way.

'You wounded bad?'

'I'm afraid I am. It's God's will.'

Two mounted troopers moved forward and he was taken to the rear, the blood darkening the yellow sash round his waist. The sight distracted some of Love's troopers and Colby went along the line. 'Look to your front! Do your duty as he has!'

But Stuart's wound had demoralised them and they began to edge back. Colby was just struggling with a soldier who was trying to hide in a culvert when he felt a blow on the head that spun him round. For a moment he thought one of the retreating men had turned on him and hit him with a rifle, but they were all moving away, and as he realised he was seeing them through a film of blood, it dawned on him that he'd been wounded.

That's a bloody stupid thing to do, he thought. Get hurt in somebody else's war!

He straightened up with an effort but as he did so there was another blow on his left thigh that whipped his leg from under him so that he was lying flat on his back in the grass half-under the fence. Alongside his face was the face of a dead man, its eyes blue, staring and covered with grit. God, he thought, if I stay here I'll die, too, and he struggled from under the fence and forced himself to his feet. His left leg seemed to be on fire and, glancing down, he saw his trouser leg was in tatters and blood was pouring down it into his boot. The men around him seemed to have disappeared and there was a general movement backwards which he tried to join. Then, thankfully, weak with gratitude, he saw Ackroyd, bent double and coming towards him at a run. He tried to take a step towards him but his leg was numb and gradually, as it buckled under him, he began to sink to the ground.

Part Two

1

'Them'll be your 'orses when you starts riding school. You look arter them and they'll look arter you.'

Listening to the sergeant, Colby allowed himself a faint smile.

'Gentle as doves, they are,' the sergeant was saying, and the new recruits listened with their jaws open, their eyes wide.

'Knows the drill better'n I do,' the sergeant continued, slapping at a sleek rump. 'It'll be your job to groom 'em, wisp 'em and make their coats shine like a shilling up a sweep's arse. Ain't that so, sir?'

Spotting Colby standing by the door, he turned to him for confirmation.

Colby nodded vigorously. 'Oh, indeed, Sergeant. That it is.'

'You'll bed 'em down on nice soft straw,' the sergeant went on, 'fill their guts with good oats, linseed, bran mash and 'ay, and lead 'em to water and to let 'em piss it off.'

Then one day, when you aren't looking, Colby thought dryly, one of the bastards'll lash out with both his hinds and kick your brains out.

''Orses never let you down,' the sergeant went on, his words coming gently as he crooned over a big bay gelding. 'Easier to 'andle than men.' He pushed across a bulging canvas bag. 'Here's a grooming kit. You'll all get one. One body brush, one dandy brush, one 'oof pick, one curry-comb, one dock sponge. The brush and comb is for groomin', the hoof-pick's for cleanin' 'is nails, the dandy's for 'is mane, tail and fetlocks, and the wisp's to shine 'is coat and increase 'is circulation so 'e'll feel more frisky. The dock sponge's for sponging out 'is mouf, nostrils and dock.' The sergeant's voice grew harsher. '*In that order*,' he pointed out firmly. 'So don't you go doing it different. His dock's his arse so don't go usin' it on that first. You wouldn't like 'aving your teef cleaned wiv a 'orse-pissy sponge and no more does he.'

Colby listened to the jeremiad patiently. He had heard it regularly ever since returning from the States.

'You was right to join the lancers,' the sergeant's voice droned on. 'Lancers is the coming thing. Lances wasn't used in the British cavalry until 1816, the decision 'avin' been taken because of the maulin' them silly people in the 'Eavy and Union Brigades suffered at the 'ands of the Polish lancers at Waterloo, from which we, with the 12th and the 16th, 'ad to rescue 'em. A fine, expert and vigorous lancer can annihilate any three experienced dragoons or 'ussars any day of the week. Lancers 'ave the longest weapons in the army an' they're always good wiv 'em. You ask the girls.'

There was an uncertain snigger, and the sergeant's voice changed again, growing harsher. 'And now – just git over there in a line! The major'd like a word wiv you. An' you just listen to 'im proper. 'E knows what 'e's talkin' about because 'e knows more about cavalry than most people ever learn. 'E rode with Lord Cardigan at Balaclava and wiv Jeb Stuart – 'oo I suppose you ignorant lot 'ave never 'eard of – in America. 'E's a brave man.'

Not so brave as all that, Colby thought, remembering his fear as Ackroyd had removed him from the field of Yellow Tavern. He'd been convinced as he recovered consciousness that he'd died and gone to hell. 'Is the death pallor in my face?' he had asked and only Ackroyd's laugh had brought him back to reality. 'You look as though you'd just come in first in the Braxby point-to-point,' he had said. 'It'll set you back a few lengths for a bit, but that's all.'

It was six years now since Yellow Tavern, and Stuart,

like Cardigan, was long dead, while he himself was known these days to the men as Balaclava Bill.

'One thing more –' the sergeant's voice grew firmer, '– when it comes to 'osses, nobody knows more'n what 'e does. Two 'undred and seventy-one kilometres across France in under thirty-two hours on the same 'orse last summer. Everybody knows about that. It was in all the papers. It's a record.'

Which, Colby thought, hadn't been quite what he'd intended. With Ackroyd to help by arranging water, oats, bran, beans and eggs, he had set out merely to show what good selection of sire and dam could do.

He cleared his throat, studying the line of youngsters in front of him in their ill-fitting stable jackets. His welcoming speech had become a regular feature of recruit training. 'First of all,' he said, 'think yourselves lucky that this regiment has condescended to allow you to join its ranks. We're a good regiment – the only cavalry regiment in the British army to wear green. And why? Because, as the sergeant's told you, we routed the Polish lancers at Waterloo and when we became lancers ourselves we decided to adopt their uniform. Goff's Greens. Goff's Gamecocks. The Widowmakers. The Clutchers. We have all those names. How did we come by them? I'll tell you. In those days our motto – motto, remember, never badge; and title, never motto – was a buffalo head. But since we became lancers we have used the French eagle we captured when we charged in support of the Heavies at Waterloo. To make it look fiercer, we gave it large claws – hence, The Clutchers, which was added to The Widowmakers, which we acquired after the Peninsula.' He paused. 'There is yet another name: The Pot Carriers, which we earned by announcing after Salamanca that we had captured Marshal Marmont's treasure waggon. Unfortunately, this name is used more often by the rest of the army than by us because we had made a mistake and the treasure waggon turned out to be his private commode, and a chamberpot is hardly the sort of thing you wear on your drum cloths.'

It raised a laugh and he was pleased. 'We have one other

distinction,' he went on. 'We are one of the only two regiments in the army to share a number. These are the 19th Hussars and the 19th Lancers. It sprang entirely from the mistake of a Whitehall clerk and has never been rectified. Now that it has become tradition, it never will be, because every regiment in the army has a peculiarity of costume or equipment or name, associated with some event in its history, and they are usually retained with the tenacity of a tigress defending her young.'

He touched the badge on his forage cap. 'Under the motto on your lance caps you'll see the words, *Aut Primus Aut Nullus*. That's Latin, and it means *The Best or Nothing*. That's what we believe in, isn't it, sergeant?'

'Sir!'

'The 2nd Dragoons, the Greys, have the motto, *Nulli Secundus*, which means *Second to None*, but of course that's rubbish because they're second to *us*. And don't believe those people who'll try to tell you we're a *junior* cavalry regiment, because we're not. We were formed first in 1642 and it was only due to the lack of foresight of someone who allowed us to be disbanded that we were a little late in the field when Joshua Goff reformed us in 1760.'

It was all nonsense he knew, but it mattered, because a man's loyalty had to be not to the Queen or the army but to his regiment, and for that he had to know everything about it as well as he knew his own family.

'It has been said,' he went on, 'that cavalry exists to look pretty in peacetime and get killed in war. What that means is that we're expected to look smart on parade but that, since we're the screen of the army, both in advance and retreat, we're always the first to bump into the enemy. In moments of crisis, the cavalry is called on to charge. To relieve pressure, to restore a desperate situation, to lead a forlorn hope, doing the things that will bring success out of failure. It's a responsible job and we must never forget it.'

He paused long enough to look at them and to let them get a look at him. 'But,' he went on, 'no matter how often you've swung your leg over a polished saddle, a trooper can't lay claim to true cavalrymanship until he has enough

118

music in his horsey soul to appreciate the majesty of "Stables."'

'This,' he continued, 'means that you will leap from your beds at Reveille, which in the cavalry sounds at 5.30 – earlier than the infantry because you have horses to attend to. To the fastidious, mucking out might seem a revolting way to start the day, especially as you'll find there are always too few forks.' He held up his hands, the fingers outspread. 'But, have no fear. I carry my personal mucking out equipment on my hands. And so do you.

'Before you get your mounts, however, you will learn to conduct yourselves like soldiers, and to remember that cleanliness is next to Godliness. Here, that means bright buttons and glistening souls. You belong in the Queen's best regiment of horse and in the best squadron in that regiment – mine!' He gave them a long hard look. 'So God help any man who ever forgets it. Dismiss 'em, Sergeant.'

Leaving the stables, Colby walked towards the Riding School. The riding instructor's voice could be heard even outside the huge shed with its outward-sloping walls and tanbark floor.

'Get up, dammit! You can get the bark out of your ear later. And sit *in* the bloody saddle, not on it! Now trot and sit straight. Grip with your knees. Head up. Heels down. AND SIT STILL! You're darting about in the saddle like a fart in a bottle!'

Recruit riding was in progress, men shaking down in the saddle in a test of grip and endurance, turning, inclining, circling, evolutions performed at a walk, trot and canter, with or without stirrups. As they finished, the order 'Bring in the jump' produced a hurdle topped with gorse, and they crossed their stirrups and swung into a canter.

'Drop your reins and fold your arms!'

As son of a commanding officer, Colby had learned to ride as a boy with the recruits and he knew the severity of this exercise as well as any of them. The tighter the arms were folded, he'd been informed, the tighter the grip with the knees, and it always seemed to be true and was valuable advice if the horse jumped big.

As he saw Colby the riding instructor came to attention. 'We got an old soldier, sir,' he said quietly, nodding to a man who was jogging round, apparently having difficulty with his horse.

The riding instructor was experienced enough to be able to tell a man's former trade from the way he sat. Carpenters, he claimed, held one shoulder forward from the habit of using a plane, while tailors, from being used to sitting cross-legged, kept their knees away from the saddle and were always the worst of riders.

''E's feigning awkwardness, sir,' he went on. 'Pretendin' 'e's a green'orn. But 'e ain't. Just watch 'im close, sir.'

Turning away, he yelled suddenly. 'Right shoulder in! Forward!'

The older man was the only one in the group who performed the movement instinctively and the riding instructor frowned.

'Only one who knew what it meant,' he said. 'I reckon 'e was discharged as a bad character from another regiment.'

On the parade ground men were marching and wheeling to the shouts of drill instructors and further away there was the heavy rumble of iron-shod wheels as guns and limbers turned and moved to the rattle and jingle of harness. The high iron gates arched over the sentry, the rifle green of his uniform dark against the drab yellow brick of the building. Tall and thin, bowed legs poured into skin-tight overalls, he exhuded cavalry spirit from every pore. As a small boy the sentry on the gate had seemed more magnificent and far more important to Colby than the Prime Minister or the Archbishop of Canterbury. As the sentry crashed into a salute, he returned it with equal fervour. He had no time for the bored flicks of some of the younger officers.

The band moved past, playing 'The Yorkshire Jockey', the regimental march, a piebald drumhorse stepping the pace in front. Dripping aiguilletes plaited in the regimental colours, the kettle drummer was seated between two barrel-shaped silver instruments draped with drum cloths bearing the battle honours of the regiment – Willems,

Talavera, Fuentes d'Onor, Salamanca, Vittoria, Nive, Waterloo, Balaclava, Bhurtpore, Guznee. Guiding his horse with reins attached to his stirrup irons, he whirled his sticks first to one drum then the other as if working himself up to the climax of a Zulu war dance. It was a lot of dressing up, Colby thought, for that most primitive of instruments, the drum.

As he swung into the mess, a loud voice was complaining bitterly about some soldier who had objected to the meat the previous day and he turned, recognising the voice. Aubrey Cosgro looked like his older brother, Claude, plump, overfed, pale-faced and pale-souled. He had been switched to Colby's squadron in the hope of working some improvement but so far it hadn't been successful. Nobody ever did much with a Cosgro.

'Did you taste the meat, sir?' Colby barked.

Cosgro jerked round. 'I should think not,' he said.

Colby's eyes blazed. 'Then you'd better do it tomorrow,' he snapped. 'And for the next seven days! I'll have a word with the adjutant.'

Leaving Cosgro red-faced and furious, he turned to find himself facing George Laughton, who ran C Squadron. Laughton had been in the regiment for ever, getting nowhere, reliable in that he did nothing wrong but also in that he never did anything very right either.

'How're the recruits?' he asked.

'Like the remounts. Hairy of heel.'

Laughton sipped his drink and glanced across the mess. 'Bit sharp with young Cosgro, weren't you?' he said.

'The officers in my squadron do their work like the men,' Colby growled. 'I don't expect 'em to leave it to the sergeants.'

Laughton sniffed. 'My squadron's a bit more easy-going,' he said.

Which, Colby thought, explained why C Squadron would never be as good as A. Anybody knew that a Cosgro – of whatever age – could be trusted no further than he could be thrown. He'd heard that Claude Cosgro had started sniffing round a farmer's wife at Hounslow.

Wonder what Georgina thought of that, he asked himself. Perhaps nothing, because he'd also heard she was seeing a captain in the Scots Fusiliers.

As Laughton turned away, unimpressed with Colby's zeal, Brosy la Dell appeared. He had acquired a well-fed look since he'd married the daughter of Colonel Markham's successor, and since his wife had announced she was expecting a baby, was full of well-being.

'How's Grace?' Colby asked.

Brosy smiled his lazy smile. 'She's fine. Baby's due in a fortnight's time. Gets excitin', this family life.'

His enthusiasm made Colby feel lonely. There must be something to this marriage business, he thought, when a man so ardently a bachelor as Brosy had been could become so absorbed by it. He seemed left out in the cold, with the feeling that he was missing something.

'Thought I might take a short break till it's due,' Brosy went on. 'Get my strength up, you might say.'

'Fishing?'

'Probably. Paris don't come within the reach of a married man.' Brosy's eyes were far away for a moment. 'Pity. It's the place to go. When Grace and I were there last year, you could feel the electricity in the air. Still, you know it better than I do. It's where you've passed most of your misspent youth.'

Colby said nothing. Since returning from the States, he'd been suffering from a deep ennui that came, he suspected, from routine, the absence of excitement and the lack of anyone important in his life. Caroline Matchett was still around, but these days she went in less for acting than for drinking brandy and it was beginning to show. And, as far as a woman with a husband whom she had obligingly discarded could be called unfaithful, he suspected she was being unfaithful to him, too. The signs were there and he had long suspected someone else was visiting her.

'Grace wants it to be called Horatio after the Old Man,' Brosy was saying.

'What?' Colby's thoughts had been far away.

'The baby, ass! Can't see it myself. One degree worse

122

than Ambrose.' Brosy peered at Colby. 'You all right? You look as if you might have saddle sores. Too much 19th Lancers and not enough anything else. You should take yourself off to Paris again. Could be exciting just now with all this talk of war between the Emperor and the Prussians.'

Colby shrugged. The recent French aggressiveness had not gone down well in England, and there had been a strong condemnation in the newspapers and in stiff speeches in Parliament. Fortunately the disturbance, a flutter of ruffled feathers that had become a foreboding beat of wings, had subsided again in the last few days and the threatened storm over some princeling the Prussians wanted to put on the throne of Spain had died to nothing more than a murmur.

'Won't come now,' Brosy said. 'For once Bismark got a bloody nose and all this big talk of war by French newspapermen's simply because they think he should be given a fright.'

'I don't think Bismark frightens all that easily,' Colby observed.

Brosy smiled. 'Well, nobody's going to pick a quarrel with France, are they? Look at the experience of war they have. All those African conquests.'

Colby thought of von Hartmann, the eager young Prussian he had met in America. 'The Prussians learn fast,' he said.

Brosy smiled. 'Well, if they do and they *are* out for war, all the more reason to go while you can.'

Colby was tempted. The previous winter he had flung himself into hunting, but it hadn't been enough and as he had studied with a fastidious eye the women he met round the shires he had come to the conclusion that old age was hurrying towards him at breakneck speed and he was growing hard to please. He was sick of pre-marital skirmishings that always came to nothing. The occasions were always boring, he found, and the women all seemed to look like Georgina.

'You could get time off,' Brosy encouraged.

Yes, he could, Colby thought, and these days too much of his time away from the regiment was spent chasing women, gambling at Deauville or roistering around London and Paris. But Braxby didn't appeal these days. With his father just clinging to life, his ancient frame knotted from old wounds, frail, nodding, shaking, and white as a corpse already, Colby didn't enjoy watching him slowly die.

There was one other drawback, too. The Rector's daughter had her eye on him. Her father was the youngest son of a peer of the realm, had a degree from Oxford, and had been a minor canon at Windsor which, she seemed to think, placed her family firmly among the mighty. She was also pretty and not too stupid and lately had taken to visiting Braxby Manor on the thin excuse that she was bringing calves' foot jelly or beef tea for his father. What was more, she rode reasonably well, enjoyed hunting and had a brother in the 11th Hussars, all of which made her not too bad a bet. Nevertheless, there remained an uneasy feeling that, brought up in the atmosphere of the church, she would never understand, as Brosy's undemanding, generous-minded Grace did, the importance of the regiment; and that, full of good works, she would grow boring in time. When he had tried to manoeuvre her into a dark corner after the hunt ball the previous autumn she had made it clear her ambition was marriage, not bed.

Brosy was watching him. 'You're cantering on the wrong rein,' he said. 'You need a wife.'

That was what Ackroyd was always saying, Colby remembered. Having smuggled him through the Federal lines to the waiting Brosy in New Orleans, where his service with Love's regiment had been tacitly forgotten and he had become nothing more than a war correspondent who had been foolish enough to get himself wounded, Ackroyd was privileged and didn't hesitate to take advantage of the fact.

'You're growing old,' he kept insisting. 'Before you know where you are, you'll be tottering about on two sticks.'

Ackroyd himself was well-married now, with a small son, and a secure position at the Home Farm, and sometimes Colby watched him with a faint feeling of envy.

He needed a home and Braxby Manor needed a woman. There hadn't been anybody who had really cared for it since his mother had died and suddenly he wondered what had happened to Gussie Dabney. By the time Ackroyd had got him home he had lost all contact with her and she with him and he had nothing to remember her by but the one urgent letter she had written, a stained yellow sash, a broken feather and a locket with a curl of her hair in it. She'd be twenty-one now, he realised, doubtless married and probably even a mother.

Brosy was watching him carefully, as though trying to read his thoughts. 'What about that Baroness you met at the Exhibition in 1867?' he asked. 'She was a goer, I'll be bound.'

Colby smiled. He couldn't remember much about the Exhibition but he could remember a lot about the Baronne Buffet de Maël. The French ballet dancer had long since disappeared into the limbo of old lovers, but Germaine Buffet de Maël, who had taken her place, was twenty-six, tall, ice-white with black hair and huge dark eyes, and, he hadn't the slightest doubt, had taken him only as the last in a long succession of lovers. She had married her baron at the age of seventeen, only to lose him on Napoleon III's ill-fated expedition to Mexico from the *vomito negro* which had decimated the French army list, and, inheriting his fortune, had joined that select band of emancipated woman who slept with whom they liked and said what they liked. But, while she was prepared to go to bed with Colby, she didn't wish to marry him, which was a complete reversal of the order of things decreed by the Rector's daughter.

As he thought about her, suddenly the mess seemed dreary, and the barracks with their surrounding mean streets and alehouses infinitely drab.

The afternoon was spent on the Common. The course was a stiff one with a variety of obstacles, including banks and drop fences, and an eye had to be kept open for NCOs who took a sadistic pleasure in contriving falls. Colby had no time for pushing his men too far. Going down the jumping lanes with arms and stirrups crossed was fine for grip and balance but to make a man do it facing the horse's tail was a sure way to destroy confidence and was worse for the horse than the man.

There was a wind and the horses were lively when they returned, kicking and squealing so that their riders learned by the hard way that bestriding an animal was less of a problem than its care and maintenance. One of them regularly resented the ministrations of the curry comb and could kick the stars out of the sky when in the mood. On occasions it even came over backwards, and it was always wiser to pass it with care.

'A horse, you'll find,' Colby pointed out dryly to the nervous recruit who was trying to handle it, 'is not only uncomfortable in the middle, it's dangerous at both ends as well.'

Claude Cosgro was sprawled in an armchair in the mess, peevish and unhealthy-looking with his plump, pale face and the taut lines at the corner of his mouth. The bugger had never been a beauty, Colby thought clinically, and marriage to Georgina hadn't improved him any more than marriage to him had improved Georgina.

'What's this about my young brother?' he said, looking up. 'He says you've given him duty officer for the rest of the week.'

'Yes,' Colby agreed briskly. 'He neglected his job.'

'For God's sake –' Cosgro's cheeks reddened '– *nobody* tastes the meat!'

'The officers of my squadron do!'

Cosgro stared at him with the dull look of a goaded bull. He'd always had too much money to spend, and his father, a baron now among the new titles that were springing up in industry, was of the same mould.

'He's supposed to be dining at home,' he grated. 'It's a family celebration.'

'In that case,' Colby said. 'I have no objection to him

being there.'

Cosgro's expression relaxed and Colby went on. 'Provided,' he continued, 'that he can find someone to stand in for him.' He spoke with grim satisfaction because Aubrey Cosgro was no more popular than his elder brother and would have the utmost difficulty in finding a stand-in.

Cosgro stared at him, his eyes hot and angry. 'Sometimes you go too bloody far, Goff,' he said.

The colonel was dining in the mess and after the meal called Colby over, offered him a brandy and took him towards the side of the fireplace. One of the younger lieutenants appeared at the other side all smiles, but the look the colonel gave him sent him blushing to another corner of the mess.

Colonel Canning, Brosy's father-in-law, was a short square man with a white moustache and long whiskers who had fought in India and he made it clear he wished to talk in private.

'Been asked to detach you to the Horse Guards,' he said quietly.

Colby's eyebrows shot up. 'Me, sir?'

'Yes. Matter of fact, I thought Brosy might like the job but, though I'm fond of Brosy and he's a good husband to Grace, he's not the man.'

Colby frowned. 'I'm not sure I want to be at the Horse Guards, sir. I'm not even sure I want to be on the staff.'

The colonel snorted. 'Then you're a damn fool!' he said. 'It's what every good officer should seek. Without staff experience you'll end up like me – just a colonel.'

'Commanding the regiment was my ambition, sir.'

'Then it shouldn't be. You've got more to you than that. Not all of us have. You'll be reporting tomorrow, so you'd better not drink any more of that brandy.'

The gloomy mood was still on Colby as he left the mess. Picking up a passing growler, he headed towards Hounslow, stopping on the way at an alehouse for something to eat.

But the alehouse was smoky and drab and the absence of

anyone of his own type made him feel lonely. It was a pity, he thought, that there weren't more women like Brosy's Grace about the world and a few less Georginas. Grace was understanding and easy-going – perhaps too easy-going for a Goff but right enough for Brosy – and suddenly he wished he could find a wife like her.

He thought nostalgically of Germaine de Maël once more. She was beautiful and intelligent and a cut above Caroline Matchett. Spoiled? Yes, but she was damned good in bed, which was something the British Housewives' Association didn't seem to think very proper when a marriage had been entered into. He'd probably enjoy being married to someone like Germaine, he thought. But – he hesitated – she'd want to live in London or Paris, and he couldn't imagine being away for ever from the beloved northern acres of Braxby – or for that matter, the 19th, which had become for him an ambition, a trust and an obsession all at the same time. She'd probably even want him to resign his commission and he didn't fancy that either. Finally, she was dreadful on a horse, though she was kindly and understanding, made love with a healthy bouncing enjoyment, and had a habit of being sorry for the middle-aged men who offered their fortunes for the privilege of her affection. It might be an idea to follow up Brosy's idea after all. If, he thought gloomily, this new job at the Horse Guards didn't preclude leave in Paris.

As he entered her house, Caroline Matchett was sitting by the fire alone, with a glass in her hand.

'You should be getting your beauty sleep,' Colby pointed out.

'It's too late for that now,' she said. 'I'm well past beauty.'

She pushed the decanter towards him and, as he poured himself a drink, he looked at her in the firelight and realised that what she said was right. Her features were beginning to crumble and there wasn't much left but the smile. As he always did, he swore to himself that when he left he'd not come back.

'Have you been drinking long?' he asked.

'About as long as you,' she retorted.

He struggled out of his coat and threw it over a chair. 'I have to go to the Horse Guards tomorrow. I expect it's some bloody awful job they've found for me.'

She was smoking, one of the few women he knew apart from Germaine who smoked regularly. As she brushed ash from her skirt, she seemed depressed.

'Do women often sit alone drinking brandy and soda?' he asked.

'This one does,' she said. 'There are a lot of bogeys about, Coll. One especially: old age.'

'It worries me, too, sometimes,' he admitted. 'And they might even eventually give the Regiment to that ass, Cosgro.'

'Never!'

His head jerked up. 'You know him?'

She paused. 'He's been here.'

Suddenly he was angry. The thought that he shared her favours with the man he most disliked seemed insulting. 'Does *he* think he'll get the Regiment?'

'He thinks he has enough influence.'

Colby scowled. 'He probably has,' he admitted. He swallowed his brandy and poured a second. 'I'll see you get another bottle,' he pointed out. 'You can't afford to keep thirsty cavalrymen in drink.'

'I get a little help here and there.'

'From Claude Cosgro?'

'He's not mean.'

'Christ —' suddenly the brandy was affecting his temper '— to think —'

She shut him up. 'You're conceited, Coll,' she said. 'Why shouldn't he come here? Why shouldn't I encourage him? I'm not wealthy and I haven't many more years before *nobody* will come.'

Her mood depressed him. What she said was right and he felt sorry for her and just a little drunk. A thought struck him. 'I heard Claude Cosgro was visiting a farmer's wife here.'

She didn't answer, staring him out.

'Is it a farmer's wife? Or is it you?'

Still she didn't answer.'

'God damn it, is it? It's been going on for years.'

Suddenly she was angry, too. 'What do you expect? He has more money than you. And he doesn't disappear into the blue like you do. Why shouldn't he be a friend?'

'I thought *I* was your friend.'

'I can't afford to have only *one* friend! It needn't make any difference. You can stay.'

'No.' He stumbled to his feet. 'I'd better go. I'm not angry. I just called – I – just to say I wouldn't be coming any more.'

She laughed. 'Because of Claude?'

It *was* because of Cosgro, but he couldn't say so. He felt deprived, cheated and ashamed. 'No,' he said. 'It's not that. I'm thinking of getting married.'

Her eyebrows shot up. 'You! The confirmed bachelor!' She laughed. 'You'll have her doubling round the bedroom like the riding master.'

He frowned, irritated. 'I'll be off.'

'I'll see you again.'

Her very certainty infuriated him more. 'I'll let myself out,' he said.

She didn't move, simply reaching over to pour herself another brandy. The maid met him in the hall and opened the door. As he fished in his pocket and laid his key on the hall table, she called his attention to it.

He smiled and gave her a sovereign. 'I shan't need it any more,' he said.

When he reached Whitehall the following day, Colby was still in a bad temper. The porter at the Horse Guards took his name and vanished, to return shortly afterwards with a young officer in mufti.

'You're for Sir Garnet Wolseley!' He made it sound like a prison sentence.

Colby followed him along a bleak brown corridor to a small drab room filled with maps, papers and books. 'This the same Garnet Wolseley who ran the Red River Expedition?' he asked.

The young man's supercilious expression slipped a little. 'Of course. I was with him. Perfect example of expert staff planning. Know him?'

'Met him in Washington during the Civil War.' Colby looked round the shabby little room. 'What's he doing here? I'd have thought he'd have deserved something better than this after the Red River.'

The young officer looked indignant. 'So he should,' he said. 'He had a right to expect important employment. Instead he was placed on half pay.'

'*The Soldiers' Pocket Book*?'

Everybody in the army had read Wolseley's compendium for officers and other ranks. It was crammed with practical advice and information, but his opinions on such touchy subjects as the capabilities of officers had stirred up regimental messes like disturbed ants' nests.

'What he said needed saying,' the young officer said stiffly.

'And now?'

'The Secretary for War brought him back. To review court martial procedures.'

Colby smiled. 'And to lead the Secretary for War by the hand with his army reforms. Professional knowledge added to political skill.'

The man who appeared a moment later was small and not much older than Colby, with a slight limp, greying hair, and a brisk manner. He didn't look much like a soldier with his receding chin and knowledgeable manner but there was something brisk and powerful about him that caught the attention at once. Like everybody else in the army, Colby knew Wolseley's reputation: commissioned without purchase, he had advanced to his present rank without spending a penny on promotion. With half a dozen campaigns and five wounds under his belt, he was full of decided opinions on all aspects of equipping, managing and training the army, and it was widely accepted that he had a tremendous career in front of him – provided he wasn't asked to resign first.

'You were to have seen the Duke of Cambridge,' he said briskly. 'But he had to go to the palace, so you're seeing me instead.'

'I'm no expert on courts martial, sir,' Colby said.

Wolseley smiled. 'Neither am I. Sit down.'

As he found a chair, Colby noticed that a map of Europe was spread out on the desk, weighted at the corners with books.

'Speak German?' Wolseley asked.

Colby shrugged. 'A little, sir,' he said. 'There were a lot of Germans in the Northern forces I was with. Even a few in the South. I picked it up.'

'Nearly did for your career, too,' Wolseley observed bluntly. 'Getting mixed up in that business.'

Colby said nothing and Wolseley went on quickly. 'How about French?'

'About the same, sir. There were Georgia Frenchmen from Roswell in Love's command. I picked it up in equal quantities.'

Wolseley placed his fingertips together in a steeple and studied Colby. 'You know France well, I believe?'

'I rode across it, sir. Last summer. Though I didn't stop long enough to study it much.'

Wolseley nodded. 'I heard about that. How about Paris?'

The words brought a wave of nostalgia back. Of all the cities Colby had visited, Paris was the most exciting and he suddenly felt an itch to see it again.

'I've spent a lot of time there, sir,' he said. 'I was there for the Exhibition.'

'What was your impression?'

What the deuce was all this, Colby thought.

'I noticed some very big Krupp guns from Essen,' he said.

'And the review? You saw the military review? What did you think of that?'

'It looked to me like the last pageant of the Empire, sir.'

'What does that mean?'

'I'm not sure it was entirely a success. The Emperor

looked old and some fool took a pot-shot at the Czar of Russia, which didn't improve relationships.'

'What about the troops?'

Colby considered. There had been a continuous stream of red and blue as the Zouaves had swung by, followed by the Guides in green and gold, the lancers with their tall schapkas and the flutter of pennons, and the Heavies in brass helmets and shining breastplates. What about them? The thing that had remained most in his mind was the acrid smell of horseflesh and the flies, the high scream of orders, the bands, the thud of kettle drums and the slow boom of guns from Mont Valérien. In the Crimea the French had seemed splendid, chiefly because the British were so awful, and nothing had pleased a British officer more than to get hold of a French frock coat in place of his brief British jacket. But that had been when the French Empire had looked good. It was beginning now to look a little aged and the glamour had begun to fade. The Emperor had got himself into trouble in Italy, and gained nothing from the Prussian defeat of the Austrians. And in Mexico, where he had set up a puppet empire with a brother of the Emperor of Austria, he had been told firmly by the Americans, whose civil war had left them one of the most powerful military nations in the world, to keep his hands off their side of the Atlantic.

He realised just what his impression had been. As the little brass guns had clanked by behind their teams and the troops had marched off in a cloud of June dust, it had occurred to him that, compared with the Americans, they seemed to belong more correctly to the empire of the first Napoleon.

He looked up. Wolseley was waiting patiently. 'I think they looked a little out-of-date, sir,' he said.

Wolseley studied him thoughtfully. 'Cross the frontier?' he asked.

'I went down the Rhine, sir.'

'Why?'

The answer seemed obvious. 'To drink the wine, sir.'

Colby's retort was inclined to be over-brisk but Wolseley

seemed unperturbed. 'See *their* troops?' he asked.

'Several times, sir.'

'Impressions?'

Jesus Christ in the mountains, would it never end? 'Workman-like, sir. When they call a class up, everybody has to report. I met a professor from Heidelberg serving as a lieutenant in the reserve. It must make for clever commanding, and in a general mobilisation you'd have companies commanded by men not only of military skill but also of high intelligence. In the French army, if you're wealthy enough you can buy yourself a stand-in, so that the ones who find themselves in uniform are merely the ones who aren't clever enough to avoid it. That's how it was in the North during the Civil War, sir, as you'll recall, and their conscripts at first were dreadful.'

Wolseley sat back in his chair. Wondering what was coming, Colby waited. 'We're very interested in what's happening on the Continent,' Wolseley said at last. 'What's *your* opinion?'

'Looks to me like war, sir.'

'That's how it looks to me,' Wolseley agreed. 'Though it doesn't appear to do so to anyone else. As you probably know, the Queen made a great friend of Napoleon III.'

Colby *had* heard. The papers had been full of it at the time. Uncertain how he was supposed to reply, he kept silent.

'She's concerned at the situation over there,' Wolseley went on. 'She's also concerned at the behaviour of the Prussians. The poor soul's in rather a cleft stick – on one side someone she admired, on the other her relations. She's anxious to know how things will go. Come to that, so are we, so for once we're all in agreement. Everybody thinks the French will win if it comes to a war. I'm not so sure. Though I know everybody beats the Austrians, any nation who can do it in six weeks must be good. What do *you* feel?'

Colby remembered von Hartmann again, with his quest for information and his supreme confidence in his own country's military system. 'I think the Prussians have better ideas, sir,' he tried cautiously.

'That's my opinion, too. And I suspect it will eventually dawn on the taxpayer of this country that our army's as far behind that of the French as I suspect *they* are behind the army of Prussia. I want you to pay another visit.'

Colby's eyebrows shot up, his bad temper forgotten. This was luck if you liked! Just when he was growing bored, too!

'Which country, sir?'

'Both.'

Better and better!

'You're one of the few men who ought to be able to get along with both sides. We're all out-of-date here and the cavalry in particular has to find a new rôle, because defensive weapons like the rifle and the breach-loading cannon revolutionised the war in America. I want you to go and report on what you see.'

'As a military observer, sir?'

'Unofficial. It's the Secretary for War's wish, because he feels there's much we might learn which will aid his reforms. But there are no funds for such jauntings, so you won't be getting any special expenses. We can hardly appoint military observers until the war starts, anyway, and if it's over as quickly as the ones against the Austrians and the Danes, they'll not arrive before peace is signed. You reported on the American War for the *Morning Advertiser*, I think. Perhaps you should go and see them again.'

'Suppose they have their own man, sir?'

'I think they won't. I've seen the editor.'

Typical of the army, Colby thought. Trying to avoid responsibility and expense.

Wolseley was speaking again. 'What you do for the *Morning Advertiser* will be your own affair,' he said. '*I* want to know about the French army. I hope you understand.'

2

Paris was different from at any time Colby could ever remember. The streets were boiling cauldrons of humanity and so packed with traffic it was impossible to cross them without picking your way through the piles of horse dung. Tartan trousers seemed to be the vogue, he noticed with a critical eye, and toppers had grown taller, while women were still wearing those damn silly crinolines.

The crossing from Dover had been calm and the train from Calais comfortable. the suburban stations were full of bustle, with groups of workmen in blue blouses, officials in pince-nez and imperials, and squads of soldiers in red trousers and snowy gaiters. Brosy had been right. There *was* something about Paris, even if it were only an air of alertness, zest and prosperity.

Leaving his hotel in the Rue Jacob, dressed by Ackroyd to within an inch of his life, Colby pushed through the mob until he found a fiacre.

'*Circulez*,' he said. 'Just drive around.'

This, he thought, was a job in a million, and he stared about him, his eyes bright, a half-smile on his face, aware of that curious excitement that being on the Continent and especially in Paris brought in him. Black against the yellow of the evening sky, he could see the great arch built to commemorate the first Napoleon's triumphs standing at the top of the Champs Elysées on the outskirts of the city.

At the other end of the avenue, the chilly dignity was lost in the casualness of narrow streets and café-concerts. Down there, under the opal globes of the gas lamps, the bars and cafés were doing a roaring trade, most of their customers outside on the pavement in the heat, the young men carrying their jackets over their arms, the girls all wasp waists and follow-me-young-man ribbons, and as much gauze from the waist upwards as they could get away with.

Following Colby's directions, the cab driver circled the Arc de Triomphe and began the descent among cabs and buses acrid with the smell of the stable. The house where they stopped was new and elegant, flat-fronted with a semi-circular porch supported by pillars at the top of a short flight of steps, its forecourt circled by railings. Hearing Colby's accent, the manservant who answered the door was not inclined to allow him to step inside. Pushing him back, Colby handed over his hat and gloves.

'And now, please,' he said. 'Announce me to the Baronne.'

As the manservant placed the cloak, hat, stick and gloves on a table in the hall and turned sullenly away, Colby barked at him. '*Et vîte, si vous tenez à la vie!*'

It was a phrase he had learned from one of Love's French troopers and, coming unexpectedly from a foreigner, it made the manservant move for the staircase a great deal faster.

Germaine de Maël was in her boudoir, in a peignoir of white lace. There was a great deal of bosom showing but somehow it managed to be discreet. Madame de Maël had been brought up in a noble but impoverished family and knew exactly what was correct, which was why the salon she ran attracted brains, wit and intelligence as well as lovers.

'Colbee,' she said softly. 'This is a delight! We must have champagne. It is so much better at this hour than your un-civilised English tea.'

'Where have you been for so long?' she went on as the maid poured the drink into flutes. 'I was devastated when your returned to your silly soldiering. Are you yet married?'

'No.' Colby regarded her with warmth and affection. She was a beautiful, highly-intelligent woman, none too

137

trustworthy but far from ruthless. 'Are you?'

She shrugged. 'No. But I am growing old. Soon I must settle down.'

'There's a man?'

'*Mais, oui*! Always. A woman can survive without love but never without lovers. His name is Narcisse and he's the Baron de Polignac.'

'Old régime?'

She made another face and smiled. 'Empire creation.'

'Doesn't even impress the servants.'

She shrugged. 'Like you, he's a soldier. At the moment, he is in Paris but he's been ordered to Metz, close to the frontier.'

'When are you going to marry him?'

'Marriage?' She pulled a face. 'There's nothing like that. He wishes to be my protector and I am happy with the arrangement. This way, I spend *his* money instead of mine. Tomorrow, I am holding a ball. You must come. Have you an English lady friend you can bring? Or are they like Englishmen – all silent and stiff and surrounded by dogs? And why are you in Paris?'

If she had a lover on the staff of the French army, Colby decided, it would be as well to be discreet. 'I came to ask you to dine.'

'I should like that. We shall be seen and then Narcisse is bound to find out, and that will make him jealous. After all, nobody owns me and I recall with pleasure our previous meetings. You have, I remember, such lovely legs.'

It wasn't difficult to find out about the French army. High-spirited, vain and intelligent, the Parisians were more than willing to talk about it and every boulevardier was certain that Prussia was the enemy. Yet, beneath the confidence, there was also a disturbing sense of anxiety. There seemed to be no plan to counter the Prussians and, above all, no method at the top. According to reports, Napoleon III was an invalid, his generals were not considered competent, and the Empress was cordially disliked for her interference in affairs. It seemed to add up to disaster and Colby didn't

138

hesitate to say so in the report he wrote for London.

'What do *you* think of it, Tyas?' he asked.

Ackroyd paused in polishing a pair of boots to consider. 'Too many bloody buttons, sir,' he said.

Colby grinned. There was a lot of sense in Ackroyd's views and he had enough experience to know what he was talking about. The army was splendid and clearly adored by the crowds for whom its bands crashed out martial music all day in the streets. Spurs and sabres clanked on the pavements and uniforms filled the squares with bouquets of colour. But like its theme music, *Partant Pour La Syrie*, a gay melody that was almost a dance-tune, it had a comic opera touch about it that didn't always seem real. Grenadiers in towering bearskins, rugged-cheeked veterans with bemedalled breasts; voltigeurs in gilded shakoes; Zouaves like part of the French flag with their blue capotes, red trousers and white gaiters; dragoons in tiger-skin helmets; hussars with pale blue pelisses; Lancers of the Guard in white tunics; and Chasseurs in olive – they were everywhere, every colour of the rainbow. Napoleon I had been well aware how to make a man proud to be a soldier and his nephew had resurrected his colour schemes. The snowy breeches, jackboots, gaudy tunics, banners, pennants and guidons, and the acres of musicians crashing out military tunes were everywhere with the tossing surf of manes, glaring eyeballs and foam-flecked flanks of cavalry. It was magnificent but Colby had a feeling it was all suspect. And certainly the conscripts were not impressive. Since the poor from the cities tended to be unhealthy, most of them seemed to be peasants.

'Not noted for initiative,' he was informed cheerfully, 'but at least they're politically reliable.'

By the simple procedure of talking to the officers from the Prince Eugène Barracks whom he met in bars, he learned that the strength of the army was a hundred thousand less than the number the Prussians could muster if it came to a war, and that there were only sixty thousand on the reserve, while the Germans had a vast mass of trained men. The Mobile Guards, supposed to be the second line of defence, consisted, it seemed, only of names on paper, and there was a lot of resentment among the men caught for conscription about also being caught for the reserve.

It made a harsh report and the British ambassador, who was charged with sending it in his diplomatic bag, didn't agree with it. Nor apparently did anyone else.

'You are the only man who has this to say about the French army,' Wolseley informed him.

The night of Germaine de Maël's ball was hotter and more sultry than ever and there seemed to be an increased excitement on the boulevards because over the last few days the talk of war in the bars had grown louder.

Bands of students and workmen were patrolling the streets, singing patriotic and revolutionary songs like 'The Marseillaise.' In front of the Prince Eugène Barracks, a great demonstration was being held, and thousands of workmen had gathered from the adjacent faubourgs to witness the departure of a regiment for the frontier. There was a great deal of drinking going on and much cheering, singing and fraternisation, more crowds in the Boulevard Montmartre, and several thousand people parading up and down the Place Vendôme with shouts of 'Vive Napoléon!'

Lacquered landaus and daumonts with matched horses were already drawing up outside the home of the Baronne de Maël as Colby arrived in a hired carriage driven by the ubiquitous Ackroyd. Germaine was dressed in white, with as much of her bosom showing as possible without being vulgar, her dark hair done in ringlets round her head. As she held out her hand for Colby to kiss, just behind her he saw a man in the uniform of the Cavalry of the Guard, slight and dandified with a moustache and a small imperial beard. His uniform seemed to consist chiefly of gold buttons and lace frogs.

'This is Narcisse,' she said quietly. 'He has to leave this evening for Metz.'

De Polignac clicked his heels, but he didn't smile, studying Colby with unfriendly eyes. It wasn't hard to guess that

Germaine, in her honest way, had let it be known what the relationship between them had been before he had appeared on the scene.

'I have heard of you, Major Goff,' he said.

The house was full of noise. Loud voices were raised in an excited chatter and the sound of an orchestra came from the ballroom in a muted thump-thump. It was a strange atmosphere that seemed confident yet somehow seemed to suffer from a dreadful doubt, as if they were all rushing to a climax at a breakneck speed and were well aware of the fact. The certainties which had founded the Napoleonist regime seemed somehow to have lost their grip and everybody seemed to be grasping at the crisis as a means of keeping up their spirits, revelling in the fact that they had forced Bismarck's climb-down, because they all secretly entertained a morbid fear of the Prussian Chancellor and felt that next day they would awaken to news of fighting along the frontier.

As the band swung into the gentle lilt of one of Waldteufel's waltzes, Colby held out his arm.

'The last time I danced to this tune,' Germaine said, 'it was at the Tuileries and you could hear the police charging the crowds outside. They were rioting about the election. They smashed windows and burned a cabman's shelter. But it turned out all right in the end and when the Emperor drove out in an open carriage the next day he was well received.' She looked meaningly at Colby. 'I shall expect you to return when this is all over,' she said quietly. 'I shall need calming. This talk of war tires me.'

'If it does come to war,' Colby asked, 'where will you see it out?'

'Metz, of course. I have promised to join Narcisse there for three weeks. That should be enough to see the armies move into Germany. I have a friend who is prepared to lend me his house. Number Twenty-Nine, Avenue Serpenoise, if you should be in the area. It's in the best part of town.'

'Suppose it doesn't work out that way?'

She looked at him with large puzzled eyes. 'What other

way could it work out?'

'Suppose the Prussians move into France instead?'

She stared at him for a moment then gave a tinkling laugh and slapped his wrist with her fan. 'You silly goose! How could that happen?'

When they returned to the salon, the lurking anger against Prussia that had been below the surface for months had risen like bubbles from the depths of a dark pond. The band had retired to eat and everybody was standing about arguing, the men in a group, the women looking nervously towards them.

'France can't stand by while a foreign power disturbs the equilibrium of Europe. In any case, the Prussians are nothing but hastily trained levies.' The speaker was a hot-eyed de Polignac and his audience, judging by their stomachs, were all civilians. He seemed to be enjoying the standing his military rank gave him and as his eye fell on Colby he swept him into the discussion. 'Don't you agree?'

Colby hesitated. 'I think the Prussian generals have profited by their wars,' he said slowly.

'And ours haven't?'

'Yours are very affable,' Colby said warily. 'And they are splendidly dressed.'

'We have MacMahon, Bourbaki, Bazaine.'

From what Colby had heard, MacMahon, Bourbaki and Bazaine were all Cardigans, elderly lieutenants incapable of running armies.

He shrugged and said nothing and de Polignac went on, his eyes blazing. 'We shall cross the Rhine and intimidate South Germany into neutrality. Then the Austrians and the Italians will come in and all that will be needed for the Prussians will be a covering force in Lorraine. Don't you agree?'

It seemed to be a plan that called for the first Napoleon and Colby forced a smile. 'I have no idea,' he said. 'I would like to see. Perhaps as an observer with the armies.'

De Polignac laughed and began to head for the door. 'There'll be no time. It will be over too quickly.' He gestured to the toadies who followed him. 'These English,' he said. 'They have no idea of the art of war.'

As Colby glared at his retreating back, a voice came quietly from behind him. 'Take care, my friend, or you'll be needing a second.'

Turning, he found himself staring into the pale face of Hans-Viktor von Hartmann.

'By God,' he said. 'You're in dangerous company tonight!'

Von Hartmann smiled. 'They think I'm an Alsatian.'

'What are you doing? Spying?'

'Not at all,' von Hartmann was quite unperturbed. 'I was invited quite properly. But a long time ago before the hubbub about the Hohenzollern Candidature appeared. I met her in Mainz. She's forgotten who I am.'

'It'll be as well if nobody finds out.'

Von Hartmann shrugged. 'I can always retreat to the Embassy. I'm there as military attaché.' He gestured at the people about him. 'Everybody in Paris is giving parties like this, this summer. I've been to dozens. I think they're all a little worried, don't you?'

It didn't surprise Colby that the Prussian had also noticed the underlying current of uncertainty.

'The Emperor's growing old,' von Hartmann continued. 'He no longer holds the balance of power and everybody knows he's lost his touch. I couldn't resist being here when they heard the news.'

'What news?'

Von Hartmann smiled. 'The King of Prussia will turn down France's demand for an apology.' He shrugged. 'After all, they *are* asking rather a lot, aren't they? Bismarck's not the man to eat humble pie for anyone. That war they're wanting is a lot nearer today than it was yesterday.'

'And if it does come to war, what will the result be?'

Von Hartmann smiled. 'We shall win, of course. We don't *play* at war. We study it. For your information, my dear Major, *our* railways run towards the frontier, not like the French – across what will be the line of march. When *ours* were built, we had a staff officer working with the builders.' The Prussian's smile widened. 'As I once told you, *our* generals don't guess. You have only to look at what happened to the Austrians at Sadowa to see that. The French army's nothing but a shop window with nothing on the shelves, and the men they will appoint to command aren't so much generals as dancing masters and court favourites. Imperial aides-de-camp to a man, picked for their ability to entertain the Empress.' He shrugged. 'Perhaps they're no worse than any others in the end, of course, but they have no staff to guide them, so they will fail.'

'How do you know all this?'

Von Hartmann's shoulders moved. 'We make a point of knowing. They also have to mobilise more quickly than we do if they're to inflict damage, but they won't because they're short of supplies and maps, and medicaments for their hospitals.' He tapped Colby's arm with his glove. 'If you are so keen on being a military observer,' he went on, 'why not join the Prussian army? We are anxious for people to see how good we are, and, after all, our countries are almost allies. With your royal family of German descent, we are even interrelated. It is the French who are the enemies.' He fished in his pocket and produced a small square of pasteboard. 'My card,' he said. 'If you're interested, go to Mainz. That's where headquarters will be.'

When Colby returned to the ballroom, it was clear that the news von Hartmann had heard had arrived. The men were drinking suddenly as though they were the last drinks in the world. There was a lot of noise and the group round de Polignac was noisy with the noisiness of the uncertain and over-excited. From outside, they could hear the roar of the crowd, which was swarming even into the Champs Elysées. Snatches of 'The Marseillaise' kept coming through the window and the excitement spread through the house as people from the ballroom joined the crowd in the salon.

'They're throwing things at the Prussian Embassy,' someone said.

The room was pulsating with noise, and the war fever was so obvious you could almost reach out and touch it. In the street outside, the bands of students and working men were now arm-in-arm, sweeping into their midst anyone who happened to be in the way. One group had a couple of soldiers in uniform on their shoulders, laughing, shouting, waving bottles and yelling '*Vive Napoléon.*'

A band arrived from nowhere, blaring out *Partant Pour La Syrie*, while the students began to chant and sing, one group against another. Tricolour ribbons and flags appeared and were draped round cabs as they picked their way through the crowd, the horses neighing with fright at the noise. They were all full of people waving bottles and offering drinks and cigars to any soldiers they saw, while the crowds spilling out of the side streets were pushing others from the pavements into the road and women were shrieking as they found themselves under horses' hooves.

Watching from the balcony, Colby saw a prostitute offer a drink from a brandy bottle to a dandy in evening dress. Then a carriage pushed past with half a dozen people inside, all yelling and laughing and waving flags. A walking stick swung, and the dandy's top hat vanished, and the next he saw of it was an urchin kicking its dented shape among the shuffling feet.

A sort of hypnotism had caught the crowd inside the de Maël mansion now and everybody began to surge to the stairs, as though they wished to be outside with the mob. Men were shouting and the ballroom was nothing but a gigantic cauldron, as people swarmed in uninvited from outside. Men holding glasses were shaking hands and kissing girls, and a woman began to sing '*J'Aime Les Militaires.*' Everybody linked arms and flung paper serpentines, then a group of young men appeared with newly-printed newspapers, whose ink smudged their gloves.

'It's war all right!' they were yelling. 'The Prussian ambassador's leaving!'

De Polignac, already cloaked and hatted, was pushing

his way to the door with his friends. They were obviously trying to make an impression and the crowd was clapping as they went. Ackroyd was waiting in the hall with Colby's hat, cloak and stick, watching the revellers with a contemptuous expression on his face.

'Come on, Tyas,' Colby said. 'We're going to take the train to Brussels.'

Ackroyd's face fell. 'Brussels?' he said. 'There won't be no fightin' in Belgium.'

'No, Tyas, my lad,' Colby agreed. 'But the French frontier will have been closed already and the only way to get into Germany now will be via Belgium and the Palatinate.'

3

The Belgian trains were crammed with Germans hurrying home to swell their army. Two of them informed Colby that they had come from as far away as New York, and they were an extraordinary mixture of American financial astuteness and single-hearted German patriotic zeal, as much concerned with their shares as they were with the wish to see Prussia win.

When they reached Cologne, working parties were already felling trees on the ramparts and repairing the forts, and a state of siege had already been declared. There was a quiet regularity about the German mobilisation, however, that compared favourably with the French frenzy. Bemedalled men called up from the reserve were mixed with young soldiers serving their first period of three years, balancing their dash with steadiness. Their shoulders were well back, their legs straight and their chins well 'off the stock.' They were gaunt, long-thighed, big-jointed men, all corners and muscle, from the mountains and plains, but they were clearly as tough as whipcord with a curious sobriety and docility, so that there were no parties out to pick drunken men out of the gutters or stop incipient riots, and there were no women hanging round the barrack gates.

The 19th Prussian Lancers were at Kaiserslautern and due to leave for the frontier, and von Hartmann was bubbling over with excitement.

'The French are having problems with their mobilisation,' he pointed out. 'Ours goes well and if they don't move in the next week, we shall have no trouble. We're to go to Saarbrücken.'

He escorted Colby to headquarters and saw him issued with passes. The place was bustling with activity but the Germans seemed occupied with a deep sense of earnestness and moral purpose that reminded Colby of Cromwell's Ironsides with their sense of justice and their Lutheran hymns.

As they took the train for the frontier, France was still playing a waiting-game and the Germans were breathing more freely with every day. Bingerbruck, the terminus from which the Rhine railway system ran towards the frontier, was totally blocked for civilian passengers but, with the passes von Hartmann had supplied, there was no problem. The regiments moving west, powdered with dust after a fifteen-mile march, had no stragglers, Colby noted, and there were only a few cases of sunstroke despite the temperature of eighty-five in the shade and the weapons, knapsacks, ammunition, great-coats, camp kettles, swords, spades and other odds and ends they carried.

Saarbrücken, where they booked in at the Hotel Hagen, was divided into two towns. Saarbrücken to the south, St Johann to the north, the bridges connecting them obstructed by casks filled with stones. The town seemed to be held only by a single battalion of infantry, though the 19th Lancers had a detachment there, and the streets seemed as normal as in peacetime, girls making eyes at subalterns outside the shops and little to be seen of the war except the pickets, the sentry on the door of the hotel occupied by the military commandant, and Red Cross flags on the hurriedly-established hospitals.

To the west the road lifted sharply towards a plateau then fell gently through densely wooded ground. In the centre of the valley was the French town of Forbach and to the left a series of heights terminating in a hill called the Spicherenberg. All along the line, pickets were confronting each other, cavalry vedettes circling in the distance, their lance pennons fluttering. A few hundred yards further on was a big blockhouse where the French had gathered in large numbers, their scouts out in front of them. Von Hartmann's lancers had already cut the railway line that connected Metz with Strasbourg, but there was nothing to see and the only excitement came when Colby went out with a feldwebel's patrol that was set upon by French North African troops, fortunately far too excited to shoot straight. As they returned, von Hartmann was looking eager. 'The French are moving cannon over the the Spicherenberg,' he announced. 'They reconnoitred it last evening. Something is clearly coming.'

Nothing did, however, beyond a salvo from the French guns which scattered a watching crowd and demolished a beerhouse, and a bout of spy-fever which resulted as often as not in the Germans arresting men of their own side sent forward to watch the French or a local yokel romping in the bushes with his girl.

As August came, a few infantry and guns arrived and the nervously-clicking telegraph at the station warned that more were needed. Armed with cigars, which they had already found an excellent introduction to German soldiers, Colby and Ackroyd headed for the front. The artillery was drawn up in line with the ammunition wagons and horses in the rear. A forge was alight and the farriers were busy shoeing, while von Hartmann's officers sat in the sunshine drinking coffee, their colour in its cover stuck in the ground with the drum major's halberd. Behind were knapsacks and rolled greatcoats in straight rows. A crowd had gathered round carts carrying beer and casks of wine, and a few men were singing, the camp kettles simmering on the fires for their meal. The whole place seemed drowzy with summer.

Crossing the valley, they climbed the slope. There was no sign of excitement, but as they neared the Exerciseplatz they saw men running about, then an officer came hurtling down the slope on a horse. Streaming down the roads from France were dense and glittering columns of troops, the sun striking sharply on bayonets and scarlet trousers. They were advancing swiftly, six abreast, with no pretence at formation, and as the head of the column reached the valley it broke apart like spray, file after file dispersing into the trees, until an unbroken line of skirmishers was drawn up in front. Squadrons of cavalry poured down after them, then, forming line at the gallop, overtook them, passed through their intervals, reformed and covered the flanks.

As the tirailleurs opened a spattering volley, the German infantry retaliated and the whole French force began to fire.

'I think we'd better get out of here,' Colby said.

As a riderless horse went careering away, its tail over its back, and the bullets began to strike the trees above their heads, they bolted for the dip. As they reached the road beneath, one of the Prussians, hit in the back, came crashing down on the shrubs at their feet. The lancers, drawn up in the shelter formed by a bend of the road, began to retreat through Saarbrücken and a knot of fusiliers hurrying after them were caught by a shell which struck down a sergeant and five men at once. By this time, the French were on the heights and driving the Germans back. As they reached Saarbrücken, shells from French guns began to crash among the houses, and, though the side streets were safe, there was a constant shower of tiles and chimney pots.

Reaching the station, they discovered von Hartmann deciding to make his final stand there and bolted instead towards the Hotel Hagen. There were three or four Englishmen inside, with several women who had been touring the frontier. As the hotel was knocked to pieces about their ears, the landlord was making sure they all paid for their drinks. A shell had burst in the kitchen to spatter the ceiling with potatoes and send gravy flowing across the floor. The landlady and the maids were having hysterics and Colby and Ackroyd helped to carry them into a cellar under the backyard. The front of the hotel was riddled by this time and they could hear the French mitrailleuses going like a policeman's rattle.

They left the Englishmen playing whist in the breakfast room, ran across an open space, crossed a deep cutting, and began to follow the railway towards Duttweiler. All around them straggling German soldiers who had lost their regiments were heading for a rendezvous at Lebach.

'Cross between a spectacle and a farce.' Colby decided he was probably mistaken about Prussian efficiency, because if the French pushed on now they could reach the Rhine without a pitched battle. There wasn't an officer within two days of Duttweiler, he decided, who wouldn't be girding up his loins for when they appeared.

Duttweiler was packed with people, and the hotel, a rambling erection with wing after wing of bedrooms on corridors along which you could drive a coach and pair, was full of foreign waifs and strays. The four Englishmen they had left playing whist in Saarbrücken were just obtaining rooms and there were several Englishwomen who were trying to get home. An officer of the American army was also there to see the fun and several British officers in mufti, as well as an English student from Bonn university who informed them that the French had not occupied Saarbrücken, had not even crossed the bridges in case they were mined, and had made no attempt to destroy the telegraph.

They didn't stop any longer than was necessary to eat a meal, then they hired horses and rode towards Pirmasens where they picked up a train to the Rhine and headed north to Cologne and into Belgium. The French newspapers there were full of the affair. 'Tremendous battle at Saarbrücken,' they announced. 'Our army has taken the offensive, crossed the frontier and invaded Prussian territory.' The British newspapers echoed the story, even the *Morning Advertiser*, which was clearly not trusting Colby's reports, so that he had to send Ackroyd to Brussels to insist that he was correct and that the 'great battle' was nothing more than a skirmish, and a very uncertain and unprofessional skirmish at that.

It appeared that Napoleon III had been present with his son, the Prince Imperial, having appeared in Metz only a few days before to lead the triumphal march of the army into Germany, so, sending two despatches to London – one to the *Morning Advertiser*, one to Wolseley – Colby joined Ackroyd in Brussels and they reached Metz the next evening.

The place was awash with soldiers and tricolours; in every square and on every one of the green islands on which the city was built, tents, horses and waggons crammed every available space. The city was still wild with excitement after the scuffle at Saarbrücken. 'Tremendous Battle,' the paper claimed. 'Frossard wins Great French Victory. Prince Imperial Receives Baptism of Fire.' But, despite the bells and the people singing and cheering in the street, Colby noticed that the newspapers were curiously empty of details and there was no sign of prisoners.

Though the army had moved to the frontier, the city was still a great camp, and a boarding house for the civilian population who had arrived to watch the war. Rattling carts and plodding companies of soldiers kept the place awake at night and military bands played all day in the Place d'Armes. It was impossible to get away from soldiers. They were everywhere, in every bar, every café, every restaurant, every square and every street. There seemed to be thousands of them – dim-eyed yokels from the Midi, boastful veterans of the Crimea, Mexico and Italy, and noisy young officers with bold eyes and tight jackets covered with braid, all eager to take advantage of the blazing emotions of the women.

Colby had managed to find beds in the hotel opposite the station. The foyer was packed with the families of officers newly arrived and desperately searching for rooms in the red-stone streets that were still strident with bugles and noisy with the tramp of feet, the clatter of rifles and the rolling of drums. Kicking, biting cavalry remounts and great Norman draught animals from the Paris buses clattered past in a bedlam of noise, and soldiers piled barrels of wine and brandy on the pavements with pyramids of boxes of navy biscuits marked with square English letters. Every alley was impeded by baggage waggons, and trains continued to chug in with lost reservists, the carriages decorated with branches of willow jammed into the lamp stanchions and wreathed round door handles. Lining up under the gas globes and spade-shaped jets in the sooty walls, the men moved off under showers of smuts from the engines, squeezing concertinas, embracing women, exchanging bread and wine and sausage, the crimson pompoms of their shakoes glowing, their voices echoing under the high, vaulted glass-and-iron of the roof. The whole city seemed to be waiting for the Napoleonic masterstroke that would bring the war to a glorious conclusion.

Among the clapping and the waving of handkerchiefs, however, Colby noticed that the dour Lorrainers, almost more German than French and never enthusiastic about Napoleon, remained curiously aloof, as if they suspected that somewhere underneath the fuss things weren't quite as they should be. How right they were he discovered at headquarters in the Hotel Europa. A hard-bitten old brigadier was storming at a young staff officer whose buttons crowded his not very broad chest.

'There are no palliasses and the blankets are mildewed,' he was raging. 'The food stinks and you can smell nothing but dishwater, rifle oil and camphor! The damned brigade's complaining and backbiting and the commanding officers are all suffering from spavins or pains in the chest! I'd like to shoot the lot of them – you, too!'

The place was filled with bustle and the slap of saluting sentries, the clatter of wheels and hooves noisy in the courtyard, the corridors a bedlam of messengers and officials moving in a great show of efficiency which to Colby's practised eye only hid a great deal of confusion. There were no passes available to watch the fighting. It happened to be one of de Polignac's duties to issue them and he made no attempt to disguise his ill-will towards Colby.

'None are being given out,' he announced. 'It will all be over before they can become effective!'

Since Colby had come across other men with passes, he could only assume that de Polignac, knowing of the relationship that had once existed between himself and Germaine, was eaten away with jealousy.

'I'm here to represent my government,' he tried. 'I have the necessary papers.'

De Polignac stared coldly at him. 'It makes no difference,' he said. 'In any case, I am suspicious of your intentions, and I would advise you to be careful. People spreading rumours or asking questions have been set on by the crowd.'

He was adamant in his refusal, continuing to claim that the war would soon be over. His manner was arrogant and confident, but the manner of the other officers made Colby suspect that headquarters was hiding facts – not only from him but from the Lorrainers and the rest of France, and he sent Ackroyd out to listen round the bars.

'Half the bloody divisions are nothing more than the expression of a pious hope,' he pointed out. 'And half the reservists who've turned up are without uniforms or weapons.'

It didn't take long to discover the plain unvarnished truth: regiments were without transport, whole divisions without ambulances. Rations, ammunition and supplies were short. The famous new mitrailleuse, the mechanical gun which was confidently expected to win the war, was useless because nobody knew how to work it. Thousands of reservists were still missing somewhere on the chaotic railways, drinking and plundering stores to stay alive, and the camps, seas of mud in the heavy showers, were full of other reservists without the slightest idea where their regiments were. 'Not –' Ackroyd added ' – that it'll make much difference. Most of 'em are badly led and worse clothed. Some of them what I've seen must 'ave had to cut their uniforms down to see out of 'em.'

Batteries were without guns, guns without horses, and horses without harness. Half the men on the muster rolls had been discharged the year before and, because its railways ran the wrong way, the French army was having to do most of its journeying on foot. Von Hartmann had been dead right, and the exhilaration of the first days seemed to be dying rapidly in an anti-climax as the young bloods of the staff, who for the first two weeks had lounged with their absinthes under the pomegranate and oleander on the Esplanade, desperately tried to bring order to the confusion.

An oasis of sanity was provided by Germaine de Maël in the house in Avenue Serpenoise. It looked over rows of little lime trees towards the Île du Saulcy, with glimpses among the steep-roofed mansions of the wooded slopes beyond the Ban St Martin. Unaware of the chaos, Germaine was sparkling with happiness and clearly enjoying the excitement, revelling in the sound of trumpets and drums that echoed across the narrow waterways cutting up the city. Intoxicated by the war and the fact that you could stand on any corner of any street and guarantee something exciting happening within a minute, she had given willingly in her warm-hearted way to the collections for the widows and orphans of Saarbrücken.

'It's all so wonderful,' she said, her eyes shining. 'More than I ever expected. When the Emperor left for the front, they had a parade in the Place Royale and I went to watch.' She clapped her hands with delight. 'The square was *filled* with soldiers! Like huge rows of flowers!'

'And the Emperor?' Colby asked.

Her face fell. 'I saw him clearly,' she said slowly. 'He was in an open carriage behind an escort of Cent Gardes.' Her expression became worried. 'Colbee, his face was grey and painted and he looked as if he were ill.'

They were still talking when de Polignac appeared. He was nervous and irritable and eager for a quarrel. His manner was subdued and over-excited at the same time, as if he had received news that depressed him but nevertheless involved him deeply in desperate events. For half an hour he and Colby glared hostilely at each other, hardly hearing what Germaine had to say, facing each other like dogs circling for a fight.

In the end, unable to make any impression on them, she shooed them out, insisting that she needed rest. As Colby stepped on to the pavement, de Polignac was waiting for him and he made no attempt to hide his intention to pick a quarrel.

'You have no right to be here,' he said. 'This is a military area and, as a foreign civilian, I could have you arrested.'

'The damned place is full of Americans, English and Scandinavians,' Colby snorted. 'You'd have to arrest the lot.'

De Polignac's dark eyes glittered. It was perfectly clear that it was less Colby's interest in the war than his interest in Germaine that was troubling him. For a moment, he seemed at a loss for words.

'It's my belief,' he finally spat out, 'that you are here for no other reason than to embarrass my government and my country!'

'And it's my belief,' Colby retorted coldly, 'that you're a stupid, posturing ass!'

He was about to stalk away when he felt the slap of de Polignac's gloves against his cheek and he whirled, red-faced and angry. 'What's that supposed to mean?' he demanded.

'Perhaps the English don't know how to behave in a matter of honour,' de Polignac said coldly. 'That was a challenge, my friend, a demand that you face me to answer for your insult.'

Colby glared, ice cold in his rage and struggling to control his temper. 'Duelling's a sport for boys,' he snapped. 'It's forbidden in my country!'

'We are not in your country, Monsieur.'

As Colby stared at the pasteboard square the Frenchman had tossed down, Ackroyd appeared, a twisted grin on his long face.

'You'll 'ave to fight 'im,' he said. 'You can't get out of it. Not and face people. Still, it's your choice of weapons, so I'd better go and see 'is second. What do you want?'

'Tell 'im fists.'

''E won't wear that. I'd better say pistols. You were never much good with a sword.'

Feeling faintly melodramatic and foolish but fortified by a stiff brandy offered by Ackroyd, Colby dressed carefully the following morning in a grey suit buttoned to the throat on Ackroyd's advice so that none of his white linen showed.

'It's misty,' Ackroyd pointed out. 'It'll make you 'ard to

see. And when you face 'im, stand sideways ' it makes a smaller target.'

'You seem to know a lot about it,' Colby growled.

'Read it in the papers,' Ackroyd said calmly. 'That time when Lord Cardigan 'ad 'is set-to on Wimbledon Common. You'll remember 'e was charged and appeared before the 'Ouse of Lords. There's nothing to worry about,' he went on, fussing like a mother hen.' It'll soon be over and 'e won't bother you after, because the troops 'ere are moving east as reinforcements any moment now.'

There had been a lot of showers during the night and, as Ackroyd had said, the morning was misty, especially in the low-lying areas among the streams and pools round the Île du Saulcy. The sort of advice Ackroyd had offered appeared not to have been given to de Polignac because, when he appeared with his second and an army surgeon, he was in full uniform, a riot of colour and gold lace. Against the misty lavender background of the bushes and trees of the Île du Saulcy he stood out like a blaze of light.

His second began to explain what they had to do. 'I propose twenty paces,' he said.

'Why not make it ten?' Colby snapped, half hoping to frighten them off with a show of aggression. 'Or even stand face-to-face? Then I'll have my pistol up his nose and couldn't miss.'

De Polignac licked his lips and his adam's apple worked.

'Twenty paces is the customary distance,' the second pointed out stiffly.

Colby sniffed. 'Very well. I expect I can hit him just as easily at that distance.'

The second blinked and glanced at de Polignac who looked ready to throw up and seemed to be regretting his hastiness.

''E didn't think you'd accept,' Ackroyd whispered. 'The second told me.'

The feeling of melodrama came again as they stood back to back and began to pace out the distance. This hadn't been at all what Wolseley had intended, Colby decided, and he could well imagine what that icy-minded cynic

157

would have thought if he'd seen him. Typical of the army he was struggling to change, he would no doubt have decided, and there would have been hasty telegrams telling him to report back to London at once.

As he turned towards de Polignac, he saw that, backed by the dark shadows of the bushes and facing fully front, the Frenchman presented a perfect target. He seemed nervous and, moving his feet to give himself a firm stance, he immediately lifted his pistol and pointed it at Colby. Standing sideways as Ackroyd had advised, Colby kept his own weapon hanging at his side. De Polignac, who seemed uncertain at the way things had turned out, kept the pistol pointing at Colby as if to frighten him, but he held it too long with his arm outstretched and it began to waver. As he pulled the trigger, Colby saw the flash at the muzzle and heard the ball whistle overhead. Watching the slow-drifting smoke, he stood silently with the pistol still at his side. Whether de Polignac had deliberately aimed high, he had no idea but, suddenly irritated by the thought that the Frenchman had expected him to back away, he decided he might as well do a bit of frightening himself.

For a long time he stared at de Polignac, the pistol still at his side, and he saw the Frenchman's second fidget nervously and the doctor lift a hand to adjust his hat. De Polignac stared back at him, his face pale.

Lifting the pistol, his arm crooked, Colby held the weapon firmly against his chest. De Polignac swallowed but he remained rigid and unmoving. At least the stupid idiot wasn't lacking in courage, Colby thought. Perhaps it would be a good idea to put the ball between his eyes to prove it. Instead, he straightened his arm quickly, deliberately lifted the pistol, fired into the air and tossed the weapon on to the grass.

De Polignac had swayed slightly but his feet hadn't moved. His second spoke to him as if to start him from the trance he was in and he drew a deep breath, turned abruptly and walked to his horse.

'The stupid little gadget can now tell his friends he's fought a duel,' Colby growled. 'It should be good for a drink or two or a kiss from a girl.'

'I think not.' It was the surgeon who was picking up the pistol and pushing it into its case who spoke. 'He's moving east with the army immediately. We all are.'

As they returned, it was clear that the anxiety at headquarters was beginning to seep into the city. A battle had been fought, they heard, but so far nothing was known and it didn't pay to enquire too deeply. The outbreak of spymania, of which de Polignac had warned, had resulted in people being crammed into police waggons merely for being blond or tall.

A few scattered detachments were still moving off as Colby headed for the Avenue Serpenoise for breakfast. Germaine's boudoir was an affair of lace, chaises longues and filmy curtains, and she didn't seem to consider it at all unusual to receive him in bed. She ordered coffee, eyeing him gravely with her huge eyes. 'Would you prefer to sleep a little first?' she asked.

Colby studied her thoughtfully as he sat down by her feet and, swept away by his enthusiasm and the thought that if de Polignac had been more determined and a better shot he could well have been dead, found himself proposing. 'I think we should go and visit the Maire,' he said.

Germaine gazed at him, her eyes amused. 'What are you suggesting?' she asked.

'Marriage, for God's sake!' he snapped. 'What did you think?'

She gave a little laugh. 'But that's ridiculous!'

'I'm the right age. So are you.'

She leaned forward to kiss him. 'I'd much rather simply go to bed with you,' she said. 'Suppose, after a week or two, I changed my mind.' She smiled and kissed him again. 'After all, with my experience I have no great admiration for men as a group. I think we would do much better to forget marriage and simply make love.'

He gazed at her, disappointed, but since he didn't feel suicidal, he came to the conclusion that he was merely being businesslike and was far from being in love.

She was lying back on the pillow smiling at him, but as she lifted her arms and placed them round his neck, the door rattled. Colby sat bolt upright. Germaine didn't turn a hair.

'It's locked,' she whispered. 'It's a precaution I always take.' She lifted her head. 'Who is it?'

'Me, Madame! Henriette, your maid. The footman's just arrived from town to say there's been another battle near Saarbrücken.'

Germaine beamed at Colby. 'How nice,' she said. 'Everything seems to be going according to plan.' She raised her voice again. 'How kind of you to tell me, Henriette! Now run away and amuse yourself. I'm rather preoccupied.'

'But, Madame – ' the voice outside the door became a wail ' – he says that this time we've lost it. He says there's also been a battle at Wissembourg, and we've been beaten there, too.'

Startled eyes turned to Colby. 'But Wissembourg's in France! That means the Prussians have invaded *us*. How *can* that be?'

Colby made for the door. 'I think I'd better go and find out,' he said.

Almost at once he bumped into Ackroyd who had come looking for him.

'The French have been beaten near Saarbrücken,' Colby said.

'That they 'ave,' Ackroyd agreed. 'Chucked off the Spicherenberg. They say the general felt a bit isolated and thought 'e'd better move back, and the Prussians thought it was part of a general retreat and set about 'im. The whole bloody shebang will be back in Metz before long, because they caught Douay's division at Wissembourg as well. MacMahon'll be next on the list.'

They didn't have far to go before they found themselves surrounded by swarms of French soldiers heading rearwards. With them were waggons, guns, ambulances, and carts full of wounded, their heads nodding to the shake and rumble of wheels. Forbach was full of them, lying in the streets in their hundreds, helped only by nuns, women and foreigners.

'It's nothing but a minor setback.' It was the surgeon who had accompanied de Polignac to the Île du Saulcy who spoke. He was bending over a wounded sergeant and seemed unperturbed by the defeat. 'The French have never been afraid to take a step backwards to enable them to take two forward. We're merely regrouping.'

It didn't look like regrouping to Colby. There seemed to be nothing but confusion and panic and there was little evidence of organisation. French intelligence had broken down and, dependent for information on the civilian population and latrine rumour, they had marched and countermarched, their orders meticulous about encampments and dress but providing nothing whatsoever in the way of information or maps. Tramping in the blazing sunshine and soaking rain, the regiments had become more and more confused as the columns crossed each other's routes and their colonels lost confidence in the high command.

There was no point in becoming enmeshed in the debris of a retreating division, but when they returned to Metz the stories had arrived before them and suspense added the beginnings of dread. The black shadow of disaster already brooded over the city and crowds began to form at the station and at the offices of the newspaper, waiting for information to come through on the telegraph. The rumours persisted throughout the day, with additional extras such as that General Douay had been killed by a shell and the Emperor had been mortally wounded. Then they heard that Ackroyd's suspicion that MacMahon was next was sound. He had been caught at Wörth and driven from the field with disastrous losses.

'They'll not get the Italians and the Austrians on their side now,' Colby said grimly. 'Not after three defeats.'

As night came, people were still waiting on the corners, worried and anxious, trying to read the latest proclamations by the light of gas-lamps. Army headquarters at the Hotel Europa was surrounded by carriages, standing in a drizzling rain that had started, all full of people desperate for news, while more aimless groups stood in the Place Royale and on the Esplanade, sheltering under dripping café awnings despite the gesticulations of the harassed waiters trying to move them on.

Ackroyd appeared. 'They've come out against Napoleon in Paris,' he said. 'Newspaper feller told me. 'E'd 'eard it on the telegraph. They're talking revolution.'

As they pushed through the city streets, they had to dodge country waggons coming from the frontier full of people, mattresses, chairs and tables. A long straggling column followed in carriages and traps, pushing small wheeled carts, carrying children, or driving a cow or a few goats or sheep. The news grew steadily worse. A hospital train organised for the wounded had been taken over at Wörth by panic-stricken soldiers, Strasbourg was surrounded, the cavalry was useless, and the Emperor too old and slow.

The first troops from Forbach arrived the following day, crossing the city to the camps on the west in an interminable stream, staggering with weariness, some of them without weapons or equipment. There was a smell of defeat in the air and the weary men were throwing away their rifles and knapsacks and stumbling into doorways to fall asleep.

The rumble of wheels and clatter of hooves went on all night and occasionally they heard outbreaks of drunkenness. The waggons were still struggling through the following morning, with the artillery trains, baggage carts, field smithies and spare horses, the soldiers begging for food and water so that women were running in and out of the houses with pails and plates. Then they heard that a train had been derailed at Commercy by Uhlans and they rode the thirty miles south to find out. It turned out that the Uhlans had had no part in it, but a troop train had run into a civilian train. As the surviving soldiers were formed up alongside the track and marched off, the dead were being brought out and laid in a nearby field. Dozens of foreigners, some of them with their own carts and carriages, the only organised help there seemed to be, were working in the wreckage and Colby and Ackroyd helped to drag out a woman with both her legs broken. Her chest was crushed and the bones were sticking out, and she was covered with blood and wailing that her child was still in the debris.

It was late when they got back to Metz where they learned that the story about the Prussians cutting the line was not so wrong after all. It was merely a different line – the one to the west that was needed for the retreat.

Every seething alley and courtyard was overflowing with troops now, every square and islet packed as the outflanked units streamed back. Obstructing them everywhere was the flood of civilians, smelling of wet wool, poverty and fear. Panic lay just below the surface and nerves seemed to be stretched until they twanged like violin strings, while the telegraph confirmed Ackroyd's story about Paris, where the government had resigned.

During the day the sky filled with clouds and it began to drizzle so that the plethora of flags about the streets grew wet and stuck to their poles. There wasn't half enough room for the troops flooding in, and fires were going in the Esplanade. Officers were ransacking their baggage among the café tables and cavalry horses picketed on the trodden lawns were dragging at the juniper trees.

Germaine was in a state of icy calm. About her the servants were throwing belongings and clothes into trunks and tying them with ropes, while the concierge was flinging dust sheets over the furniture and locking the shutters. The house was filled with gloom.

'Colbee –' As she saw him, Germaine quietly poured him a drink and handed it to him, her hand shaking ' – you must save us. The army is defeated! The Empire is collapsing about our ears! The Emperor has been shot and the Marshals have all gone over to the enemy!'

'Not yet!' He tried to calm her. 'It's not as bad as that.'

'Where is Narcisse?' Her eyes grew moist. 'Why doesn't

he come to help me? This is the moment I need him.'

'He's probably busy,' Colby said. 'I think a lot of people are busy just now.'

'Then please do something! I can't stay here. I should be back in Paris where it's safe. It is up to you to take me!'

4

The slow shifting of troops from the east into the city continued – deep columns of blue, white and red, the metallic August sun on unsheathed bayonets. The soldiers were shouting that they had been betrayed, and sullen eyes stared from under shakoes and brass cuirassier helmets. A rancid smell of sweat, fear and anger rose amid the clouds of grey dust stirred up by thousands of shuffling boots.

During the day, news came in that Napoleon had turned the command of the army over to Marshal Bazaine and there was a marked lifting of spirits, because the French hadn't been badly hurt, despite the defeats, and were still strong enough to hold off a few Prussians.

Walking back from the empty station, Colby heard that the Emperor had arrived in the city and was attending Mass in the cathedral. Quickening his pace, he arrived just as Napoleon came out. He looked haggard and shabby. A cloak was thrown over his uniform and straggling grey hair escaped from under the gold-encrusted red képi. The Prince Imperial, just behind him, seemed only a frightened boy struggling to hold back his tears. The square was filled with a brooding suspicion that Metz was being betrayed. There were no cheers, and the heavy faces of the Messins were hard and unforgiving as they watched the Emperor, his eyes desperate in a face that had been painted to hide his illness, climb heavily into his carriage.

Late in the morning, they heard the mutter and rumble of guns from the east again. As the sounds came, the westwards movement halted and everybody stopped to stare back to where the cathedral spire shone golden in the sun.

A few frantic staff officers appeared, forcing their way through the mass of men and trying to turn them back the way they had come.

Ackroyd popped up from nowhere. 'Prussians 'ave bumped into the rearguard,' he announced. 'They've 'alted the retreat to face 'em.'

As they rode towards the fighting, they could hear the rumble of guns growing louder and the ugly grinding sound they recognised as the mitrailleuses. When they arrived, the ambulances – most of them still foreign – were at work. Through the halo of mist, they saw what appeared to be miles of dead and wounded, lying where they'd been caught by the guns, French on one side, Prussians on the other. Carts full of straw were jolting them across the slopes towards Metz.

Deciding it was wiser to get on the road to Verdun before it was too late, they returned to pack Germaine among the trunks in the carriage, still calm and clear-headed but protesting loudly that she was not in the habit of travelling like a servant. It was impossible to move, however. The whole French army, a hundred and sixty thousand strong, with all its guns, pontoon bridges, horses and four thousand supply waggons, their numbers swollen by the vehicles of escaping civilians, were struggling out of the city by the Longeville route. It had been going on for two days now in one huge ill-policed convoy.

With the aid of a few bribes, Colby managed to halt the stream long enough to force the carriage into the throng and they began to move at a snail's pace out of the city, surrounded by a winding straggle of peasants and people sitting in carriages filled with china and furniture. The last information Ackroyd had brought from the station was that there was no guarantee that any more trains would arrive from the south either to bring reinforcements or carry away refugees. It was clear that organisation had totally collapsed.

During the morning the sky filled with clouds and the day grew dismal with drizzle. The flags hanging from abandoned houses slapped and smacked in the breeze over

166

the columns of men plodding up the hill, their clothes filthy, their boots heavy with mud, the driving storm beating at their backs. Zouaves, the spoils of robbed hen-roosts hanging at their belts, threaded in and out of hay-carts filled with women and children. Grenadiers of the Guard mingled with stocky Lignards, and hussars and lancers jostled each other in an attempt to pass to the front. Furious staff officers cursed and gesticulated, while men edged to the side of the road from the path of the towering train of pontoon barges that had been intended to bridge the river to make the passage of troops more easy.

As the afternoon came, the rain stopped and the sun appeared, hot, stifling and exhausting. The rumour passed down the ranks of the slowly-shifting column that the troops defeated near Strasbourg were retreating on Chalôns and that it was hoped that the Army of the Rhine would join them there. But the news was vague and no one knew where the Prussians were.

'The French cavalry,' Colby observed, 'seem to think their only job's to spruce up their bloody millinery. The whole army's mesmerised and like a lot of undertakers creeping round a corpse. If that damned carpet-bagger, Bazaine, stays in Metz much longer he's never going to move until they cart him off a prisoner to Germany.'

As it grew dusk and torches appeared, tempers grew worse, then they heard guns rumbling to the west and heads came up as ears cocked. From a mounted officer covered with mud who was trying to fight his way through to headquarters, they got the information that Uhlans were on the left bank of the Meuse and to the south of the road, and that the French cavalry screen, feeling its way gingerly forward, had been stopped near Mars-la-Tour. As the head of the column halted, the whole bewildered strug-gling mass concertina-ed to a stop. The civilians climbed from the carriages trapped among the carts, fourgons and guns, and sat wearily at the roadside, eating their picnic meals and waiting for the route to be cleared.

'You must find a hotel – an inn,' Germaine said firmly. 'I can't sleep upright in a carriage.'

She was still calm but her insistence on comfort made Colby feel like hitting her over the head with something.

Point du Jour was crammed by the convoy carrying the Imperial household, huge fourgons and carts in the Imperial colours marked with 'N' and guarded by Cuirassiers and Dragoons of the Guard. The royal comforts congested the whole road and the soldiers filing by made no attempt to hide their feelings. Moving sullenly, their silence was in sharp contrast to the cheers of a fortnight before. Occasionally, even, one of them raised his voice. 'A cheer for the Emperor,' he yelled, and the cry came back immediately with a 'One, two, three, merde!' that spoke of constant repetition.

Reaching Gravelotte, with a great deal of difficulty and a lot of bribery they managed to get a room in the inn. It was hardly up to Germaine's standard and consisted of a bare uncomfortable attic.

'Stay here with me,' she pleaded.

'I can't,' Colby pointed out. 'Bazaine's bound to bring up troops to clear the road ahead. It can't be held by more than a couple of squadrons of Uhlans, and I ought to go and see what's happening so we're ready to move on in the morning.'

'Stay with me! I beg you!'

'Germaine, be sensible!'

'This isn't a time for sense!' The calm shivered and broke. 'It's a time to lose ourselves in despair! You can sleep in my bed. I shall not take up much room.'

He backed hurriedly from the room as the maid struggled in with a suitcase containing the thousand and one bottles of unguents and powders Germaine used to keep her skin creamy. Downstairs, he fought his way to where the landlord of the inn was beating off hysterical customers.

'There is no food,' he yelled at Colby. 'It has all gone! We don't expect such numbers!'

Colby slipped a handful of silver across. 'Bread and cheese will do,' he said.

The landlord glanced at the money and gestured to a

door behind his bar. 'In the kitchen,' he said quietly. 'I daren't bring it out here.'

Collecting the food in a handkerchief with a bottle of thin wine from the frightened wife of the proprietor, Colby headed outside to where Ackroyd was guarding the horses.

'You ain't leavin' me with 'er, are you?' Ackroyd said indignantly. 'She's got a maid and a manservant.'

'Just for the night, Tyas, old son,' Colby said.

Climbing into the saddle, he began to head westward, taking to the fields and picking his way between the weary civilians standing in groups near their vehicles. No one stopped him or told him he had no right to be on the road the army was using. Soldiers were quarrelling everywhere. Having expected orders to continue, they were bewildered and angry because none had arrived. Tents had been erected and the cavalry had unsaddled, with long lines of horses with their heads down at streams. No patrols seemed to have been sent out.

Eating the food he had brought among the trees alongside the road, Colby struggled on again before daylight, aware of a stirring about him and eyes turned towards the west. A rumour had spread that French troops were approaching on a converging route from the south. Near Vionville, a cavalry mess was being erected and bivouacs set up in the growing daylight, and there was a smell of coffee in the air. The only discordant note came from an over-keen officer who was asking that he might be permitted to take out a patrol to investigate small bodies of troops which had been seen on high ground to the west.

'It's Ladmirault's corps coming up.' The general he approached shook his head firmly. 'There's no need to worry.'

The Emperor had got through, it seemed, with an escort of dragoons and chasseurs, insisting that Bazaine should push on after him, but nobody seemed to be aware of any urgency, and in the increasing heat officers' servants were unpacking shaving kits and trotting off towards Vionville to find rooms where their officers might wash and brush up. Jacketless soldiers had removed their heavy brass helmets and unslung their sabres, and were laying blankets on the ground and placing saddles for back rests.

There was some activity ahead but the army seemed in no hurry, so, begging coffee from the mess, Colby watched a string of chargers being led past to water at a nearby pond. Tables had been set among the trees and officers were breakfasting, while the narrow village streets, acrid with the smell of horses, were jammed with waggons, carts, pack animals, and soldiers buying eggs and vegetables in the sunshine.

Colby had just finished his coffee when he heard faint distant popping noises followed by growing whirring sounds. As he looked up, there was a series of crashes in the trees beyond the road and he realised that what had been believed to be Ladmirault's corps was in fact the Prussians, and they were opening the ball.

As he headed for his horse, an officer came thundering between the tents, his arm flung out towards the south.

'*Les Prusses!*' he was yelling. '*Les Prusses!*'

Probing along the flanks of the retreat, the German cavalry had discovered that Bazaine's left lay unguarded and, establishing horse batteries on the hills, were already coming into action. Other troops, heading for the sound of the guns, were barring the Verdun road, and the whole jam-packed mass of people, horses and vehicles just heaving into movement, had come to a standstill again.

Officers had appeared, their jackets unbuttoned, their faces half-shaved and, as they stood in a group, staring bewilderedly to the west, the first shell burst on the outskirts of the village. As more shells crashed down there was a hasty scuttle for shelter. Men jumped barebacked on to their horses and galloped off; officers began to run wildly backwards and forwards, trying to rally them, searching for grooms or chargers, buckling on sabres and shouting orders nobody seemed willing to listen to. The transport drivers were fleeing in a body across the fields, followed by the inhabitants of the village, the civilian refugees, and several dragoons whose heavy knee boots were not designed for such an occupation. In a matter of minutes, the whole brigade had disappeared over the horizon, crashing through the infantry which had turned out as the firing had started.

The cannonade was not followed by an attack, however, and the French infantry began to take up their places behind walls and buildings. The sun was hot by this time and the ground was steaming, and a few stampeded chargers were still galloping across the fields, their tails up, their stirrups swinging, as the French hurriedly tried to face left. There were so many of them in so small an area, however, they were getting in each other's way. Several houses were already in flames and it was possible to see rolling clouds of smoke and dark blue blocks appearing out of the valleys to the south. Determined to halt the movement west, the Prussians had committed their infantry, but their numbers seemed few compared with the mass of men waiting for them along the road.

Heading back to Gravelotte, Colby passed Bazaine's headquarters. The Marshal, an unprepossessing figure with his paunch and his podgy, piggy-eyed face, sat outside his tent with a napkin at his throat and a knife and fork in his hand, calling for horses to be saddled. A few minutes later he set off down the road to see what was happening, pushing between the stream of refugees trying to bury themselves among the army. There was no panic and the hedquarters staff seemed to regard the German attack, with the whole French army of the Rhine in front of them, as suicidal. Certainly the Prussians were making little impression and, committed piecemeal, their infantry was already being flung back with heavy losses.

As Bazaine disappeared, an aide with blood on his cuffs started arguing in the middle of a group of staff officers. The man he was addressing was being helped into his coat and his head was bare, his sparse grey hair stirred by the wind.

'A determined attack would drive them back into the ravine,' the younger officer was shouting.

'Then tell your general to get on with it,' the staff officer snapped, holding up his arms for a sergeant to buckle his sword round his waist.

'He needs support!' The aide was growing frantic at the casual attitude. 'He has neither reserves nor resources for such a move, sir!'

The staff officer hitched at his belt and held out his hand for his scarlet-and-gold képi. Slamming it on his head, he turned to his horse. 'You must wait until the Marshal returns,' he said. 'Or rely on local counter-attacks. There's nothing I can do!'

The firing had grown intense now and smoke was covering the road. An attempt by the Prussians to post guns on the heights was driven off and the infantry on the open slopes were scattered with heavy losses. The French looked uncertain, however, chiefly because the Prussian advances were so confident, and by midday the heights to the south were packed with German batteries which were beginning to dominate the French positions. As the Prussian attacks grew stronger, Vionville, the point of junction between two French corps, fell; and the French artillery fire was directed on to it to make it impossible for it to be held.

It was clearly impracticable to head back to Gravelotte, and, forced to wait behind a row of cottages whose tiles and chimneys were being systematically knocked off by German guns, Colby was surrounded by French soldiers loaded with pots and pans like tinkers. As they began to move forward, a shot struck a tree, showing him with leaves. Bugles screamed and in the distance, a half-battery of Prussian guns hurtled over a rise, the great weapons bouncing.

As the Prussian infantry began to advance again, extending their intervals to cover the French front, drums and fifes were squealing and flags fluttered in the centre of the line. The French gave a defiant yell and rushed forward. The Germans halted and began to fire volleys by alternate platoons, the lieutenants and sergeants counting the drill, precise, mechanical and inhuman, and after two or three minutes of volleying through the powder smoke, the French centre dissolved. As the attack flowed round the Germans, men rolled on the ground, kicking and clubbing and stabbing. Cavalry appeared, sabres jingling, sparks flashing from iron-shod hooves as they crossed a patch of stony ground, then as they cantered forward the retreating Germans broke into a run.

Glancing about him, Colby saw that Bazaine had reappeared and was with his staff in the field nearby, his Chinese face impassive as he pointed to the east. It was obvious he wasn't contemplating a general advance because he was looking over his shoulders towards Metz, thinking not of defeating the Prussians so much as how not to be defeated himself.

As he waited, a harassed staff colonel told him that Frossard, having borne the brunt of the attack all morning, was in a precarious position. 'Bataille's down,' he said, 'and his division's crumbling. They've asked for cavalry.'

As he spoke, the high silver note of trumpets cut across the noise and a regiment of Cuirassiers of the Guard moved across the road, the sun catching their snowy gauntlets and the sky blue of their tunics. Picking their way over broken agricultural land and abandoned equipment that spoiled their alignment, they began to sweep down on the German infantry, horse-hair tails blowing from their helmets, embossed guidons flapping. As the Prussian skirmishers ran together to form a line, the sabres lifted and the riders threw back their heads to fill the air with shouts of '*Vive l'Empereur!*'

More Prussians had thickened the line and they showed no inclination to budge. There was a crashing volley and the line of horsemen sagged and heaved, then burst into fragments, moving to the right and left of the infantrymen. A second volley stopped the charge dead, and a third and fourth disintegrated the formation. As the horsemen galloped wildly about, German dragoons and Brunswick Hussars with black uniforms galloped up to a counterattack and drove them back to their lines, only to be caught in the French fire in their turn and also driven off.

Spectacular, invigorating and entirely ineffective, Colby thought dryly.

To the north of the road a wide grassy sward stretched

westwards towards the valley of the Yron. It seemed a standing invitation to more attacks and, as the smoke cleared, Colby studied it carefully. It was perfect cavalry ground and, deciding that before long someone was going to take advantage of it, he began to pick his way round it back towards Gravelotte.

Prussian infantry were pushing forward again now, their flags against the sky, then, bursting from the trees, the outline of men, horses and cannon appeared abruptly as a French battery raced across the brow of the field, opening fanwise as it went. Guns, caissons and carts jolted over the rutted ground, leaping like gigantic grasshoppers, the drivers plying their whips and spurs. As they swung, bouncing over a shallow ditch, they gouged great ruts from the earth.

As the great weapons were unlimbered and the horses trotted back out of sight, there was a moment of frantic activity, then a wall of yellow smoke that cracked and bellowed and was streaked with red glare. Splinters flew like knives, howling and humming into the mass of advancing Germans to dot the grass with squirming bundles that gave off a low moaning pierced by high, tearing screams.

It was the Prussians who were struggling to hold their positions now but, as Colby watched, a brigade of German horsemen emerged, taking their time to get their alignment and put their flank guards in position. Partially concealed by a depression, they were moving towards the French batteries, clearly intending to hold them until further troops could come up. For a moment, smoke hid them from sight, then as they lifted in a colourful wave out of the depression, they came down on the batteries in a charge as effective as anything Murat had ever attempted. German shellfire had already driven off the French infantry supporting the batteries and, with no time to fire, the guns were caught in the open. The Prussian horsemen swept over them like hounds over a fence, their riders sabring the gunners at will. Only fifty or so horses had gone down, but as the remainder faltered, their order lost and blown after the gallop, fresh French cavalry, outnumbering them five to one, came thundering down on their flank.

Trumpets screamed the recall and, breathless, thinned, without reserves, the Germans swung away. Officers yelled for a rally and as the French were checked, they were able to cut their way out of the mêlée in small hunted groups. The batteries had been thrown into confusion and the threat to the German positions had been smashed.

In the lull that followed, Colby pushed further round the broad area of grassland to the north of Vionville, and as he moved through a belt of trees he found himself among a regiment of lancers just cantering into position as the German cavalry retired. At once, several of them detached themselves and surrounded him, chivvying him towards the officer in command. It didn't surprise him in the slightest to find it was de Polignac.

'What are you doing here?' he demanded.

'You know damned well what I'm doing,' Colby snapped. 'I'm an official observer for my government.'

He was half expecting to be arrested, but de Polignac was gesturing towards where the remnants of the German cavalry were still withdrawing.

'Did you see it?' he asked. 'It was magnificent, was it not? The Magdeburg Cuirassiers and the 16th Uhlans. How I wish I could have done that! They tell me the correspondent of *The Times* of London rode with them. Did you see him? He took his place alongside one of the troop leaders, and even carried back a wounded officer.'

He was elated, excited and fidgeting in the saddle, itching to be in the action. But the Prussian infantry was being driven back now and it seemed that at any moment they would be forced from the field. As the French continued to hesitate, however, they again risked everything by rushing forward every man they had. Fresh troops appeared and were thrown into the fight, but they were in close order and with no advance guard as they blundered through Mars-la-Tour into the thick blue lines of French infantry coming from the north. Caught in the bottom of a valley, they had to crouch, exhausted and immoveable, for ten minutes while the French fired into the inert mass.

Then, roused by their officers and drummers, the French hurled themselves forward to drive them back up the slope at the other side of the valley.

'Now!' de Polignac said. 'Now is when Marshal Bazaine will launch our cavalry!'

'He'll never do it,' Colby said. 'He hasn't the experience.'

De Polignac gave him a bitter look, but the enmity seemed to have gone from him, as if they were both professionals discussing a point of war.

Colby was quite right, and the opportunity was missed. While the French waited, five German squadrons came through the smoke. As they swept forward, the French infantrymen flung themselves down and the cavalrymen, finding it impossible to use their swords on them, wheeled their horses in frustrated fury, yelling for lancers to be brought up.

'Now it will be our turn,' de Polignac said, his eyes alight.

But no orders came and, as the German cavalry circled, other French horsemen moved forward from the right to meet them. The shock was tremendous. It came across the air like a great clash of cymbals, while, as the dust rose, the shapes of riders flickered against it in a curious sort of shadow show.

De Polignac was almost beside himself now with impatience, shifting in his saddle and circling his horse to look for the galloper he confidently expected to bring his orders. Lacking the experience to know when to strike on his own, he was angrily watching the horsemen in front, still struggling in small knots. In the distance a sombre line of woods stretched towards the Yron and across the grass lay a trail of wreckage, overturned artillery limbers, smashed guns, thrashing horses and the red-trousered shapes of dead French Lignards. Then, on the left, a half battery of Prussian horse artillery began to move into position, the crimson hussar facings of the drivers clear in the sunshine, and Colby found himself urging de Polignac forward.

'Now's your chance,' he said.

De Polignac glanced at him, eager but uncertain, his eyes questioning.

'This is your moment. They're unprotected. I'd better be going.'

De Polignac's mouth twisted in a reluctant smile. 'You won't be in the way, Monsieur.'

Colby hesitated. It was an invitation and a challenge at the same time, an effort to forget the bitter feelings that had existed between them. If he retired, as he ought to, the Frenchman would consider him either afraid or still full of hatred.

'Very well,' he said. 'I'll ride with you.'

De Polignac's smile grew firmer and he gestured. 'Perhaps you'd like to take up your position alongside me,' he said. Then, as he turned to his line of troopers, his sabre came out with a metallic screech. Lifting it high in the air, he swung it down until it pointed to the struggling artillery-men in front.

With the snort of excited chargers, the lancers leapt at once to the gallop. De Polignac had moved ahead of his men, his cap lost, his dark hair floating in the breeze created by the speed of his mount. A gun fired and, as men and horses went down in a tumbled heap, the riders near them streamed in ribbons to the right. But de Polignac screamed at them and they recovered to crash over the Prussian guns, only to find themselves facing a thin line of Prussian dragoons, who went down in a tangle of rolling horses before them. A fresh line of French hussars, seeing their success, emerged from the woods and swept over the brow of the slope to join in. In reply, more German horse-men appeared and de Polignac's line caught them in the flank, sending horses to the grass in a growing mêlée. There was so much dust and smoke it became impossible to tell friend from foe, but the figures that loomed up in front of Colby all seemed to swerve to right or left. The air was thick with the cries of men and the neighing of horses as the line was swallowed up. As they crashed into the enemy squadrons, the battle seemed to heave and sway, surging this way and that, then the two wings began to wheel inwards, so tightly locked it was impossible to have any wish in the matter of where to go.

Seeing the growing battle, both sides poured men into the struggle. Cheers sounded but it was impossible to see why, and all control on both sides was lost. A French lancer came at Colby from the flank, his weapon at the Point, saw that Colby wasn't wearing uniform and swerved away, to lift a German hussar out of the saddle. Then he found he was thrusting off a Uhlan who seemed equally startled to find himself facing a civilian. As the German swung away, his horse crashed into the heavy mount of a French cuirassier and went down under the hooves of another line of riders bursting out of the smoke. Several of the oncoming horses leapt over the thrashing charger but others, following close behind, were brought down and a group of French lancers began to prod at the screaming mass until they were driven off by a charge of German hussars. Riderless horses were bolting, half-demented at the noise and excitement of the battle, neighing with fear, their eyeballs bulging, blowing crimson froth from their nostrils. Their riders, blackened by smoke and maddened by thirst, were reeling in their saddles with fatigue.

The field had broken up now into a medley of smaller actions which swept backwards and forwards across the open downland, degenerating into a welter of furious charges, regiment against regiment, squadron against squadron, troop against troop. Across Colby's front, a grey horse careered, screaming from the wounds that smeared its flanks with blood. It was dragging the lifeless body of its rider, his foot caught in the stirrup, until the leather broke and the body rolled away. A squadron of Prussian lancers appeared, their weapons levelled, their bodies hunched to take the force of the blow. The French were caught looking the wrong way and Colby saw them recoil under the impact.

De Polignac's regiment had been broken up now and somewhere a bugle was sounding the rally. The Prussian battery was still firing into the mass of horsemen, killing its own side as well as the enemy, and as the whole area filled with smoke again, Colby saw a flash of flame as a shell sent horses and riders to the ground. There was no thought of rallying, no control, no order and no sense and, collecting a group of his men round him, the excited de Polignac, flushed with his success, drove into a wedge of cuirassiers, only for his men to be caught in the flank themselves by a group of Prussian hussars.

'*Nun, Kinder!*' the German officer screamed. '*In Gottes Namen, nun!*'

As the Prussians crashed into them, the Frenchmen whirled to face the new threat, only to be caught from the other side by an entirely new attack by Uhlans. Their blue and yellow uniforms dimmed by the smoke, the Germans came in at the gallop, their lances down. A sword opened de Polignac's jacket from shoulder to waist and, as he cried out and the blood flowed, a lance caught him under his sword arm. The Uhlan was moving at a gallop and Colby saw the Frenchman's body bend backwards under the thrust. The sword dropped from his hand and, as he rolled from the saddle, Colby saw the lance point protruding from his ribs at the other side, clawed by the dying man's frantic fingers. As he fell, his horse stumbled and the Uhlan's horse almost went down, too, as it became entangled in the kicking legs. As he recovered his mount and struggled to shake the body from his lance, the Uhlan was caught by a French lancer whose point took him in the middle of the back and pitched him over his horse's head.

Animals reared and plunged, kicking and screaming as they fell. Sabres chopped like great knives, hacking men from the saddle in a frenzied butchery. Guns were crashing out along the fringe of the fight, filling the air with drifting blue smoke. Groups of riders broke free, turned and plunged back into the mêlée. Horses, shot through the lungs, spurted purple foam from their nostrils, plunged and fell with kicking legs to smash the brains from their riders. Dismounted men hewed and shot at each other.

Colby saw a sword carve across an officer's arm and a

flash of crimson spray as the arm, still holding a sword, whirled into the air. There was no gentility about this sort of fighting. This was face-to-face butchery on an enormous scale, with dozens of regiments involved. A horse fell backwards on to its rider even as he slashed at an opponent, crushing him. Alongside him, a German dragoon neatly parried a cut but, as his sword came down, the French trooper dodged and the blow fell across his mount's spine just behind the saddle. The horse screamed and a cascade of yellow liquid spurted from under its tail as it sank like a dog run over by a brewery dray, dragging its haunches, its eyes rolling, its jaw loose, tongue hanging out, and forelegs trembling.

Trumpets were going all round the fight now and there was a distinct movement to the rear by the French. Gradually the huge mass of horsemen shredded itself out and, as the German squadrons fell back in their turn, the field was left to the dead, the wounded, and the riderless horses. Some of them were cantering away through the smoke, others were quietly waiting by the bodies of their riders. One of them, its stomach opened by a lance thrust, moved slowly across the field, treading on its own entrails but still stopping occasionally to nibble at the grass as if nothing had happened. Others lay on the ground, struggling to rise, lifting their heavy heads then letting them fall back with a thump and a jingle of harness. Dismounted riders were streaming away, small knots and flecks of colour, staggering in high jackboots, their heads unhelmeted, heavy cuirasses thrown aside to allow them to scramble to their feet.

As the field cleared and the vast mêlée separated into drifting flurries of horsemen, Colby found himself in the middle of a group of German lancers. Stumbling horses and staggering men streamed past, some of them helping desperately wounded comrades, some with other riders up behind them, some dragging limping mounts. One man had been run through by a sword, another kicked in the chest as his horse had gone down, so that with every breath he took his shattered ribs collapsed. The face of a third had been carved by sabre slashes, the teeth laid bare, one bulging eye floating in a shattered socket that was filled with thick black blood. With its unkempt hair, the mutilated head looked like a crimson mop.

As Colby passed, a shouted order halted them, and as the panting horses came to a stop, steaming, their heads drooping, they were shouldered aside by a blond officer wearing the black facings of the staff. It was von Hartmann and he stared at Colby with a twisted smile.

'So,' he said. 'It seems you and I are always meeting on the field of war.'

He paused, while Colby stared at him silently, still shocked by the enormous battle that had been fought around him. 'I hope –' von Hartmann began to speak, then he gestured at the remains of the lancer regiment with a hopeless movement of his hand. There was a wound on his face and he looked exhausted. Pointing at the blood on Colby's jacket and smeared along his leg, he raised his eyebrows.

'Are you hurt?'

'No. I'm unharmed.'

The Prussian turned in the saddle and indicated the carnage. 'I think cavalrymen the world over will have to think again after this day's work, Herr Major,' he said. 'Rifles have made the defence too strong, and I see no future for this sort of idiocy.'

A gun spoke in the east and as the shell arced over them towards the Prussian lines, von Hartmann looked round at his men. 'Too many good fellows have fallen today,' he said. 'But, then, it is always the tallest poppies that are picked.' He lifted his sword in salute. 'I think it's time we left. *Hals und Beinbruch*, Herr Major. Perhaps we shall meet again.'

5

The day was coming to a close as Colby rode slowly towards Gravelotte. There was a smell of smoke in the air and about him was that feeling of anti-climax and dying excitement that always followed a battle.

Dead horses made mounds on the turf, their stirrup irons catching the last of the sunshine. The whole area smelled of crushed grass and in the distance he could still see the stumbling figures of unhorsed men.

This was never the way to use cavalry, he decided. Perhaps the Americans weren't so far wrong in their methods after all. There was no longer any place for massed charges, because rows of rifles made mincemeat of horsemen armed only with swords or lances, and the tremendous losses had achieved little. Death rides, he decided, didn't really suit him and they were getting to be too much of a habit.

He passed through one of the batteries. A gun had burst and several soldiers were grouped round an officer who was holding his head and groaning in agony with shattered ear drums. Men, horses and wheel fragments were strewn across the grass and the blast had injured men for yards around. One corpse was hanging in a tree, its entrails showing, its clothes torn off, a few sick-looking men standing beneath it, wondering how to get it down. Stretcher bearers were moving past them into the fields, looking for those who might be saved from among the hundreds who were dead. A carriage passed, carrying the body of a general, his gold-encrusted képi over his face, his body dripping blood from the door at every step of the horses.

Rezonville was full of wounded. Many of them had been laid on the soft surface of dunghills and the huge forms of dead cuirassiers stared at the sky with sightless eyes, flies gathering on the blood on their jutting imperials and moustaches. A vivandière with a torn skirt hanging in loops over soil-stained breeches, her spurs twisted, her eyes streaming with tears, moved among them with her barrel of spirit.

A colonel shot in the foot, his leg propped up on a cushion, moved to the rear in a landau, driven by a civilian wearing a red cross brassard. 'Five times,' he was saying. 'Five times they charged us and five times we sent them back.'

The Prussian attacks seemed to have been fought to a standstill but both armies were worn down and the cavalry on both sides had been shattered. The French artillery was still holding Vionville, though, and, even if the army could not move forward, it could at least move back towards Metz.

Supply had broken down completely, however, and the long undisciplined convoy of waggons, carts and carriages had dissolved into confusion. Some of the civilian drivers had already turned back, others had cut the traces and bolted. Yet others had unloaded their waggons of supplies and filled them with wounded, so that the whole road was littered with abandoned boxes and tins and crates, and biscuits were being ground to dust by feet, hooves and wheels. The confusion in the French Intendance was equalled only by the confusion in the army itself. Nine infantry divisions, three cavalry divisions and a vast amount of artillery were crammed into the two-mile stretch between Rezonville and Gravelotte and, with no hope of sorting out the chaos, the tail of the army had been turned round. To their bewilderment and fury, men who thought they had won were now marching back towards Metz, looting the convoys of supplies for food as they went.

As Colby moved along with them, thirsty, dusty and grimed with smoke, Bazaine and his staff rode by. Bazaine's expression was as opaque as ever but it was clear from the faces of the men around him that they entertained little hope of pushing forward through Mars-la-Tour.

Night came with no orders and no attempt at organisation. Flames showed where Vionville still burned and, as Colby headed north of the village in the late dusk, he came on the scattered corpses of Prussian cuirassiers in white tunics and polished breast plates, the remains of the first charge against the French guns in the early afternoon. Past him along the road dragged a procession of ghosts, French soldiers shuffling and straggling in groups. Through the darkness he could hear the soft trample of hooves on the grass and the clink of bits and scabbards as a long line of French dragoons in scarlet cloaks rode back on their tracks. There was no singing and a crestfallen droop to shoulders, while the mournful thump of a single drum gave time to a regiment of voltigeurs, their officer riding behind, slashing angrily at the bushes with his whip.

Battery after battery clanked and jolted after them, the drivers arguing and disputing the way. In the fields, more horsemen passed with the same lifeless look, slumped in the saddles. The air was full of the smell of burning stores and the sulphurous fumes of artillery smoke that still seemed to hang about. Behind them the death-wreath of burning houses and trees lifted into the air.

Colby's mood was thoughtful. He had seen what was probably the greatest cavalry battle in the world since the days of Murat. Thousands of horsemen had been involved on the slopes and valleys round Mars-la-Tour, regiment upon regiment, brigade upon brigade, division upon division, all caught up in the most appalling slaughter. The day had brought over ten thousand dead, and a large proportion were cavalry. Lifeless horses lay everywhere, scattered over the fields where they had been brought down by shells; among the smashed hedges and fences, in farmyards and gardens, blocking the road; hundreds of them, both French and German, in such numbers as would take weeks to clear.

The wind died, shrivelled to nothing, as he reached Gravelotte. Every house had become a hospital and the lights of feeble lamps glowed in the windows. Discouraged men crouched round fires or under the trees, watching as the wounded were laid on straw which had been spread in yards and gardens and fields. Men and women stumbled about with pails of water while a surgeon from an American ambulance worked over an oilcloth-covered table dripping blood.

The wounded were packed into every space available. Those who had died lay in corners and, under a blanket was a pile of amputated limbs. Other men had succumbed to their weariness and simply stumbled to a halt, laying down to sleep among the dead and the dying. The street was littered with abandoned rifles, knapsacks and greatcoats, while those still on the move licked around the abandoned vehicles and the halted gun limbers like a flood from a burst dam. It was like the vast charnel house of Waterloo all over again, the desolation of a battle that had been equally splendid and just as out-dated.

As Colby reached the inn, Ackroyd appeared. He looked worried and his expression showed his relief as he recognised Colby.

'What 'appened?' he said. 'Nobody 'ere seems to know 'oo's won.'

He had a letter for Colby from Germaine. Thrown on her own devices, she had shown more sense of self-preservation than Colby had credited her with. The letter was written on one of the scented sheets she carried in her toilet box. It smelled faintly of musk and the scrawl was hurried, but it made it quite clear where she was going.

'*As far as possible,*' she wrote. '*To the Mediterranean. To Marseilles or Perpignan or Toulouse. I shall probably even leave France for Corsica.*'

There seemed no alternative but to follow her to Metz. In the Avenue Serpenoise, Sisters of Charity, like great moths in their wide winged caps, were carrying food and drink and binding wounds with strips torn from sheets and curtains, and even as they reached the centre of the city in the growing daylight they heard the guns start again and learned that yet another battle, greater even than Mars-la-Tour, had started at Gravelotte.

'Three battles in five days,' Ackroyd said wonderingly. 'Where in God's name will they put the wounded?'

By evening the first of them were arriving in Metz with the last from Mars-la-Tour. The scene was nightmarish as the stream became a flood and finally a stampede. Every courtyard and open space was full of men too tired or too weak to walk any further, and the air was filled with a high ullulation of complaint and sorrow. Ambulance men were struggling to remove the wounded towards the Place Royale where marquees had been erected in the gardens of the Esplanade, and, as more long convoys appeared from the west, a priest waited by the roadside to give them a blessing as they passed. There were so many it was clear nobody knew what to do with them. The Palais de Justice had a Red Cross flag at each corner and other public buildings overflowed with them until they were pushed into convents, barracks, hotels and even private houses. The hundreds of tricolours flapping in the gusty air left wet smears on windows and walls, the waiting rooms of the station were occupied by the medical staff and the floor was packed with stretchers. In the dim glow of the gaslight the red cross on its white background glowed like blood.

'It's time we were leaving, Tyas,' Colby said. 'This place is going to be besieged. The Prussians are already moving round it and the French staff haven't the foggiest idea what to do.'

'Where are we goin'?' Ackroyd asked.

Colby gestured. The sky looked tortured, with green and gold thunderheads building up in the east. The wind coming from the north made the telegraph wires hum with what sounded like ominous messages of war. On the gusts, they could hear the muttering of guns.

Colby sighed. 'Belgium,' he said. 'Then home.'

'They had them in tents,' Colby said. 'And in marquees on the Esplanade. They dragged railway waggons off the rails into the Place Royale and slung hammocks inside for them.

But the weather changed and they started to die in hundreds. The North African troops didn't even seem to wish to live, and the stink of pyaemia and gangrene from the Coislin had to be smelled to be believed.'

Wolseley's rooms were full of the same books and plans, and on the wall hung a map of France that was better than anything Colby had seen in the hands of the French staff. Wolseley sat in a leather chair, watching as Colby's hands moved across it. There was a strange reserve of vitality about him that indicated a firm will and a strong sense of knowing what he wanted.

'Bazaine had no plan and nobody knew what to do,' Colby continued. 'The troops wandered about and nobody attempted to do anything with them. The army had split into factions – Imperialist, Republican and Monarchist – and they were all blaming each other for the defeats and doing nothing about breaking out, although the Prussians were already erecting long-range batteries on the hills. We got out without any trouble at all towards Plappeville and there were hundreds of troops up there, pushed north by the fighting at Gravelotte. The whole army could have got clear and fallen on the southern flank of the Prussians at Sedan, but they didn't even try.'

As Colby became silent, Wolseley shifted in the chair. 'And Sedan?' he said. 'Tell me about Sedan.'

Colby's hand moved. 'It stuck out a mile that the Prussians would try to stop MacMahon and the Emperor joining up to rescue Bazaine. But the French made no attempt at a feint or any effort to draw them away from their path. As they were forced further and further north, they found themselves pushed into the angle of the frontier near the Belgian border where they hadn't room to manoeuvre.'

'Then?'

'Mixture as before, sir. There was little wrong with the ordinary soldier or even with his weapons. The confusion was all at the top. The disaster was colossal. The Prussian army's now heading for Paris.'

'Will Paris come to an arrangement?'

'Not yet, sir. But I think eventually. When I passed through on the way to Calais, they were preparing for a seige but there was no plan and no order.'

Wolseley was silent for a moment then he lifted his head. 'What's your view of the Prussians?' he asked.

'They made a lot of mistakes, sir, but they had one quality that saved them again and again. They marched to the sound of the guns. The French seemed to march away and seemed only to think of using their cavalry when in trouble – as if it were the effort of despair. To me there seemed no place on a battlefield dominated by breech-loading rifles for masses of horsemen.'

Wolseley's eyebrows lifted and he gave a thin smile. 'If that's your view, how do you propose to handle it if ever you succeed to the command of your regiment?'

'I intend to give it a great deal of thought, sir. There's still a need for horsemen, but not used in that way.'

'That's a crafty retort if ever there were one,' Wolseley said. 'So what's the answer?'

'Train 'em to use their carbines, sir.'

Wolseley permitted himself another slow smile. 'I think you'll be highly unpopular with some of our mounted regiments,' he said. 'Go on. Tell me more about the Germans. What makes 'em so able?'

'Their army's a machine, sir. By the use of railways and telegraphs they manage numbers not known up to now. I think we shall have trouble from them in Europe before long. I suspect that they like war. But it's not the old kind of war, sir. The French provided that. Their doctrine was always that they wouldn't win by defence. They never went anywhere but forward. I think their success lies in the fact that their staff is trained. Bravery isn't enough. A staff officer needs to be more clear-headed than brave, methodical rather than dashing.'

'Are you suggesting we recruit scholars?'

'No, sir. Just the more intelligent of what we have. I think this war shows the trend of future wars and it'll be a good idea if we take note of it.'

Wolseley was silent for a long time, staring at his fingers

as they rested on the brown wood of his desk. 'I read the pieces you wrote for *the Morning Advertiser*,' he said at last. 'They were well-written and succinct. Can you write all that again? For me. In a report.'

'I think so, sir.'

'Then you'd better get on with it. You'll be found a room and a couple of secretaries. I want it setting down with as much clarity as you showed in the reports for the *Morning Advertiser*. You have a gift with a pen and the Secretary for War will be very interested.'

Colby hesitated. 'Sir, it was not my intention that I should be away from my regiment for good.'

'Nor is it ours,' Wolseley snapped back. 'The best leaders of the future will be men who have done alternate spells on the staff and with troops. We shall all be seeing a change in a year or two when the reforms we plan take effect. The purchasing of commissions will go. It has to go. It's illogical, iniquitous and indefensible in these modern times, and when it does go we shall perhaps be able to push a few of our more capable men into ranks commensurate with their ability.'

He paused, his eyes bright with enthusiasm. 'I have no time for politicians,' he said. 'They're nothing but a race of drones, and Cardwell stands head and shoulders above the rest for the forwardness of his ideas. But – ' he hesitated ' – they *all* act in accordance with the national tradition of starving the army of brains and then complaining about the hidebound military mind when it comes to war.' He paused again. 'You ought to learn a lot here that might be good for you, because politics and military leadership are very closely connected.'

Brave, brilliant, ambitious, unpopular at court but popular with the press, Wolseley clearly had his finger on the pulse of the army. He turned to the window again. 'Have you got rooms in London?' he asked over his shoulder.

'No, sir.'

'Then you'd better get some. Got anybody trustworthy to look after you?'

Colby didn't think Ackroyd would object to being away from home a little longer. 'I think I can manage that, sir.'

'Then you'd better get on with it and get yourself settled in. You may be going back to France. I'm interested to know what the Prussians will do about Paris.'

'I can answer that now, sir,' Colby said. 'They'll besiege it.'

'Starving 'em out won't win the Prussians the love of the civilised world.'

'I suspect that won't worry Bismarck too much, sir. I met General Sheridan, the American, at Sedan. He and I had a few things to talk about. He's got a reputation for ruthlessness, but I suspect the truth is that he's just a clear-thinking man. Moltke had come to the conclusion that wars could be won simply by the movement of troops. Sheridan pointed out that this was only the first requirement of victory and that the way to end a war was to cause the inhabitants of an invaded country so much suffering they'd force their government to demand it.'

'And?'

'I think Moltke took it to heart. I think the Prussians will bombard.'

London had a wintry look about it and the cabbies shivered in their high seats on the hansoms. There were a few men Colby knew at the Cavalry Club, including a captain who had been at Balaclava. He was thinking of selling out before the purchase system was brought to an end and was in a gloomy mood. There was also a note for Colby from his sister Harriet who had been on a visit to her father and been surprised to hear he'd been entertaining a young woman.

'He said she was asking after you,' she wrote. 'She refused to give a name because she wished to surprise you. What have you been up to?'

Colby decided he'd better go home and, catching a train the following morning, he was in York by the afternoon. At Harrogate, a trap from Braxby was waiting for him, driven inevitably by one of the Ackroyd family. Harriet met him at the door, grave-faced, to announce that his father had been put to bed with a chill.

'I don't think he has the will to fight it,' she said.

Despite the grey day there was something about Braxby that nudged at Colby's heart. This was where he belonged, where the bones of his ancestors rested, where he, too, would eventually rest, God willing, and that knowledge was surprisingly important.

The pleasure at coming home was spoiled by the frailty of his father. Grey-faced, his white hair like a wispy halo round his head, the general lay on pillows in the bedroom. A huge fire burned in the grate and the housekeeper sat by it, knitting. As Colby entered, she rose, bobbed a curtsey and disappeared.

The old man's face lit up as he saw his son but he found talking difficult. 'Been in France, I hear,' he murmured. 'Involved in the war.'

'Not involved, Father,' Colby said, bending to kiss the fragile-looking skull. 'I was sent by the War Office. Wolseley sent me.'

'Don't like Wolseley. Stirs things up too much. How'd you find the French?'

'Not as good as when you were fighting them, Father.'

'Weren't even then. Marshals were a poor lot on the whole. Even Napoleon was past his prime. How about this other Napoleon?'

'Also past his prime, Father. And *his* marshals are even worse. Most of them, as far as I can see, shouldn't have been in charge of a corporal's picket. They got their rank because they went down well with the Empress's ladies.'

The old man sniffed. 'Well, that's all finished now,' he said. 'Napoleon's a prisoner in Germany and the Empress is a fugitive in England. Got a place in Kent, I heard. Would have done better in Yorkshire. Still, I always did think the French lacked backbone.' He was silent for a moment, exhausted by talking. 'Who's this gel?' he ended.

'Which girl, Father?'

'The one who came here.'

'I haven't the faintest idea, Father.' The only person

Colby could think of was Germaine.

'Time you were married.' The old man's muttering was barely audible now. 'Hoped I might see a grandson before I go. Nothing odd about you, is there?'

Colby laughed. 'Not on your life, Father. You were none too young yourself when I was foaled.'

'True, but things are different these days.'

How, Colby wondered. Men and women still went to bed together. 'Who was she, Father? Didn't she say?'

'No.'

'What was she like? Tall? Good figure?'

'Dunno. You'd have to trot her up and down a bit. All she did was sit in a chair. Seemed intelligent, though. Pretty. Dark hair. People without dark hair look as if their faces have faded. Always had dark hair in our family. Good breeders.' The old man moved restlessly on the pillows. 'Better go now. I'm tired. It's bloody awful when you're old. You're always tired.'

Harriet was sipping a sherry in the library when Colby went downstairs. 'How's Henry?' he asked.

'My husband,' Harriet said briskly, 'is bursting with health. I wish to God sometimes he were a little more pale and wan.'

Colby wondered if he chased Harriet round the bedroom at night. Harriet was no wilting lily herself, however, and he suspected she enjoyed her life as much as her husband enjoyed his. It made him feel lonely.

'Making money?'

'By the thousand.'

'Children?'

'All snotty-nosed at this time of the year. But they're well. George is starting to ride and doing rather well at it. Sarah's got a pony.'

Seemed to be following the family tradition, Colby thought. He himself had been stuck on a pony at the age of three and expected to stay on. He hadn't, of course, but he'd learned quickly enough through falling off.

'This girl –' he began.

'Which girl? The Rector's daughter? I hope you're not

thinking of marrying her, Coll. She's an awful bore.'

'Damn the Rector's daughter!' Colby snapped. 'I know she's a bore. No, this girl who came looking for me. Who the hell is she?'

'God knows. Father said she didn't have an English accent.'

'Jesus Christ in the mountains!'

'That's a splendid oath!'

'Picked it up in the States.' Colby poured himself a whisky and sank it at a gulp. 'What was she like? I couldn't get more out of him than that she had dark hair.'

'That's about all he told me.'

'Pale skin? Dark eyes?'

He didn't say.' Harriet sighed. 'He's getting a bit old to notice females.'

'He wasn't too old to notice she was pretty.' Germaine for a quid, Colby thought. After all, he'd asked her to marry him and she'd probably decided, with France in its present mess, that it was a good idea. 'Did he say what she wanted?'

Harriet smiled. 'You, I think,' she said.

6

London seemed empty. There were few people Colby knew and Caroline Matchett seemed to have vanished. He'd heard she'd been taken ill and, because he'd once been fond of her, he went to see if there was anything he could do. But the house at Hounslow was shut up and there was no sign of either her or the maid.

Wolseley's report, a bulky wad of paper written out by a procession of War Office clerks, was almost finished when Colby's father died and the telegram that arrived at his rooms sent him post-haste to Yorkshire.

A detachment of the 19th had already arrived and were billeted in Braxby under a lieutenant and a sergeant-major. The old man's horse, with his boots reversed in the stirrups and covered with a black cloth, was brought from the stables as the gun carriage arrived. As it moved off, followed by the carriages of the mourners, it was escorted by the bearers, six lancers with black armbands, their dark uniforms sombre against the light of the winter day.

'Wrap me up in my old stable jacket –' the words of the song he'd so often heard his father singing rang round Colby's head like a dirge 'And say a poor devil lies low. And six of the lancers will carry me. To the place where the best soldiers go.'

It was only a short distance to the churchyard and a band from the local militia provided the music, the solemn thump of the 'Dead March' giving the beat for the step. The rooks in the oaks were filling the air with their harsh cries, and the steady thud of the drums beat against the chilly day. The village street was filled with people of all ages, and the militia had lined the verges for the passing of the coffin, covered by the Union Jack and bearing the dead man's hat and sword. Behind walked the sergeant-major of the 19th, bearing a cushion covered with decorations, and the officer and escort of lancers, their legs curiously thin-looking in the green overalls, their eyes sombre under the lance-caps, their cheeks brushed by the plumes fluttering in a breeze that set the trees creaking.

'Man that is born of woman hath but a short time to live, and is full of misery . . .'

It didn't seem to fit, Colby thought. His father had been the least miserable of men, and he suspected even that he'd enjoyed every minute of his life until the last few months.

'He cometh up, and is cut down, like a flower . . .'

The Rector had a voice like the bass pipes of an organ, and he enjoyed using it. Glancing up, Colby saw his daughter standing opposite him. She was dressed in unrelieved black. She was watching him and, as he looked up at her, he saw her cheeks grow pink.

The sergeant, holding the folded Union Jack under his arm, lifted his head. His order, screamed at the top of his voice, brought the escort of lancers to the graveside, fortunately without falling into it, and they raised their carbines. The volley – a little ragged, Colby thought professionally – sent the rooks into the air. The second one was better and the third got it almost right. Then the soldiers filed away and waited to one side as the mourners filed round the grave. The thump and rattle of soil on the coffin lid sounded hollow and mournful.

As they moved for the carriages, Colby caught sight of Brosy and Grace, and then of the Cosgros, Claude all pink and white, Georgina tight-faced and hard-eyed in a way he'd never noticed before. They were no friends of his father's but, he supposed, because they were neighbours they had to put in an appearance.

Afterwards, in a subdued murmur of conversation as the maids handed round the sandwiches and the port, the Rector attached himself to Colby, murmuring commiserations. 'So sad, so sad,' he announced.

'Not sure he'd have thought so,' Colby pointed out sharply. 'He enjoyed his life more than most people and probably didn't begrudge dying.'

The Rector looked shocked and, as he backed away, Georgina appeared in front of Colby, pale-faced, more bosom than ever since she'd produced three children.

'Colby, I'm so sorry,' she said.

There seemed to be a speculative look in her eye and he wondered if she were making eyes at him again.

'He had a good life,' Colby said. It was a safe cliché. The old man *had* enjoyed his life, though he suspected he wouldn't have complained at the chance of a few more years of it.

'Are you married yet, Colby?'

'No, Georgina. Still fancy free. It seems to be suiting you, though.'

She pulled a face that was meant, he supposed, to be noncommittal. 'Are you staying home for long?'

'Few days. That's all. I have a job in London at the moment. Temporarily on the staff.'

'That's where Claude belongs. He could bring his intelligence to bear.'

Claude, Colby thought, hadn't got any bloody intelligence. Put him on the staff and the whole army would fall apart.

'Somebody has to do it, I suppose,' he said.

She touched his arm. 'Claude returns to the regiment tomorrow,' she said. 'You must come for tea. Two lonely people –'

She left the words hanging in the air as she moved away, and he stared after her.

'What are you grinning at?'

He swung round at his sister's voice. '*Was* I grinning?'

'Near enough. What about?'

He turned and smiled at her. 'I think Georgina's after me again,' he said.

Before returning to London, Colby had to visit the solicitor in Harrogate over his father's affairs. The weather was cold with a hint of rain in the air and there was a strong wind that sent the clouds scudding across the sky above the tops of the bare trees. Harrogate station was petrifyingly cold and full of people with pinched cheeks and red noses. A draft of infantry was heading south and were clasping their womenfolk alongside the train. As the whistle went they all climbed aboard and the train drew out, sprouting a forest of scarlet-clad arms.

Back in London, everybody seemed concerned with Paris. Besieged for several weeks now, it was clear it would fall before long. The Prussians had poured westwards, so sustained by French wine, it was said, there was a continuous line of broken bottles all the way from Sedan. Within a fortnight, they were seizing trains as they tried to escape and within three weeks had thrown a ring round the capital. The French had learned nothing and the Prussians had established their headquarters at Versailles where Bismarck, in a white uniform, indulged his curious mixture of gluttony and spartan simplicity, and the German Emperor, august, courteous, always in uniform, fussed about the level of the wine in the bottles at the end of the meals.

With the increasing cold, it soon became clear that hunger was beginning to take its toll inside the city, and a bitter Christmas came and went with the Prussians still outside. It was obvious their leaders were growing worried by the protraction of the war and by the fact that the contempt the rest of Europe had felt for the popinjay Empire was now directed against the ruthless Prussians. Bismarck developed varicose veins and the Crown Prince – probably for the benefit of his mother-in-law, Queen Victoria – was expressing himself weary of the fighting. Clearly something had to be done to end the siege and there was only one way to do it. What Colby had predicted became a fact, and the first shells fell on the city two days after Christmas. In no time they were falling at a rate of three and four hundred a day, killing men, women and children. Demoralised, half-starved and on the point of revolution, Paris capitulated in less than a month.

Wolseley gave Colby the sort of look he would have directed at a major prophet.

'Well?' he asked, gesturing at *The Times*. 'What do you think will happen now?'

'There'll be the usual victory march through the city, sir, I expect. To make Paris know it's been beaten. I see the Germans are demanding enormous reparations. That ought to help quieten them down a little, too.'

Wolseley shrugged. 'And that, I suppose, will be that. The Germans will go home and Paris will return to having a good time as it did after Waterloo.'

Colby paused. 'Not this time, sir,' he said. 'This time there'll be no return to the old days. At least not for a long time.'

Wolseley's eyebrows lifted. 'Are we about to be treated to more prophetic wisdom?' he asked. 'Why not?'

'There'll be trouble, sir.'

'What sort of trouble?'

'Insurrection, sir.'

'What!' Wolseley looked startled. 'Another? They've already had three revolutions since 1789.'

Colby shrugged. 'There are to be elections, sir, and when they come the Empire will be blamed for starting the war and the republic for prolonging it. France will elect monarchists to be on the safe side and Paris, which has always considered itself the brain of France, won't stand for that.'

Wolseley looked at him steadily. 'That's a startling suggestion,' he said.

'I believe it to be true, sir.'

Wolseley gestured. 'If you prove right, then I should say you're way ahead of all your contemporaries in a sense of situation. It should stand you in good stead. You'd better go and get it all written down.'

The news from Paris very quickly followed the pattern Colby had suggested. The place was revictualled after its months of starvation, but the elections had struck it like a

198

thunderclap. Only a handful of the militant extremists of the left had been elected.

As Colby had predicted, they had been routed at the polls by the Monarchists, and Adolphe Thiers, a ruthless little man with a round head, steel spectacles and a predilection for dictatorship, had been elected President, something which immediately started the hotheads in Paris talking of self-government. What made it worse was that as the armistice talks with the Germans dragged on, it became clear that France was to lose all Alsace and most of Lorraine, including both Metz and Strasbourg.

'It'll mean war in perpetuity,' Colby said. 'The French will never lie down under this and, as soon as they're strong enough, they'll try to get it all back.'

Despite their rage, there was little the French could do but accept the terms, and they had to suffer the march past of thirty thousand Germans through their capital and endure the sound of German trumpets and German bands. Shop windows were shuttered and draped with black, and savage retribution was dealt to civilians who appeared to be too friendly. As soon as the Germans left, the Parisians made the derisive gesture of scrubbing the pavements with disinfectant.

'Well,' Wolseley said, 'it seems your talk of revolution was a little off the mark. But the Foreign Secretary's interested in France and so is the Secretary for War, so I think we ought to go and take a look. How do you feel about another visit to Paris?'

The French capital seemed to be haunted by the half-sweetish, half-foetid odour of cooked horseflesh, and its wounds were still visible in smashed and desolate houses and the fading signs outside the shops, *Boucherie, Canine et Féline*. There seemed to be battalions of women in black, and small portions of siege bread, framed and glazed, were on sale in the novelty shops. Faces were bitter and Colby wasn't surprised to hear talk of undying hatred for everything German. But the revictualling of the city was almost complete and, as Colby and Wolseley occupied their rooms in a hotel at the bottom of the Champs Elysées, herds of cattle were still being driven in and it was already possible to order a meal in a restaurant.

With Wolseley invited to spend a few days in the country with the American ambassador, Colby was left to himself, and, walking about the city, it didn't take him long to become aware of a dangerous ferment that was bubbling up. Food had done much to restore the damage done to bodies but there was more than that to be repaired, it seemed. The humiliation of defeat, the peace terms, the drabness of the city and the dangerous French ennui after the drama of the siege were working and the population was existing in a vacuum. The city was still licking its wounds and, under the feeling of peace brought by the warm weather and the spring blossom, there were sharp anxieties and fear. Blood-red posters spattered the walls and, with soldiers everywhere, an alarm from the direction of Montmartre sent him in a hansom to see what was happening.

When Wolseley reappeared, he announced that he was returning to London but was leaving Colby in Paris for another week or two to keep an eye on things.

'I think everything's quietening down nicely,' he said. 'The American ambassador feels it's all over now and that, with the prospect of good business and an abundance of food, Paris is recovering.'

'I disagree, sir,' Colby said.

Wolseley's eyes glittered. 'You have a great gift for telling me I don't know what I'm talking about,' he said testily. 'Why do you say that?'

'The poorer classes don't seem to be benefiting from the food, because they can't afford it, anyway, and I don't think the new government's helped them by deciding to end the pay of the men of the National Guard. To most of them it's been a form of dole. They demonstrated in the Place de la Bastille yesterday. It was nothing but a march past, but it went on from ten in the morning until six in the evening, with bands and their colours draped in black. All the speeches were anti-government.

200

The mood was ugly, sir.'

Wolseley listened quietly, gesturing to him to continue.

'They also took away from the artillery parks about two hundred cannon which were due to be handed over to the Germans. They claim they were paid for by public subscription during the siege so that they've never been the property of the government to hand over. They've got them up in Montmartre.'

Wolseley was silent for a moment then he rose and stared out of the window. 'You must be due for leave,' he said unexpectedly.

'I hardly think so, sir.'

'You'd better take some, nevertheless. And you'd better spend it in Paris. I want to know what happens and so will Cardwell and the Foreign Secretary. But I can't keep you here officially. You'd better take leave until the business resolves itself. I want someone with an ear to the ground. But this time don't get involved. If anything happens, come home.'

Within forty-eight hours of Wolseley departing, Ackroyd arrived from London and Colby moved from the expensive hotel at the bottom of the Champs Elysées to an apartment in a flat-fronted block near the Luxembourg. It was so brown it looked like the inside of a cardboard box but Ackroyd had come prepared with summer clothing, money orders on Paris banks and his usual unflappable manner.

'Your sister was in London, sir,' he announced. 'She asked me to tell you that the young lady had called again.'

Colby frowned. 'What young lady?'

'The one that called before.'

'Who is she, dammit?'

'Your sister didn't tell me, sir.'

'Was it the Baronne de Maël, Tyas?'

'I couldn't say, sir. I never seen her. And your sister seemed to be playin' careful. An' if it *was* the Baronne, sir, then I should point out that she ain't there any more because at the moment she's in Paris.'

Colby jerked round. 'How do you know, you bloody old rogue?'

Ackroyd allowed himself a superior smile. 'I took the precaution of directin' the 'ansom from the station via the Champs Elysées, sir. The 'ouse was used as a 'ospital durin' the siege, the cabby told me, but now the war's over she's back in it.'

'How do you know it's her, Tyas?'

'I seen 'er, sir. There was a carriage outside so I instructed the cabby to stop and wait, and eventually she came out.'

There was an unexpected kick at Colby's heart. He had enjoyed good times with Germaine.

'How does she look?' he demanded.

'Beautiful, sir.'

'Think I ought to go and see her, Tyas?'

'No, sir,' Ackroyd said firmly. 'She ain't your cup of tea at all.'

Colby glared. 'What the hell *is* my cup of tea?'

'Not 'er, sir. I can't imagine 'er ladyin' it at Braxby or thunderin' across a field after a fox, covered with mud. Can you?'

Paris seemed almost to be listening for an alarm. The horse-buses were running as usual but people had formed the habit of talking earnestly in cafés and bars and at the corners of the streets. The air was full of excitement and not much business was being done.

Tempted by the knowledge that Germaine was back, Colby toyed with the idea for some time of going to see her but he had a shrewd idea that Harriet would not approve of her. Despite her impeccable breeding, she would not go down well in Braxby and, as Ackroyd had said, he couldn't really see her smashing through the weather-beaten haw-thornes of North Yorkshire after a dog fox in the middle of a misty November day. Nevertheless, there was something about her that drew him. Remembering how once he would have liked to have sunk a hatchet in her head at Gravelotté, he couldn't imagine why, but he was sufficiently interested to dress himself in tails, cloak and top hat in the hope that he would be more attractive to her.

Ackroyd had just arrived back at his rooms after a day sniffing round the bars and he looked at Colby with alarm. 'Where are you going?' he asked.

Colby tried to appear nonchalant. 'Thought I'd call on the Baronne de Maël.'

Ackroyd gave a low laugh. He seemed highly amused. 'Shouldn't, sir,' he advised. 'Not now.'

'Why not?'

'Because it's starting.'

'What's starting?'

'Paris, sir.'

Colby tossed his hat and gloves down. Ackroyd had an uncanny gift for absorbing a political situation quickly.

'Out with it,' he snapped. 'What's happened?'

'Them guns they took up to Montmartre – they sent the army up to bring 'em back. Only they were as efficient as usual and forgot the gun teams. The troops went over to the mob and they've shot the general in charge.'

The news Ackroyd had brought turned out to be incomplete. The mob had shot not one general, but two, having found another who'd been foolish enough to poke his nose in out of curiosity. They'd been killed in a garden in the Rue des Rosiers, their bodies mutilated by a mob shrieking like lunatics, and other senior officers, including the Minister for War, had barely escaped with their lives. Now, with their nerves far from good after all that had happened since the previous September when the Empire had fallen, Thiers' government, anxious not to lose their grip on the country even if they lost it on Paris, were withdrawing to Versailles. Behind them went what was left of the Regular army, jeered at all the way through Paris by the amazed but delighted Parisians.

Curious, Colby took a cab to Montmartre, but everything seemed quiet. There were crowds of people about and a lot of men in the uniform of the National Guard. The guns were still where they'd been parked, but there was no sign of trouble and dozens of sightseers were strolling about.

The following day the newspapers announced that the city had been taken over by a commune. What a commune was nobody knew. The word had been murmured under the Second Empire and shouted during the siege, but even those who had shouted it loudest weren't sure what it did. Memories also still recalled the revolution of 1848 and the bombs thrown by crimson-hued left-wingers, yet there seemed remarkably little excitement. Shops remained opened and the theatres were still playing, while the trains in and out of the city still ran. Business even continued to pick up and, unable to resist the strange sensation of being part of a carnival, Colby headed once more for the Champs Elysées, only to find that Germaine had bolted again.

She was worse than a bloody weathercock, he decided. It would be no good thinking of marriage with her. She'd be off to Marseilles or Perpignan at the first hint of thunder.

For once, however, she seemed to have guessed wrong and the reign of terror that had been expected in a city taken over by a mob had not occurred. Apart from the fact that left wing journals, which had lapsed under Thiers, were allowed to re-open, there was little to suggest change. But, though the streets were quiet and curiously empty, it was impossible to telegraph reports to Wolseley because there was no postal or telegraph service out of the capital. Then, as the days passed, the absence of communication with the outside world suddenly began to seem ominous and, hearing there was to be a demonstration in the Place Vendôme, Colby decided to go and watch it.

The groups of people moving from the Opera and the Bourse seemed to consist chiefly of retired officers, shop-keepers and elderly gentlemen. They carried banners – 'Time Presses For a Dyke Against Revolution', 'For Peace' and 'Reunion of the Friends of Order' – and were marching towards the Rue de la Paix where a barricade had been erected. The National Guard waited in front of it and a shouted order stopped the column.

'We're unarmed,' one of the elderly men shouted back, though Colby noticed bulges in the pockets of a few of the more nervous-looking.

'Go back,' the Guard commander ordered. 'My instructions are that you should disperse.'

'We're French,' an old man at the front yelled, waving his stick. 'We're Parisians! We have every right to be here!'

When the shouts of 'Socialist canaille' started, Colby decided it was growing a little tense and started to look for a doorway where he could shelter. As he edged past, it was obvious that a few of the other sightseers were growing nervous, too, and there was a general movement rearwards by the more doubtful demonstrators and men bundling away their womenfolk. It was difficult to get clear, however, because the pressure from the rear was forcing the leaders closer to the line of National Guardsmen. Rifles were raised and the soldiers were in an ugly mood, and Colby had just found himself a shop doorway when a shot rang out, echoing among the tall buildings around him.

Almost immediately it was followed by a volley, and the square was filled with smoke and the screams of women. The crowd heaved and lurched, as those pressing forward at the back turned and began to run. As it began to crumble, the yelling mass dispersed, bolting for the Rue de Rivoli. Another volley roared out and, in front of the shop doorway where Colby was sheltered, an elderly man wearing the Légion d'Honneur stumbled and fell, his fingers clawing at the wall. As he slowly subsided to the pavement, blood from his breast daubed a red smear across the stonework.

The crowd was bolting now as fast as their legs would carry them. Above their heads, faces were hurriedly withdrawn from windows and, as Colby dragged the wounded man into the shop doorway, he saw the shutters of Worths', the couturiers, fall into place. The square seemed to be filled with bodies but as the smoke cleared many of them clambered to their feet and began to run. Immediately there was another volley and several of them fell. As the National Guard moved back, their weapons still held at the ready, a few shopkeepers and uninjured moved out to help the dying.

Stretched on the shop floor, the old man was breathing in a heavy snoring noise and as Colby bent over him, opening his shirt to find the wound, a woman knelt alongside him and lifted her dress to wrench at the white cotton of her petticoat. Tearing it free, she tried to staunch the blood with it, but an artery seemed to have been severed and her fingers became reddened with it. Sitting back on her heels, she put her hands to her face and began to sob.

'It's too late,' she said.

It was indeed, Colby thought. Blood had been spilt. The people he had seen laughing on the boulevards, feeling that the Commune could not affect their lives, now knew different. The rift between Paris and Versailles had gone beyond reconciliation. There would be no terms now and precious little else but hatred.

It seemed to be time to go home.

7

There was a great deal of speculation. The threat to established order which had risen in Paris seemed clear heresy, yet travellers returning from France showed a surprising sympathy with the fact that the Commune was trying to provide liberties the British had been enjoying for generations.

Watching the newspapers at Wolseley's request, the only thing that drew Colby's attention was a name he recognised among the newly-elected leaders, and it didn't take long to discover that the 'Citizen Paul-Gustave Cluseret', who figured among the military officers of the Commune was that same Cluseret he had saved from being lynched in America. Enquiries revealed that his career since had followed a predictable path. He had acquired the American citizenship he had so much desired and had even got himself into American politics, but he had been unable to keep his fingers out of dangerous pies and, involved with a group demanding Irish freedom, had been forced to leave America and had turned up in England to take part in an attack on Chester Gaol. With the British police also after him, he had fled to France where he had been arrested for sedition against Napoleon, but, claiming American citizenship, had merely been deported, only to return when the Empire fell, to take his place in the ranks of the Commune.

There was still no sign of Germaine and Colby could only imagine she was enjoying herself in the South of France once more. Caroline Matchett had disappeared from the face of the earth and, with nobody else on the horizon, he was even beginning to eye the Rector's daughter with a measure of speculation. He wanted to get married and was conscious that she was not unaware of his interest. Since his great-grandfather had founded the regiment, it was not unlikely – Claude Cosgro's ambitions notwithstanding – that, because tradition demanded it, he would in time become its commanding officer, and wife to a cavalry colonel carried a lot of weight in the shires.

His job in London finished, he was due to return to the regiment, but Wolseley seemed unwilling to let him go, claiming that he hadn't yet finished with France. Certainly London still lapped up stories from Paris. By comparison England seemed remarkably dull, with nothing to raise the eyebrows beyond the scandal of Lord William d'Eresby fleecing his mistress of thousands and then eloping with her maid, and the Prince of Wales being accused of adultery with Lady Mordaunt and having to go into the witness box to deny it. *The Illustrated London News* and *The Graphic* both had correspondents and artists in France, all making the most of the extraordinary situation of a capital city defying its own government, but they seemed able to find remarkably few incursions into civil liberties and no commandeering of private property beyond the seizure of two right-wing newspapers. But, Colby noticed, there were other, more private, reports that landed on his desk that mentioned soldiers and policemen shot without trial for no other reason than that they had served the Empire. Justice, in fact, seemed to have come to a stop because, like the postal officials, the Paris judges had wisely disappeared.

It was still possible to move in and out of the city without trouble, however, food was available, and the hatred engendered by the shootings in the Place Vendôme seemed to be dying. The Commune had been established and correspondents were even beginning to suggest that Thiers would have to climb down and treat with its leaders. But then, in the first days of April, Thiers' cavalry fell on a Communard outpost and shot the lot, and a massed sortie in retaliation showed that the Commune was no more efficient than the Empire. Utterly smashed, its leaders were caught and shot out of hand, and at once hostages were arrested, among them the Archbishop of Paris, his Vicar-General and a host of priests, nuns and foreigners.

Immediately Paris was under siege again. The gates clanged shut and, after the failure of the civilian 'generals' who had led the disastrous sortie, Gustave-Paul Cluseret, from being an unimportant military man, became leader of the Commune's army.

'Didn't you know the fellow?' Wolseley asked. 'In America or something?'

'Yes, sir,' Colby admitted. 'I wasn't impressed.'

Unexpectedly, the discussion became an invitation to dinner at Wolseley's club. Wolseley was inclined enough to keep himself to himself for the invitation to be intriguing, and Colby wondered what it entailed, because he suspected that it certainly entailed something.

There was another guest, and his presence raised Colby's eyebrows, because he hadn't known Wolseley even knew him or, if he had, could possibly like him. The meal was served quietly in a room separate from the other members, which immediately put Colby on his guard and made him suspect there was dirty work somewhere in the offing. It didn't take long to bring the talk round to politics and finally to France.

'Thiers has persuaded the Prussians that it's in their interest to squash this revolution.' Wolseley's guest spoke in a quiet voice, an amused worldly smile playing about his lips. 'And, since Bismarck's started to consider it might spread to Berlin, he's returning four hundred thousand French prisoners of war to help him do it. This time Thiers means business.' The faint smile came again. 'He seems to be assuming that if the army couldn't defeat the Prussians, at least they ought to be able to defeat their own countrymen.'

Colby said nothing, aware that somewhere in this roundabout chitchat there was something unpleasant for him.

'Does it affect us, sir?' Wolseley said, affecting a bland disinterest.

'Yes.' His guest smiled. 'If nothing's produced a reign of terror in Paris so far, this shooting of prisoners will. It will be 1791 all over again and the Commune will doubtless be frightened enough to butcher a few prisoners of its own.' He smiled at Colby and sipped his wine, clearly not expecting to be among the unlucky ones. 'They might not *all* be French either,' he ended and Colby began to at last see where the conversation was leading. 'There are British people in Paris wanting to get out.' The smile had given way to a sombre gravity now. 'Andrew Gordon, for instance, who's a Methodist minister. You may have heard of him. Prates a little, but he's given to holding mass meetings and there'd be quite an uproar if he weren't saved. George Clarendon –'

'Fortieth Foot,' Wolseley put in.

'– the American Minister's family.'

'Friends of mine, as you're aware,' Wolseley said.

'– Lord Wane. Lady Ecclesfield.'

There was a long pause then Wolseley's guest put his fingertips together and looked at Colby. 'Lady Ecclesfield's about to be married to a distant cousin of the Queen's,' he said. 'Can't imagine why. It'll do the Queen no good. And Lord Wane's part of the Royal Household. What he's doing over there just now, I can't imagine.' He looked at Colby again. 'But you see the problem, I'm sure.'

Colby saw it only too plainly. 'What about the Foreign Office?' he asked.

The smile this time was faintly contemptuous. 'The Prime Minister refuses to be involved, particularly where Lord Wane and Lady Ecclesfield are concerned. Gladstone's no favourite of the Queen, as you possibly know, and doubtless he sees no reason to concern himself with favourites of hers. The Queen has therefore turned to me.' The friendliness returned to the smile. 'I turned to Wolseley here.'

Colby said nothing.

'They have to be brought back to England,' the quiet voice went on. 'We've approached Washburne, the American Minister, and he's more than willing to help. But he insists that they're not his concern really – which indeed they're not – and that we should have someone there of our own to handle it.'

'Can't the Embassy?'

There was a shrug, a gesture with slim white hands and a moué of sadness. 'The Embassy is functioning at half-throttle at the moment. The ambassador, Lord Lyons, is not the most enterprising of men. As for his staff, like Washburne's people, they seem to be spending more time in Versailles than in Paris. After all, that's where the French government is, and I think they have their hands full. What we need is someone able to handle the business without being hampered by any other responsibilities. Wolseley said *you* might help.' The quiet friendly smile came again. 'The Queen would be grateful to me for solving her dilemma. Grateful to you, too, I suspect.'

There seemed little more to be said. Certainly not by Colby. As they left the club he realised the matter had been settled with hardly a word from him.

Wolseley watched the carriage carrying his guest disappear into the darkness, the clip-clop of hooves slowly fading.

'Not a bad fellow, Disraeli,' he observed. 'For a Jew, that is.'

It was no longer possible to get into Paris by train and Colby and Ackroyd had to hire horses. At the Porte Maillot, they were stopped by men of the National Guard, all fiercely whiskered but curiously uncertain of themselves.

Nobody was prepared to take the responsibility of letting them through and several officers and NCOs went into committee for twenty minutes before announcing that they would have to send the request for entry to the Commune – which wasn't due to be in session until the following day.

'Send my name to the military commander, Citizen Cluseret,' Colby suggested.

'The military commander is far too busy.'

'Not to see me.' Colby's card and a handful of silver

changed the sergeant's mind and he agreed to send a runner at once.

There was a café handy and Colby and Ackroyd sat in the sunshine, drinking cold chablis until the sergeant reappeared. 'The military commander instructs us to allow you to pass,' he said.

Cluseret looked older, his beard streaked with grey, his handsome face a little flabbier. He removed the cheroot from his mouth as he saw Colby and rose to shake hands.

'You once did me a favour,' he said bluntly. 'I was in a very difficult situation. What do you want?'

He listened carefully as Colby explained why he was there, then he shrugged. 'Why not?' he said. 'I don't wish to detain anybody, whatever my comrades might think. Every foreigner eating food in the city leaves just that much less for the Parisians. Perhaps it would be as well to avoid some sort of international incident, too, so let me 'ave the names and they will be issued with passes.'

He escorted Colby to the door. 'These *crapauds* 'ave no idea 'ow to conduct things,' he observed quietly in English as they walked down a corridor lined with slovenly National Guardsmen. 'Am I supposed to make these objects into soldiers? The ineptitude of the people who run the Commune is quite incredible. They are good for nothing but thinking up resounding titles for their private armies and dressing in a way that would do credit to the Empire. I 'ave ordered no lanyards, no glitter, no gold braid. They will be better for it.'

He was the same cynical Cluseret Colby had met in America, saying what he thought about his colleagues with a recklessness which seemed suicidal.

The apartment near the Luxembourg was still free and Colby paid the rent in advance and moved in quickly. The Embassy, working at half-cock with many of its staff in Versailles, was able to supply the names of stranded Britons, and Washburne, the American Minister, provided those of several Americans. It wasn't difficult to persuade Cluseret to permit a train to pass through the lines, and the Reverend Andrew Gordon, scourge of the unbelievers, George Clarendon, of the 40th of Foot, Washburne's family, Lord Wane and Lady Ecclesfield were all unearthed.

A second batch of travellers was also allowed through, but this time their departure was more hurried, because Neuilly, the prosperous village to the west of the city which had largely been spared by the Prussians in January, was close to the railway line and the shells beginning to come from Versaillese guns manned by returned prisoners of war were starting to fill the hospitals with injured. Shattered bedding, furniture, mirrors and glassware lay in the streets and people were living in cellars praying for the fighting to finish. As the shells reached further and further into the city, haphazardly killing Communards and anti-Communards alike, the splinters were even striking the United States Legation near the Etoile, and Ackroyd, carrying a message to Washburne, brought back a stone foot knocked off a bas relief on the Arc de Triomphe. The Champs Elysées was deserted these days and there were barriers by the Rond Point beyond which no one but soldiers was permitted to go. It was clear that the great attack Thiers was anticipated to launch with his returned army was expected soon and there was a new flood of applications for passports or protection papers, and the Second Secretary who appeared to be running the British Embassy put out a notice that British subjects remained in Paris at their own risk. If the bombardment was achieving nothing else, it was at least encouraging people to leave.

Thiers was generally regarded by the British still in Paris as an ass but they were all well aware that when his attack came he would know where to aim because he had been the Minister responsible for building the city's defences in the days of Louis-Philippe, and Issy was suggested as the place. That they were dead right was proved at the end of the month when, after a tremendous bombardment, Fort Issy fell. A new request to Cluseret to permit foreigners to leave via the German lines to the east was brushed aside.

'Later,' he said. 'First I must regain Fort Issy.'

213

Reporting to Washburne that evening, Colby found him looking worried. He had a strong face and wore his long hair swept behind his ears, a typical American with steady eyes, a strong nose and jaw, and a Puritan sternness about his manner and clothes.

'Cluseret saved Issy,' he said. 'Thiers' army was as slow as usual. The place had been evacuated but Cluseret got his men there before they thought of moving in. Unfortunately, we'll get no more help from him because he's been arrested. They say it's lack of ability, but it can't be because he's the only one who has any. There's a rumour he was planning to sell the Commune to the government.'

'It would be in character, sir.'

Washburne gestured. 'I think it's just the Commune being nervous,' he said. 'His successor's no safer. He's already being accused of not having the right political spirit, whatever that might be. I guess the Jacobins are in control and they're talking of shooting the Archbishop and a few hostages – foreign ones if necessary.'

From that moment, Colby's work, shared with two or three Englishmen and Americans, became more secret, and the removal of people from the Champs Elysées area was done at night. They were hurried to the north-east of the city where the Prussians still lay, and all those young enough to be active were taken inconspicuously on buses to the Jardin des Plantes, from whence they walked to the Porte d'Italie and thence to Sceaux on the road to Orléans. The carriages were kept for the elderly and infirm.

Nobody argued, because by this time it seemed that half Paris wanted to get out and stay out, not only foreigners but Parisians threatened with conscription. The National Guard were entering houses to arrest anyone who failed to answer the call, and thousands of Frenchmen were going into hiding. Some escaped in baskets of dirty linen, some were smuggled out on British or American passports, some disguised themselves as peasants and pretended they were returning to their farms. The city was beginning to look like a city of the dead.

Curiously, the behaviour of the rest of Paris remained surprisingly phlegmatic. Labourers worked at their little plots of ground under the blossom trees and fishermen still sat fishing beneath the bridges of the Seine as cannon balls and shells roared and rattled nearby, and, near the Madeleine on their way to the Luxembourg, Colby and Ackroyd passed a weight-lifter entertaining the crowd.

All those who wished to go had gone by the middle of May, and Colby was thinking once more of leaving himself when a note from Washburne summoned him to the United States Legation.

'We have two more American citizens, Major,' he announced. 'And I'm afraid it's up to you. Our people are occupied getting as many priests to safety as possible. This Raoul Rigault, who's running the Committee of Public Safety, has announced his intention of shooting everyone in holy orders, so we're fully occupied. They're at Number Seventy-seven, Boulevard Pereire on the way to Neuilly. They couldn't leave before because one of them was ill and the other was doing the nursing. We were told of them by a family who left yesterday. The name's Putnam and though they've expressed their willingness to leave, they have no transport and are unable to find any.'

Obtaining a carriage was not as easy as it seemed. With the Versaillese on the point of attacking, all horses had been commandeered for guns or escape, and carriages and cabs had disappeared from the streets. It was Ackroyd who remembered the owner of a stables in the Rue de Rennes which they'd used on their previous visit. His horses were old and he was having difficulty feeding them, so that it didn't take long to persuade him to sell them a carriage, lock, stock and barrel, to be picked up the following morning.

Colby was just finishing his evening meal, half-heartedly listening to the firing from Mont Valérien, when he lifted his head, conscious that the guns seemed nearer. As he listened again he realised that it wasn't guns he heard, but drums. The sound was growing louder and, as he crossed to the window, the street filled with soldiers heading for the barricades in the west. A cart full of gunpowder rattled along after them and long teams of ragged men, women and children trailed behind, pulling a gun.

At that moment, Ackroyd pushed his head round the door. 'The Versaillese 'ave got inside, sir,' he said. 'By the Point du Jour. Somebody opened the gate for 'em. They're fighting near the Avenue des Ternes. Any moment now the Boulevard Pereire will be in the line of fire.'

As they left the apartment, people were standing on street corners and in the doorways of shops and bars, staring towards the west. Every now and then they were brushed aside by workmen wearing officers' swords and sashes, as swarms of ragged troops rushed past to take up defensive positions. The sound of firing was growing louder and, as the traffic towards the west grew to a flood, they had to push their way through it to the Rue de Rennes.

The owner of the stable had vanished but the horse and carriage were there. Colby backed the animal into the shafts and harnessed it himself, then climbing to the box, drove it into the street to be met by a cavalcade of ragged horsemen, followed by half a dozen guns rumbling over the cobbles. He seemed to be across the route of the Versaillese advance and as he neared the Boulevard Pereire, he saw a young man holding a white flag start to wave it frantically. Immediately, one of the men on horseback stopped his horse alongside him, drew out a pistol and placing it against his head, shot him dead. Further down the street, a group of Communards were driving a monk and three nuns in wide-winged starched hats towards a barricade that had been built across the street. More troops were running up, their weapons swinging, their red banners tilted forward, and one of the men fell. Bullets were clipping the top of the barricade, puncturing sandbags and striking splinters from stones and boxes and old doors as the nuns were forced to climb to the top in an attempt to stop the firing. As they watched, two of them were hit and collapsed, rolling down the other side out of sight.

There was a lot of smoke now and they could hear the thud of artillery, the rattle of musketry and the grinding roar of mitrailleuses. Men were yelling that a Versaillese battalion had broken through and they saw men running back, some without weapons, yelling they had been betrayed.

Number Seventy-seven, Boulevard Pereire, was untouched by artillery fire but not far away there was a house with a large hole on the first floor and rooms riddled with shell splinters. Inside, the flying wreckage of the windows had ruined carpets and curtains and furnishings. Number Seventy-seven was unlocked and appeared to be empty. As they entered, the firing increased and the roar of musketry sent them to the top floor windows to watch what was happening. As they looked out, shells began to fall among a column of marching Communards which immediately broke and began to head back at full speed. As it crumbled into a horde of terrified men and women, tumbling and rolling under the wheels of carriages and ammunition carts, frightened horses bolted, dragging empty vehicles or the fragments of broken shafts, then men began to throw down their weapons and bandoliers and shout the same old vicious cry of betrayal with which they had heralded every defeat since the war against the Prussians had started the previous year.

'Generals', their horses lost, came running back among the shouting workmen and the limping old men and women carrying dead sons. Here and there a body sprawled on the pavement, or a shattered carriage lay lopsided in the gutter with the equipment that had been thrown away by the fleeing troops. The trees in the Boulevard Pereire were being cut now by flying shell splinters and the ground was covered by grape, canister, shot, broken shells and flattened bullets. There was a gun in the garden of the house opposite and the men working it had knocked down the wall to allow them to pass through. Near the hole were the bodies of four National Guardsmen.

Thinking the people they were seeking might be hiding, they searched the house from attic to cellar. There was no

217

sign of them and the terrified horse in the street was snatching at the reins. Thinking it would break free and bolt, they were just on the point of leaving when Colby's eyes fell on a group of brick-built outhouses at the bottom of the garden and it occurred to him the Americans they were seeking might have hidden there. Through the dusty window, he saw a wheelbarrow and tools and plantpots on a bench. There was no sign of life but, as he turned away, he heard a cry that sounded more delighted than scared, and the door burst open.

As he swung round, his jaw dropped and his eyes widened, as memory raced back at a stretch gallop.

'Jesus Christ in the mountains!' he yelled. 'Gussie Dabney! What in God's name are you doing here?'

8

'I'm always meeting you hiding in outhouses,' Colby said. 'Why in the name of Heaven didn't you get away before it was too late?'

Ackroyd was helping a moaning Mrs Dabney into the carriage as Colby hurried Augusta down the path with a couple of Gladstone bags, the only luggage they had been able to pack.

'Father was heading a trade delegation to the new government, so we all came.' Augusta looked up at him. 'I guess the reason for his visit disappeared with the government's removal to Versailles.'

She hadn't grown any taller and she was still so slender he felt he could span her waist with his two hands. But she had filled out and now clearly had a behind under her bustle and a before in front. The peaky elfin face had rounded into smooth curves and those enormous violet eyes of hers had taken on a new beauty that was enhanced by the lavender dress she wore. Despite the din and the flying metal she seemed less frightened than excited at having found him again.

'Where's your father now?' he demanded, reaching for the reins.

'He's in Germany. We've been everywhere since we crossed the ocean in February.'

'Why in God's name didn't you go with him? It would have been a damn' sight safer.'

'Because Ma got ill and we had to stay. She was real bad, too.'

'I was told the name was Putnam.'

'That's the owner of the house.' She gave him a nervous smile as if she thought he might make it an excuse to abandon them. 'They're friends of Pa's. We rented it.'

As he reached for the whip, she scrambled from the tonneau of the carriage to the driver's seat alongside him, treating Ackroyd, who had to climb into her place, to a view of a length of leg as she did so.

'We were in London,' she went on excitedly. 'A friend of father's at the Embassy looked you up in the Army List and I even found out where your home was. But when I arrived there you were in London. And when I reached London you'd gone back home. When I went there again you'd come to France.'

'So *you* were the mysterious female who was always asking after me?'

'I swore your sister to secrecy. I think she thought it was a good idea. I felt that she approved of me.'

By God, Colby thought, gripping the reins, so do I. She was beautiful, she was brisk, she sounded intelligent and she had the most honest eyes he had ever seen. Brosy la Dell's suggestion that it was time he married came into his mind at once.

'Where are we going?' she asked.

'Only one place *to* go,' he said. 'Apartment I've rented. Not very big but safer than here. Yesterday I could have got you out of the city. It's too late now.'

She said nothing but she gave him a glance that looked remarkably like one of triumph.

A burst of firing broke out behind them and fragments of brick and stone were chipped from the walls above them.

'You must have been mad to stay in Paris,' he yelled as he lashed the wretched horse into a half-hearted gallop.

'Don't snarl at me, sir,' she snapped back. 'It wasn't my fault!'

'Why didn't you get a protection pass then?'

'The man wouldn't give me one. I think he had his eye on me.' She gave him a quick grin. 'He told me his name was Rigault and started talking about sexual promiscuity and concubinage and saying I was too pretty to leave.

When he suggested dinner, I thought I might suffer something far worse than the refusal of a pass so I left and didn't go back.'

'You damn near left it too late. There's talk of shooting the Archbishop and rounding up all foreigners as hostages. We may have to go over the ramparts.'

Finding a cross street where there was no firing, they stopped at an épicerie to buy food, wine and a bottle of brandy. The landlord told them barrels of gunpowder were being stacked in the sewers with men waiting with lighted torches to blow the city sky-high if the Versaillese got in. As they climbed back into the carriage, the rifle fire began to grow in volume and ragged men and women began to appear with mattresses which they piled on top of a barricade that was being built. Manoeuvring the old horse through them, the carriage bouncing in the potholes where the paving stones had been ripped up, they reached the end of the Boulevard St Germain. There was a small group of soldiers under a mean-looking sergeant who seemed no more than a child. Stopping them, he came to Colby's side and demanded that he hand over the carriage. Before he knew what was happening, he was staring down the barrel of Micah Love's huge LeMatt.

'Get out of the way, mon petit,' Colby murmured. 'Or I'll blow your head off.'

The boy's eyes glittered and he waved a hand. 'Pass, friend,' he croaked.

Colby passed the gun back to Ackroyd. 'If he changes his mind, Tyas,' he said. 'Shoot him dead.'

Despite being in a state of near-panic, Augusta was studying Colby with pride mixed with alarm. The biggest part of civilised life came within a woman's sphere and most occasions were dominated by them. But this one, she realised, was clearly not one of them. Colby was not a big man but at that moment he seemed strong enough and capable enough to deal with anything, and her heart almost burst with happiness. Overcome by curiosity, she was just glancing back to see what was going to happen when she felt her head pushed down between her knees, then, grasping the whip, Colby brought it down savagely on the horse's rump. Hurt and startled, it leapt straight into a gallop.

It was only a few yards to the corner and, as they turned it, they heard a shout behind them. The huge LeMatt exploded near her ear with a sound like a cannon firing, then a volley of shots splintered shutters and whanged against iron verandah railings. At the other end of the boulevard there was another barricade and Colby wrenched the horse into a side street leading to the Luxembourg. Another volley and the sound of bugles made him swing into another street, just as a flurry of men dived round the corner and bullets started to chip stone from the walls in a shower of sparks.

'We're in the middle,' Ackroyd yelled.

With a swing of his arm, Colby swept Augusta off the driver's seat into the tonneau of the carriage in a flurry of white petticoats and flailing legs, and Ackroyd pushed her to the floor where her mother already cowered. As they reached the door of the apartment block, a volley stopped the old horse dead in its tracks. For a second, it stood trembling, its head up, blowing crimson spray through its nostrils, then it collapsed with a crash to the cobbles, the taut reins dragging Colby in a nose-dive from the box on top of it. As he sat up, sprawling across the dead animal, Augusta was alongside him, clutching him in an agony of apprehension.

'For God's sake, Tyas,' he yelled, disentangling himself from the reins. 'Get 'em into the doorway!'

'I thought you were dead,' Augusta was shrieking at him over the din.

'Of course I'm not bloody dead!' he yelled back. 'It takes more than a few dirty Froggies to kill me!'

Ackroyd had got Mrs Dabney out of the carriage and leaning against the door. But it had been locked from inside and, as they struggled with it, a swarm of ragged men carrying a red banner ran past them towards the barricade. Another volley sent several of them sprawling, one of them falling right in front of them, a pool of bright blood spreading under his chest.

'Oh, my God!' Augusta said.

A gun banged in the distance and stone and splinters of wood rained round them, and leaves began to drift down from the trees. Men with rifles were crouching in the angles of the wall firing down the street and bullets chinked and whined overhead. The barricade burst into flame as a line of rifles fired, and a woman standing in a doorway opposite with her head out, watching what was going on, spun round as if she'd been snatched away by an invisible hand.

The doorway where they sheltered was shallow and Colby was standing with his arms round Augusta, who was clutching his jacket in terror, trying not to scream. Ackroyd managed to kick the door open at last, but there was no sign of the concierge. His apartment was unlocked, however, and Colby began to drag a sideboard into the hall. To his surprise, he found Augusta alongside him, her hair coming down, leaning her small body against the sideboard, red-faced and panting as she worked with him.

Jamming it against the smashed door, he added a table and chairs, then grabbing her hand, pulled her after him down a curving flight of stone stairs to a cellar where men, women and children from other apartments were sheltering. Outside a gun was banging away monotonously, close enough to bring plaster down every time it fired.

They got Mrs Dabney lying down on a mattress Ackroyd dragged down from upstairs, and Augusta bent over her, crooning encouragement, her small face taut and strained but showing no sign of fear. The firing was still going on outside as it grew dark and, under Colby's direction, they dragged an old tallboy full of apples across the cellar and jammed it across the grill that opened on to the street. One of the men went upstairs and produced blankets and, as they settled down for the night, Colby found Augusta next to him.

'Frightened?' he asked.

'Of course not,' she said, her voice shaking and uncertain. 'Why should I be, with you here?' She paused. 'I suspect you saved our lives, Mr Goff.'

'Micah Love's gun,' he said. 'It's enough to frighten an elephant.'

There was a long silence. The cellar was damp and smelled of decay and, after a while, Augusta's voice came through the darkness.

'Mr Goff,' she said quietly. 'May I come a little closer? I guess there'll be mice. I don't like mice.'

They lived off wine and apples and stale bread for three days as fighting raged up and down the street. When it seemed safe to move out of the cellar and everybody vanished to their own apartments, they helped Mrs Dabney up the stairs and Augusta put her to bed. When it was safe to go outside and they emerged, stiff and dirty and tired, the barricade down the street lay in a heap of broken paving stones, sandbags and torn mattresses, with here and there a body sprawled among the bushes in the gardens alongside. The old horse that had brought them home still lay in the shafts of the carriage, its blood dried to a brown crust, its stomach swelling as the heat lifted its legs. Charred papers kept drifting down from the buildings the Communards had set on fire and, against the redness of the sky, the Butte de Montmartre stood out like a dark hump. As the last Communard resistance was blasted into tears of blood against the wall of Père Lachaise, summary courts martial were already being held in the theatres, the Communards condemned in batches and taken outside to be shot at once in the streets round the Panthéon.

It was like coming into daylight after being through something from Dante's *Inferno*. As he stood in the street, staring up at the smoke-filled sky, Colby felt Augusta's hand slip into his and he drew a deep breath. It was summer now and the weather would be good in England. In France they were already looking round for scapegoats, and parliamentary weasels in France were even more spiteful than they were at home. He suddenly wanted to see Braxby. To hell with Wolseley. To hell with Disraeli. To hell with the Queen, come to that. He was going to take some leave – real leave – even if it meant going on half-pay.

He turned to find Augusta watching him. It was as if she knew what he was thinking and, uncomfortably, he suspected she did. Why not marry the damn girl, he thought. He wasn't so sure he wouldn't let her down because, after thirty-five years of freedom, he had a feeling he would notice the reins more than she would, but at least he felt she would never let *him* down.

Mrs Dabney was in no state to be moved so he made his way cautiously across the city to the American Legation, where Washburne informed him that the Archbishop and other hostages had been shot. 'I think it was as well the Dabneys weren't left where they were,' he said. 'I'll see that a carriage's sent round for them.'

Returning to the apartment, he found Ackroyd, with an apron round his waist, polishing the glasses, and Augusta over the stove in the kitchen preparing soup.

'It's mostly vegetables,' she admitted.

It was curiously reassuring to see her busy. She seemed quite unperturbed and the place had a cleaner look about it that indicated she hadn't wasted her time.

'It's not even our apartment,' Colby pointed out.

'It doesn't matter,' she said. 'If anyone calls, it's right that you should appear to be properly looked after.'

There was a strange possessiveness about her and at the same time a comfortable feeling that she belonged there. They were polite to each other, greeting each other like old friends as she emerged from where her mother lay in what had been Ackroyd's bed, and Colby began to find he was even enjoying it.

Gradually the noise outside died down and, as Washburne's carriage arrived, Augusta collected her belongings together. As Ackroyd helped her mother down the stairs and tucked her in with a rug, Augusta studied Colby.

'I guess it's a good job Ma was here with me,' she said nervously. 'I have a reputation for wildness and Pa would have been highly suspicious.'

Suddenly he didn't wish her to leave. 'Where are you going?' he asked.

'We have friends in Versailles.' She paused as if she were

waiting for him to protest. 'Then home, I suppose.'

She looked small and forlorn and was clearly hoping he would ask to see her again.

'I still have the locket you gave me at the Burtle House,' he blurted out.

The forlorn look vanished and her eyes shone. 'Why did you keep it?'

'Thought it might come in useful. I also have the turkey feather and the sash. They didn't protect me much. I was wearing 'em all when I stopped a piece of shell at Yellow Tavern.'

She said nothing and he went on. 'I also have the words you spoke when I left. I've never forgotten 'em.'

As her eyes widened and her cheeks reddened, he swallowed, feeling remarkably nervous and unsure of himself. She was only twenty-two and thirteen years' difference could prove too much. Yet life was empty and he could see it stretching far away into old age, until he grew crusty and fat like George Laughton. He felt she could fill the emptiness and knew suddenly that more than anything else in the world he wanted her to.

'Since you always said you were going to marry me,' he managed, 'why not let's get on with it?'

She stared at him. For a long time neither of them spoke and he thought he'd done it wrong.

'Is that a proposal, Mr Goff?' she asked quietly.

'Yes, dammit! I have to hurry because you move around like a streak of lightning and if I don't act now you'll probably disappear back to the States.'

She seemed to hesitate. 'We've not known each other long, Mr Goff.'

'We've known each other years! I doubt if we've ever been apart.' Her eyes shone, and he went on hurriedly, feeling suddenly desperate. 'Marry me. I'm just a horse-smelly cavalry type and I'm not wealthy. But I'm not too much in debt. Just to my tailor and bootmaker and the saddler. You'd have to live in a garrison town, which consists of mothers and their daughters and then the army, but you'll get to know countries you'd never heard of. I want you for my wife. I want you to say you will be.'

Her eyes were like stars and made his head swim a little. For a second longer she stared at him as if she couldn't believe her ears, then she flung herself into his arms.

'Oh, yes, Mr Goff,' she said. 'Please! It's something I always dreamed of.'

9

Braxby was very different from Virginia. Instead of towering tulip trees and wooded rolling slopes, there were dry-stone walls and grey houses hugging the shelter of the valleys in twisting curves. Instead of bluejays and blood-red cardinal birds there were rooks, harsh-tongued in the oaks that formed a wind-break for Braxby Manor. The days were darker, too, and the riding was harder, and they hunted over stone walls and banks, nine feet of which you descended before falling the rest, but there was beauty too, she discovered, and a grim sort of charm about the empty uplands that were devoid of everything except low, wind-blasted heather.

'There've been Goffs in Braxby since the Dark Ages,' Colby explained. 'One was a judge. Another was beheaded during the Wars of the Roses. Mostly they've been a mixture of farmers and soldiers, and men from Braxby have been joining the 19th for a long time. I love the place. For me soldiering's just one sortie after another from here.'

There was not the slightest doubt that Augusta was welcome. The Ackroyd family – who seemed to fill a whole row of Home Farm Cottages – were all turned out on parade by Ackroyd to meet her, all the women sturdy country types, the men a mixture of straight-backed ex-soldiers and stoop-shouldered farmers who had followed the plough.

The big house had a neglected look, because there had been no one to look after it for so long, but in spite of fireplaces that created enough draught to draw a cat up the chimney, it had possibilities. Oh, it had such possibilities, she thought delightedly.

The fact that she could ride and understood animals got her off on the right foot straight away as they all trooped round the stables, accompanied inevitably by Ackroyd grooms and Ackroyd stable boys. It intrigued her to watch them all together, startled to realise that her husband-to-be had a supreme confidence in the correctness of his behaviour that came unquestioned from his background. He wasn't acting a rôle and she realised that his family had behaved throughout all their history exactly as he was behaving now. He belonged to a privileged group and he paid for the privilege by accepting the responsibility for the people around him, treating them all with good humour and consideration, exactly the same with a dark-visaged horse dealer trying to sell him a horse and kicking its fore-legs into a more becoming position as he was with the bishop, who was some relation and had agreed to marry them. It warmed her heart. The family – Colby, his sister, her husband – all seemed so unaffected by jealousy, envy, greed or anything else, they made her own entirely normal relations seem trivial by comparison.

Intrigued at having a foreigner in an area which had fought all its life to avoid having 'foreigners' – even from other parts of England – the neighbours called in ones and twos to meet her. A plump, pale-faced woman with too-red lips who introduced herself as Georgina Cosgro claimed with a comfortable possessiveness that jolted her, to be one of Colby's old flames. Brosy la Dell's wife, Grace, as kindly, good-humoured and easy-going as Brosy, put her at ease.

'He had a crush on her as a boy,' she said. 'That's all. Don't worry about her. Concentrate on the regiment. It'll be quite as much part of your life as Braxby. Perhaps even more. It's something you have to get used to.'

It sounded terrifying, but Grace was reassuring. 'It's a restless life,' she pointed out. 'All ups and downs. But you develop a philosophical attitude to it. There's one thing, though: You'll never be without friends. You'll be sad, happy, homesick, ill or well, but it'll always be in the company of other army wives who understand. I grew up in the regiment and, though I sometimes hate it, I wouldn't exchange it for anything.'

Quite obviously, Colby considered she should become involved in the mystique that was the regiment as soon as possible, and almost the first thing he did was take her to the regimental chapel at York Minster and let her stand for a while beneath the tattered banners that hung in the vaulting silence. They were dusty and torn and hung in nets to preserve them, and she found it hard to understand why they appeared to mean so much.

From York, he took her to Ripon, where Harriet lived, and from there to the regimental depot where he showed her the instrument with which Trumpeter Sparks had sounded the regiment into action at Balaclava. It was an ordinary-looking trumpet in a glass case, with a fading coloured cord, and it was dented and bent because Sparks' horse had been shot and he had fallen on it. Though it seemed to be regarded with awe by everybody who stopped in front of it, she found it hard to see the reason for the reverence.

'I shall never belong,' she said. 'It terrifies me. All the worship of those old flags –'

'Colours,' he corrected her stiffly.

'Very well – colours. The way you put the names of your batttles on them, remembering all the blood and all the misery.' She gestured helplessly. 'Why do you set so much store by it?'

He gestured. 'A soldier can only be brought to the highest efficiency by making him believe he belongs to a regiment that's superior to all others. That's the army's strength. They don't fight for the Queen. They fight for the honour of their regiment.' He smiled. 'You're lucky. You've married into a good one. Not so good as to be snobbish, but good enough to be concerned with its people. In some regiments you have to be inspected, checked for breeding, and promise never to let the side down.'

'Do you think I might?'

'It's sometimes hard to keep up,' he admitted. 'But army

wives are a tough lot and they've had to endure capture, wounding, imprisonment, kidnapping, shipwreck and God knows what.'

She looked at him, alarmed, and the smile became a grin. 'But,' he added, 'a surprising number of them have lived to tell the tale and bore their grandchildren with it.'

Since Augusta's family were already in Europe, it seemed easier for them to stay there and the wedding was brought forward with a haste that set a few tongues wagging.

For a change, Yorkshire's rugged soul relented, and the weather was not only fine but actually warm, though there were clouds building up over the Pennines and a strong wind sending shredded whisps across the Brack to change it from blue to a leaden purple as they covered the sun.

The detachment from the 19th arrived early, waiting outside the church in a splash of rifle green, red and gold among the dark suits of the men and the gay dresses of the women. Augusta appeared from the house that had been lent to her family for the wedding, riding with her father round the village green in a smart borrowed carriage, decorated with white ribbons and lace and driven by one of the Ackroyds in his best tweeds, with a bunch of white flowers in his cap and holding a whip decorated with a paper frill that looked as if it had come off a lamb chop.

The wedding dress had been made in a hurry and was a fraction too tight, so that she knew that all through the ceremony she would have to keep drawing deep breaths to survive. Her father was in a sombre mood and when she taxed him with it, he shrugged.

'What can any father feel, Gussie,' he said, 'When he knows he's going to leave his daughter in a foreign country.'

'Colby'll look after me, Pa.'

'I hardly know him!'

'I do. That's enough.'

'Augusta Dabney, I'm still worried.'

'Pa, I'm not. I love Colby. I've loved him ever since the day I first saw him. I'm very proud that he's seen fit to ask me to be his wife.'

'He's a soldier, Gussie.'

Augusta looked at him with a mixture of pity and anger. 'Then, Pa,' she said, 'I'll be a soldier's wife.'

As they entered the church in an atmosphere of ancient stone and candlewax, the sight of so many uniforms startled her. The whole damn church seemed to be full of soldiers, she thought, all in green, red and gold, their plumed lance caps lined up together on a spare pew by the door like a lot of eggs on a table. When she saw Colby waiting alongside Brosy la Dell, she gasped. He had an ideal figure for a cavalryman, medium height, lithe and spare, with flat thighs and strong hands, and she had never seen him in uniform before, let alone in full dress. Taller in the tight-fitting jacket and narrow overalls with their double gold stripe, he seemed a blaze of colour and manliness. In his right hand he held a black lance cap ornamented with brass and surmounted by a square frame covered with cloth coloured to match the facings of his jacket.

Ackroyd had worked hard on him and the buttons, brassware, gold cord and pipeclay shone. As he turned to look at her she felt her knees go weak. He didn't smile, however, and she wondered wildly if he were as scared as she was.

There was an archway of swords as they left the church and a shower of rose petals and a fiddler to lead them across the green to the carriages. The guests all seemed to be either soldiers, local bigwigs, farmers or farm workers, their red Yorkshire faces shining with soap. Augusta's mother wept on her shoulder, unable to decide whether to be proud or miserable, and as Harriet dragged her round, introducing her, she was aware of a few searching looks and a few embarrassed smiles as harsh Yorkshire accents clashed with soft Virginian.

The storm which had been threatening all day arrived as they scrambled into the carriage that was to take them to the station. Because it was October, they had rented a house at Melton Mowbray to get in some hunting and they ate their evening meal together quietly, both of them a little nervous of their new estate. Dammit, Colby thought, I feel worse than I did when I joined the regiment, all thumbs and elbows. Opposite him, Augusta was eating quietly, her face pale in the candlelight, and he was surprised to see how confident she looked. When she said she felt tired and was going to bed, he stayed downstairs long enough to let her get organised. Women needed time to do their hair and titivate themselves, he knew.

He found it strange to think he was going to share his bed with a woman for the rest of his life. For a moment he toyed with the idea of having a drink but decided in the end not to bother, and tried instead to read the paper. Somehow none of it made sense. There was trouble on the Gold Coast, he saw, where tribal factions were quarrelling among themselves and the Europeans were yelling for somebody to come and stop them. It would be a nasty business, he decided. The Gold Coast was a sickly set of problems, he'd heard, and British control was limited to a few coastal strongholds, with a garrison that consisted mainly of coloured troops and a few unwanted naval vessels, while the Europeans spent most of their time recovering from one illness or another. He was on the point of lighting a cigar when he remembered that Augusta was still waiting, probably nervous over her initiation into the married state. He'd heard it said that some women didn't even know what they were supposed to do and some men had to wait weeks before they finally managed to consummate the marriage. Good God, he thought, why didn't mothers tell their daughters what it was all about?

He felt pleased with himself, however, self-consciously proud of his new wife and feeling that, with a little help, he ought to be able to shape her into a good soldier's wife. Dammit, she knew already what battle was all about.

The wall-paper in the dressing room was deep red, covered with purple flowers, and it seemed to suggest all sorts of dangerous intrigues. Cleaning his teeth at the wash hand stand, he stared at himself in the mirror. He had never gone in for weeping whiskers like the Cosgros. After the fashion of Wellington's soldiers, his father had always been clean-shaven and the habit had passed to his son. Not a bad figure, either, he decided. Good chest and shoulders. Strong legs. Nose a bit lopsided where he'd broken it coming off a horse as a boy, but no sign of baldness yet, thank God.

He was curiously nervous. Dammit, he thought, *fathers* ought to tell their *sons* what it's all about, too! Slipping into his nightshirt, he brushed his hair and opened the door. All the candles were still lit and he was surprised because he'd heard that new brides always liked to meet their husbands for the first time in bed in the pitch darkness.

Augusta's nose was poking over the top of the sheets and her hair was a black cloud on the pillow. Dammit, he thought, she was more beautiful than he'd realised. She smiled at him then her eyes widened, and she sat up abruptly. To his surprise, she was unclothed. No damn nightdress or anything!

'Mr Goff, why are you wearing a nightshirt?'

He gaped at her. 'For God's sake, why not?'

'This is our wedding night. I'm not a shrinking violet, Mr Goff, and I think two young people going to bed together should be fun.'

As he stared, she went on earnestly, her eyes bright like an angry kitten's. 'There's a lot of talk about morality these days,' she said. 'But from what I can gather, it isn't all that different from any other time; people just talk about it more, that's all. Your Queen has nine children –'

'Eight,' he corrected. 'And she's *your* queen, too, now. How many are *you* contemplating?'

'Seven.'

He'd been thinking of one – eventually – a son to carry on the family name as his father would have wished.

'Seven?'

'Yes. And they'll never arrive if we go to bed together with twenty yards of flannel between us.'

He looked down at her. Sitting up in bed, she didn't seem much more than a child saying her catechism, small-framed and large-eyed in the candlelight, and she seemed as unaware of embarrassment as a child taking a bath. By

God, he thought, she was right! There *was* too much bloody humbug about this business of going to bed together! It was all right, apparently, for a man and woman to prance about naked if they weren't married, but if it was respectable and all above board, the whole thing had to become shifty and hidden from the day.

'By God, Mrs Goff,' he said enthusiastically, wrenching at buttons, 'I think you're right.'

Part Three

1

The clouds which had been building up all morning had filled and rounded and, by the afternoon, were heavy with rain and moving across the sky like the grey galleons of some celestial armada. Cantering towards the Common, Colby glanced upwards, hoping the storm would hold off just a little longer. Aubrey Cosgro's troop was at exercise and he could see no sense in them getting wet through and having the unnecessary work of grooming and cleaning after galloping in the mud. He had half-expected to meet them on their way back to barracks, in fact, and as the rain finally came, his temper overflowed.

This was not the day for bad temper either. Balaclava Day was celebrated in the regiment by free beer for the men, free spirits for the sergeants, and a slap-up dinner in the officers' mess. The occasion was always tinged with a measure of excitement that even the newest-joined recruit could feel. Work was done normally, but there was always a tendency to go easy on everybody, and the fact that Cosgro had taken his troop to the common in a threatening storm was enough, on this day of all days, to spoil Colby's happiness.

It was a good job, in fact, he thought, that the army reforms everybody had been expecting for so long had finally gone through, so that stupid young nincompoops like Aubrey Cosgro couldn't pick themselves in wherever they wanted, simply because they had enough money and knew the right people. What had happened to the French in 1870 had scared Whitehall and, though they'd been preaching reform ever since the Crimea, nothing had been done about it until now, and snot-nosed fartlets like Aubrey Cosgro had still been able to bring influence to bear. He suspected Cosgro even enjoyed working the men in unpleasant conditions because it gave him a sense of power.

The houses were left behind as he approached the area of gorse and bracken and as he passed the first clump of scrub, Cornet Lord Ellesmere appeared with a sergeant and a trumpeter from a dip. He was a likeable young man with acne who was so shy he could barely give an order.

'What the devil's going on'' Colby snapped. 'Where's Lieutenant Cosgro?'

Ellesmere turned in the saddle, a blush reddening his cheeks. 'He has the men at mounted sword practice, sir.'

'In weather like this? Where is he?'

Ellesmere pointed. 'Beyond the trees, sir.'

As he gestured at the jumps and dips over which the regiment exercised its horses, Colby heaved at the reins and, kicking at the flanks of his mount, galloped across the turf, ironshod hooves flinging up the clods behind him. By this time the rain was coming down heavily enough for puddles to settle in the folds of the ground.

Cosgro's troop was drawn up in a double line, and long before he reached them Colby could see they were in a resentful mood. They were in the dark green regimentals edged with red, the plastrons reversed as if on campaign so that the cherry-coloured breasts had become mere edged piping. Cosgro had them done up to the nines, with lance caps and everything, the elaborate lines drooping to their chests in complicated founders and tassels, the dyed plumes hanging wetly over their ears. God damn it, Colby thought savagely, this was no day to wear their best uniforms! Two days away buying horses and the bloody idiot was behaving like a colonel, and a bad one at that.

The water dripping off their chins, their jackets black with damp, the horsemen had thrust their lances into the ground, points together, the pennants sodden and heavy. They were at a dip where a bank-jump had been constructed and just beyond were dummies on poles and wooden

Turks' Heads for cutting and thrusting practice. The horses were muddied to the girths and the riders's eyes were bitter at the thought of the hours of cleaning and grooming that lay ahead. Three men stood to one side, holding their horses' bridles, all three showing signs of having been unseated. One of them had blood on his face as if he'd had a nose bleed and another was bent over his horse's hocks, rubbing gently, calming the trembling animal.

Aubrey Cosgro, in a forage cap and well caped against the rain, sat his horse with the sergeant-major. 'Go on, Sergeant-major,' Colby heard him shout. 'What are you waiting for? Next man.'

The troop sergeant-major was obviously trying to protest but was clearly ineffective and Colby saw Cosgro gesture angrily with his crop. 'War doesn't stop for rain,' he yelled. 'Get on with it!'

The troopers began to head for the jumps one by one. The slippery going and the rain in their faces made it difficult to keep their correct distances and several of them missed their thrusts. Colby's face was like thunder. Even at that distance he could see the horses were having a bad time of it and he knew the jump well enough to be aware that unless they changed feet at the top of the high bank, they were badly placed for the descent. Only the more sure-footed animals were making anything of it. As he drew nearer, a young trooper, who seemed no more than eighteen and – with the depression that was bringing men into the forces to avoid unemployment – could well have been younger, kicked at his horse's flanks. The animal was clearly tired and Colby wondered how long Cosgro had had them at it. Its head was down and, rather than leaping up the bank, it scrambled up. Foam at the bit, its eyes frenzied, it pulled up in a flurry of mud and scattered turf and tried to change feet. But it lost one leg down the far bank and as its rider tried to heave it up, it went down on its side, turning a complete somersault to land with a sodden slithering thump on the turf beyond.

The sergeant-major spurred forward to snatch at the

241

reins as it scrambled to its feet, and held it, trembling, as its rider dragged himself to his feet. He was limping and had cut his lip, but he jammed his lance cap back on his head with a sullen glare at Cosgro.

'Again,' Cosgro yelled at him. 'And this time, make sure it's done properly!'

He was so occupied with his anger he didn't hear Colby arrive, and it was Colby's furious shout that brought him up sharp.

'What in God's name's going on here?' he yelled and, as he dragged at the reins, he was aware immediately of the different looks on the faces of the watching men. The sullenness vanished at once and a delighted expectancy took its place.

'Mr Cosgro! A word, please!'

Frowning heavily, Cosgro yanked savagely at his horse's head and trotted up to Colby.

'You're improperly dressed!' Colby snapped. 'When the men are wearing lance caps, *you* wear a lance cap. The men have also not been allowed to cloak. Why not? Take yours off, too, sir!'

Glaring, Cosgro dismounted, unfastened his cloak, rolled it and secured it to the saddle, then mounted again, frowning at the rain that started to soak his tunic.

'And now what the devil are you doing?' Colby's whip jabbed out. 'That man, there: What's happened to his horse?'

'Nothing, sir.'

'Get down, sir, and have a look.'

Sullenly, Cosgro dismounted and went to the trembling animal whose hide was black with rain and smeared with the mud of the fall. He felt along its leg and rose with blood on his hand. 'It's gashed its fetlock, sir,' he announced.

'Then why the devil are you insisting it go round again?' Colby turned to the sergeant-major. 'Send these four men back to barracks, sergeant-major. They aren't in a proper condition to be on parade. Get 'em away.'

'Yes, sir.' A look of satisfaction on his face, the sergeant-major turned away and a moment later the four horses were moving slowly back to barracks.

'You'll have to answer to the colonel, sir.' Colby turned back to Cosgro. 'He doesn't like horses returning injured from parade. Have you been round the course?'

'No, Sir.'

Colby's mouth twisted in a tight smile. 'Then, I think you'd better, don't you? We mustn't ever ask the men to do something we aren't prepared to do ourselves. You'd better get on with it.'

Cosgro glared. 'In these conditions, sir?'

'If the men can do it, so can you! Off you go. And don't dawdle.'

Cosgro mounted, drew his sabre from the scabbard with a look that suggested he'd be only too pleased to use it on Colby, and yanked at his horse's head. His mount was quick and clever but Cosgro wasn't a good or a bold rider. He missed his thrust at the Turk's Head and almost unseated himself, then, on top of the bank, his horse, seeing the danger, tried to turn and jump back the way it had come. Cosgro rolled in the saddle, his leg came up, the stirrups flew loose, and down he went into the mud. He climbed to his feet, tears of fury in his eyes and spitting the rain from his lips. As he shoved his cap straight, Colby was pleased to see there was mud on his overalls.

'Go on, Mr Cosgro,' he said gently. 'You haven't finished the course.'

The rain was coming down more heavily than ever as Cosgro remounted, and he made heavy weather of the ride, taking the hurdles slowly and carefully. He was taking far longer than any of his men and when he finally halted in front of Colby he was spattered with mud, soaked with rain, and crimson with humiliation and fury.

Colby stared coldly at him. 'I said a moment ago, Mr Cosgro, that no officer should ask anyone to do something he isn't prepared to do himself. Corporal, give me your sword.'

Holding the weapon easily, he made for the nearest jump, hoping to God that the gelding he rode wouldn't fall and make him look a fool. But the horse completed the round quickly, slithered over the bank without accident and galloped back to the line of watching troopers.

'Sergeant-major,' he said. 'Take the men back to barracks. Mr Cosgro –' his voice rose as Cosgro turned to follow '– a word with you!'

As the troop moved off, the atmosphere had changed perceptibly and Colby heard one of the corporals mutter. 'One up to Balaclava Bill!'

'Mr Cosgro,' Colby said quietly, turning to the furious-faced lieutenant. 'In future, whenever you bring the men out on exercise, you will do the round yourself. First. To prove it's safe. If *you* don't like it, you'll perhaps remember that the men won't like it either. Thanks to you, they have hours of work ahead of them. That won't make you popular but, while *that* doesn't worry me one jot, it also doesn't make the army popular and, in case you haven't noticed it, there's a move on foot to encourage a better class of men to enlist, something they'll never do if they hear of fools like you! One thing more: I can hardly order you to groom your own mount or clean your own uniform like a trooper, and your servant will have to do it for you. But you will give him a thundering good tip. If I find you haven't, I shall want to know why. Now, join your troop.'

He sat his horse, watching as Cosgro cantered off after the disappearing men, his mind seething with rage. Damn Cosgro, he thought angrily. Damn the whole bloody tribe of Cosgros!'

The rain had stopped as they reached the first of the houses, and despite their sodden uniforms, the troop brought a stir of colour to the mean streets. Van drivers halted to let them pass and one or two of the horses appeared to have recovered enough to be skittish. Colby knew very well that they hadn't and that their riders were deliberately making them shy to draw the eyes of passing girls and frighten the older men and women who took such a delight in writing to the paper when the streets round the soldiers' alehouses exploded into fights. It was an old trick and one they'd not have tried if Colby had been up with them, but at least it showed their spirits had returned.

As they topped the rise towards the barracks, he could see the town in front of him. Set in a valley below the Pennines, it was expanding rapidly, its steelworks lighting the sky with their devilish colours every night as the furnaces blazed, the little streets of flat-fronted houses scarring the land round the chimneys with their narrow-gutted ugliness. It wasn't a place to be recommended for its beauty, and hardly seemed a propitious place to station a regiment of light cavalry. But the barracks were new, spacious and airy, and the men liked it, which was something. Even for the officers the town wasn't the backwater it seemed because there was a great deal of money in industrial England these days, and the new magnates with their watch chains and fancy waistcoats were eager to show off and generous with their entertainments.

An engine, pulling waggons loaded with supplies into the sidings nearby, hooted suddenly, and a big chestnut known to everybody as 'The Bolter' took fright. As its hooves beat a tattoo on the cobbles, a patient nag in a milk float heard the call to arms and, as the charger went past at full tilt, lifted its head and joined in, cart and all. Nobody was hurt, and the owner of the milk float tipped his hat to Colby, having enjoyed it like everybody else. It produced a few grins, too, which made a change from the earlier sullenness.

Turning in at the stables, Colby's nose was full of the ammonia smell of horses, and his ears were full of the jingling of rowels, the clanking of scabbards, the champing of bits and the anticipatory rattling of collar chains as expectant horses threw up their heads, waiting for the trumpeter to sound 'Feed.' He was aware now of bright eyes and cheerful faces.

The young trooper who had fallen at the bank had a dark mark down the side of his face and, as Colby approached, he stiffened and stared at him with a rapidly closing eye.

'How's that peeper?'

'S'all right, sir. Nothing much.' The boy managed a

twisted smile. 'No worse than you get in a Saturday night maul at The Gun, sir.'

Colby gazed at him intently. 'Your face's familiar. What's your name?'

'Sparks, sir. 504, Sparks, Joshua.'

'My trumpeter at Balaclava was called Sparks. His trumpet hangs on the wall at the depot. Any relation?'

'My uncle, sir.'

'Was he, by God? I'm glad you're in my squadron, Sparks. He was a good soldier. Let's hope you'll be equally good. How long have you been here?'

'Two months, sir, since I finished my training.'

'Well, you'll not find much time for extra-mural activities, because parades, drills, stables and the care of saddles and harness will take a a lot of your time. Know what your embouchure is?'

Sparks grinned. 'Yes, sir. Me mouth.'

'How's yours?'

'S'all right, sir. I've got all me teeth.'

'Good. Would you like to be a trumpeter, like your uncle?'

The boy's eyes glowed. 'That I would, sir.'

Colby nodded gravely. 'The trumpet had its origin in heaven,' he said. 'Everybody's aware of a good trumpeter. A poor trumpeter cuts the air like slashes from a sword. A good one sounding the Last Post fills the air with pride, loneliness and nostalgia. I'll have a word with the Trumpet-major.'

As he turned away, he saw that several of the men had stopped to listen and he rounded on them sharply. 'Well,' he snapped. 'What's of interest to you? When you can keep your saddles up to the standard of the 19th, that'll be the time to stop. You especially, Threader –' the soldier he addressed stiffened '– I want that horse cleaner than your own horse-smelly hide. You work as if you had strangles and your riding's nothing to write home about. If you confined it to horses and not girls you'd be a better horseman.'

Threader grinned sheepishly and someone yelled from the other end of the stable.

'That's put 'im back a few horses' lengths, sir.'

The scowls had gone and the men were hissing and cooing over the curry-combing as Colby walked down the line of stalls, stopping here and there to run his hand down a hairy fetlock.

'Legs should have been done by now,' he pointed out briskly. 'Get the order of grooming from the sergeant and see you follow it.'

'Tail wants pulling.' He stopped this time by a vast horse with hips like book-ends. 'And if this brute can't get any fatter we'll have the vet see him or have him put down.'

At a third, he stroked and patted. 'She's turning out well, Sergeant. Might get a foal out of her. We'll see about sending her to the farm.'

Occupied with the business of the regiment, the breeding of sound horses, the cost of saddlery, the fit of a lance bucket, the quality of picketing rope, Colby reflected that he would much have preferred to be on his way home. But this night of all nights belonged to tradition. Tradition was a fine thing and he believed in it.

As he bathed, he found himself thinking about Augusta. She had adapted quickly not only to a new country but to a new kind of life. This was hardly the place to live after Virginia, but she never complained, seemed to be happy, and had taken to hunting like a duck to water. Her first ride had been on an enormous horse that had run away with her but she had not lost her head and had sensibly steered it into a haystack which had brought it to a sudden sullen stop.

The mess had been made splendid for the occasion. Over the fireplace the portrait of Joshua Goff, his great-grandfather and founder of the regiment, had been draped in the regimental colours, as were the portraits of former colonels which hung round the room. At the opposite end were three other portraits, of the men who had led them at Salamanca, Waterloo and Balaclava. The officers were already gathering, splendid in dress tunics, ornamental daggers, highly polished mess boots and gilded swan-necked spurs.

Brosy la Dell was waiting for him, holding two schooners of sherry. 'Time for a quick one at a good cavalry drinking pace,' he said, pushing the glass forward. 'I've got a thirst like an ostler.'

'Nervous feel about the mess tonight,' he went on. 'All these reforms Parliament's pushing through. Hear we have a special guest. Grace told me. She'd heard from her father.' He glanced across the ante-room to where Claude Cosgro and his younger brother were glowering in Colby's direction. 'Heard you had another set-to with the pup,' he said.

'I'll always have set-tos with the likes of Aubrey Cosgro,' Colby said. 'Claude's nothing to write home about, but Aubrey's beyond the pale.'

As Brosy drifted off to speak to the adjutant, Claude Cosgro appeared. He was growing fat and there was a petulant look on his face.

'You've been picking on Aubrey again, I hear,' he said. 'Can't you leave him alone?'

'I'll leave him alone when he starts to behave like an officer.'

'Dammit –' Cosgro's brows came down '– he's only a boy.'

'All the more reason why he shouldn't try to behave like a man. If you're so concerned, Claude, why not give him the benefit of *your* experience.' Colby almost added 'such as it is,' but he bit his tongue in time. There was no point in exacerbating the quarrel.

As the trumpeters, marched in by the trumpet-major, entered the mess and lined the wall by the door like living statues, the conversation fell silent. On the signal, they came to life and lifted their instruments, lapping and licking their lips.

'Sound!'

The call shrilled across the room, echoing from the walls and the chandeliers, and as they filed out for a drink in the kitchen, the officers put down their glasses and headed for the dining room. The corridor was lined with the regimental drummers who were sounding a long roll as they walked past. At the head of the table, more drums had been piled. The table carried no cloth and polish had made it jet black. It was big enough to seat every officer and all the guests and was piled with silver. Among it was the loving cup made from the silver pot de chambre taken from Marmont's baggage after Salamanca and the goblet found in Napoleon's coach after the rout at Waterloo. They stood together on the green, red and gold strip that ran down the centre of the table.

About the walls were other trophies – swords, lances, strange brass helmets and plumes, together with ancient accoutrements and colours taken from enemies way back into the distant darkness. Behind the colonel's seat was the guidon with every one of the battle honours embroidered in stitches of gold. Alongside it were two troopers, the best in the regiment, picked for their smartness and rewarded later with drinks in the kitchen.

As they waited by their chairs, Colonel Canning, Brosy's father-in-law, appeared in the doorway. He was looking old, Colby thought, and would be due for retirement in a few years. Glancing across at Claude Cosgro, he suspected he was still hoping, as senior major, to take his place. Perhaps the powers in Whitehall would think differently, however, and since Cardwell was trying to abolish purchase, Claude could no longer use his wealth to make sure.

Behind the colonel, as he moved to his place at the head of the table, was the guest of honour, wearing the uniform of the Inniskillings. Nothing special about him, Colby thought. Noted chiefly for a cantankerous concern with saddlery. Then another figure appeared, small, limping and noteable for the absence of chin.

'By God,' Brosy breathed. 'It's Wolseley!'

There was a murmur of interest as they took their seats. Cardwell's reforms hadn't left Wolseley very popular and the murmur that ran round the table sounded indignant.

'See he's made major-general,' Brosy whispered. 'Only forty-two, too! Cardwell, I suppose. Not popular in London, I hear. Reads too much.'

Colby grunted. 'Some people don't read enough,' he murmured. 'I'd be surprised, in fact, if the Cosgros can read at all.'

'Wonder what he's doin' here,' Brosy went on. 'Ain t a four-legged job, is he? Light Infantry, I heard.'

At a nod from the colonel, chairs were scraped back and they all sat together in one movement. It was all, Colby thought, really quite pointless, though perhaps its very pointlessness made it worthwhile. Cavalrymen were a definite species, and though the rest of the army tried hard to tell them they were merely ordinary soldiers like the rest of them, they knew they weren't.

As the claret and the champagne flowed, he found himself listening half-heartedly to Brosy. He was watching Wolseley who was talking animatedly with the guest of honour, obviously putting some point he felt strongly about and, judging by the expression on the other man's face, not pulling any punches.

'Not sure I like the man,' Brosy was saying. 'But I suppose things *have* to be changed. The army's in no state for a European war if one comes along. They say we're behind the Germans.'

'We are,' Colby said. 'In their army, they conscript for two or three years, then send the men back to civilian life – where they help increase the national wealth instead of being a drain on it. We enlist for twenty years, by the end of which they're too old for active service, have nothing to offer as civilians, and leave no reservoirs of reserves.'

Brosy popped a potato into his mouth. 'Different now,' he observed. 'Cardwell –' he gestured with his fork '– and that feller at the end of the table – they've brought in a shorter service with the colours. Much better than it was. Like this business of grouping regiments in pairs, so that while one's serving abroad the other can be bringing up its numbers.'

'Won't work,' Colby said.

'Why not?'

'The British Empire covers too much of the globe. There'll always be more battalions serving abroad than at home and those ordered overseas'll exist in name only and overseas drafts'll continue to be filled with last-minute enlistments who'll be useless in action.'

Brosy chewed slowly and turned to look at Colby as if he were some strange sort of sage. 'Where *do* you get these ideas, Coll?' he asked.

As the meal ended, the colonel rose and lifted his glass. 'Gentlemen! The Queen!'

Everyone leapt to their feet and stood in frozen silence. Movement stiffened to the rigidity of a plaster frieze.

As they sat again, the glasses were refilled and the colonel tapped with his gavel and pushed his chair back again.

'Gettin' stiff,' Brosy whispered. 'Grace says he ought to retire.'

'Gentlemen! The Regiment!'

As they sat again, Cornet Lord Ellesmere rose to his hinds, blushing so scarlet his acne disappeared. He was shaking with nervousness and Colby could see his hand trembling as it clutched the edge of the table.

'My Lord,' he stammered. 'Colonel Canning. 'It is my duty to give you the plague toast. It has always fallen to the youngest cornet since 1763 when one Jeremiah Harkness was the only man left on his feet after the plague had decimated the regiment in India. Gentlemen – may we rise as many as we have sat down.'

They drank it solemnly and it was then the turn of the guest of honour to propose the Balaclava toast and the health of the survivors. At this point the rough-rider sergeant and the quartermaster-sergeant were brought in, the only other ranks survivors still with the regiment.

Seated with Brosy, Colby glanced at Claude Cosgro and saw his frown as he raised his glass. He always liked to pretend he, too, had ridden in Cardigan's charge and Colby had actually heard him perpetuating the legend in bars. He'd even had the nerve, in fact, to turn up at the first dinner held in London after the Crimea, but more men had appeared then than had actually set off down the valley and after that there had been a stricter watch on the names and he'd never managed it again.

As senior survivor, Colby rose and waited until the two sergeants had been handed glasses.

'From the survivors, Colonel, sir, to the Regiment – with whose name I couple one more – Major Cosgro who, but for the ill-luck of being on other duties, would have led the representatives of the regiment instead of me.'

It was a blatant lie but he hoped it would help to heal the growing breach between them. Cosgro looked pleased and even managed a smile, but Colby noticed that his younger brother scowled and didn't even bother to drink.

The formalities over, they moved to the ante-room. The colonel drew Colby on one side. Over his shoulder Colby could see Claude Cosgro sinking a large brandy and demanding another, and his brother in a fierce argument with Ellesmere.

'I believe you know General Wolseley, Coll,' Canning said.

From the way Wolseley, who was standing with his back to them, turned as his name was mentioned, it was obvious the meeting had been pre-arranged. Wolseley stood eyeing him for a moment. He didn't beat about the bush with pleasantries.

'Heard of King Coffee, Colby?' he said.

'Yes, sir. Gold Coast, I believe.'

'Actually, his name's Kofi Karikari.' Wolseley talked with the self-satisfaction of a professor addressing a pupil. 'You'll have read how he sent his Ashantis into the Protectorate to harry the Fantis, attack Elmina and worry the missionaries and the Europeans?'

'It was in *The Times*, sir.'

Wolseley nodded. 'The government's decided it's time he was knocked on the head. They've given me the job.'

Now we're coming to it, Colby thought. He watched Wolseley carefully. He had an enormous capacity for work, he'd heard, and there was a peculiar buoyancy of mind that gave his undistinguished frame a strange vivacity. He was speaking now to Colby in a way that was surprisingly gracious.

'A tricky job, sir,' Colby ventured. 'His capital's over a

hundred miles inland behind the Prah River and the climate's only bearable from December to February.'

'How do you know?' The words were barked at him.

'Looked it up, sir.'

'Why?'

'Matter of interest, sir.'

'Hm!' Wolseley was studying him keenly. 'I think I can do it,' he said. 'I've been given civil as well as military authority. It's a combination that appeals to me and I've decided on a new kind of campaign. I shall land at Gold Coast Castle at the beginning of October with a group of hand-picked officers and no troops. I shall raise units from the coastal natives, build a road inland to the Prah, then call in the three battalions of Regulars I've been given. They'll arrive in mid-December, and by the end of the month I shall be ready. I shall dash inland, holding my troops in camps which have already been prepared and fending off any Ashanti resistance along the road.'

'I see, sir.'

'I don't persuade myself it'll be easy because the road will be little more than a tunnel through the rain forest. At the end of January I shall blast the spirit out of King Koffee's Army – probably at Amoaful – burn his capital and by the beginning of March be on my way back to England.'

'It sounds a good way to do it, sir. Soundly conceived.'

'And,' Wolseley said, 'it recommends itself to the Government, because it'll be quick and cheap and won't tie up Regular troops for long. It depends entirely on the specialists I've picked. Many of them are colleagues from the Red River. I want you to join me.'

Colby said nothing. Now he had it. On the mat.

'I've got Evelyn Wood to drive the road inland,' Wolseley continued. 'And Redvers Buller for Intelligence. There'll be little cavalry, but it will need to be handled by someone with imagination.' He studied Colby's face. 'I don't want elderly major-generals. I want *young* men. With the local rank of colonel. It's something you can't afford to turn down, I think, because it'll be a successful campaign and there'll be a great deal of kudos attached to it.'

He was quite right, of course. There was something about Wolseley Colby didn't like. He suspected he was arrogant, self-satisfied and an intriguer, but there was no doubt he was skilful, highly intelligent and lucky.

'I quite agree, sir,' he said, smiling. 'I *can't* afford to turn it down.'

When he reached home, he wasn't quite sure how to lay the news before Augusta. Having her husband snatched from her so soon after marriage wasn't something he imagined she'd welcome. She'd settled down well to being a soldier's wife and, even if she had no love for this chilly northern town and the rented house they occupied, she showed no signs of discontent.

She was in bed when he arrived, but as soon as he appeared, she turned up the lamp and sat up, wide awake.

She delighted him, whether she was running the house, organising some charity or up to the front with the local hunt as the hounds poured over a hedge with the field strung out across half a mile of grazing behind. Though he didn't know it, she tried to model herself on him, determined to be as capable, as beautiful and as brave as he wished her to be. He decided for the umpteenth time that he was the luckiest man alive.

She was beaming at him. 'You look so splendid in full dress, Mr Goff,' she said. 'I'm always so proud to see you.'

'So'm I, Ma'm, to see you.'

'Especially in bed, I think.'

He grinned, unembarrassed. She made no bones about her enjoyment of making love.

'I hope you didn't drink too much,' she said as he kissed her.

'No.' He felt as sober as a judge, and twice as sober because of the news he brought. He suspected it was shattering and couldn't think of anything that could possibly be of greater moment to a young wife.

'Dull dinner on the whole,' he said. 'Wolseley was there.'

'Wolseley?'

'Little feller with one eye and a face like a piece of stale bread. Met him first during your war. He had something to tell me.'

She studied him. 'I have something to tell you, too,' she said.

He hardly heard her, busy wondering how best to break the news. On their wedding night she had told him that, since she was a soldier's wife, wherever he had to go he had to go without looking back. It had cost her a lot, he knew, but he also knew she wouldn't break her promise. 'He wants me to go to Africa,' he blurted out.

She stared at him and he saw her face fall. 'To Africa? What on earth for?'

He explained. 'It's this feller, Koffee,' he said. 'He's got to be put in his place. They've given the job to Wolseley and he wants me to handle the horses.'

She was silent for a moment and he saw moisture in her eyes. 'It's only for a short while,' he pointed out quickly. 'He hopes to be away within the month and back by the end of April.'

She stared at him and suddenly the tears flowed.

'It's something I can't afford to ignore,' he argued. 'And you promised never to stand in my way.'

'I won't,' she sobbed.

'Well, then! A matter of months, that's all. It's the best news I've heard for a long time, the best I shall hear this year, I expect.'

Her sobs grew stronger and he put his arms round her, wondering what in God's name was wrong.

'Yes,' she said bitterly. 'It's the best news you'll hear all right! It's the only news you want to hear! *My* news is nothing in comparison!'

'Well, it can't be, can it? This could –' he stopped dead. 'Your news? What news do you have? Are your parents coming to visit you?'

She looked at him, her small face tense, a lock of hair falling over her nose so that his heart swelled with love for her. Fear and loneliness seized her and she pushed his hand away in a fury of anger then immediately relented and snatched it back, and instead began to beat his chest with her small fists.

'No, you idiot,' she wailed, spraying tears in all directions. 'I'm going to have a baby!'

2

Robert Waldo Yorke Goff was born just as his father was being carried half-conscious, in a high fever and apparently dying, from a camp just south of Kumasi to the West African coast.

He had been hit by a bullet fashioned from a bent nail and fired at point-blank range into his back as he rode on a track through the jungle that was hung every few yards with decapitated bodies. When the surgeon's probe had reached the region of his heart without finding the bullet, it had been decided it was time to stop. Given up for lost, he was pushed into a cart for the coast where another surgeon decided that a bullet fashioned from a bent nail might well not have gone where it could be expected to go and, by a little exploring managed to find it. Within a matter of days, Colby was on his feet, feeling not a great deal worse in health than he had felt throughout the whole humid, enervating campaign, and, about the time his new son – of whom he was as yet unaware – was first showing the facial muscle spasms that his delighted mother was convinced were smiles, he had decided he disliked the hospital – which was full of men dying from fever or the jagged wounds caused by crude native weapons – and had staggered from his bed. On a borrowed horse which itself was in a state of collapse, he rode through a night of torrential West African rain which turned the road into a muddy track, to rejoin his unit, and was present at the burning of King Koffee's kraal at Umkasi.

Wolseley had been right. His detailed planning had brought success and, by the end of March Colby was on his way back to the coast, with the 'Ashanti Ring' – the narrow group of officers round Wolseley – already born, and the phrase 'All Sir Garnet' newly part of the English language.

Wolseley had surrounded himself by a remarkable group of young men – Pomeroy-Colley, Evelyn Wood, Redvers Buller, Baker Russell, George Morrow, Maurice, Butler, Brackenbury – and it had seemed at first a privilege to be one of them, because they were the possessors of ideas and proven courage. On second glance, however, Buller seemed sound only as far as his voice would carry; Colley was inclined to underestimate his enemies; Butler was too willing to champion an enemy's point of view; and Morrow was a narrow staff theorist and a toady of very dubious ability. As the campaign advanced, it began to seem less and less of an honour and, from the way Wolseley was using them, Colby could see them, as they increased in rank and stature, splitting the army down the middle. No army could function with clever theorists alone and he suspected a few had even attached themselves to their brilliant chief for what they could get out of him and were not as sound as Wolseley thought.

Perhaps it was the bullet in the back that brought it forcibly home, because it was thanks to bad dispositions and over-confidence on the part of George Morrow that he had been where he was, and the dislike he had already begun to feel for Morrow was actively increased when he dodged the responsibility and laid the blame on Colby.

Left behind to tidy up the affair, when he arrived home, his son was three months old and Augusta had long since got over her disappointment at his disappearance. Because of her size it had not been an easy birth but her mother had appeared from Virginia and, with the aid of Harriet, by the time Colby arrived home, yellow with fever, she was completely recovered.

By this time the regiment had moved to Brighton, and Augusta had proved her intelligence and drive by acquiring a home near the sea which, she claimed, was ideal for the health of her new son and her weakened husband. With the aid of Grace la Dell, she had packed all their belongings into trunks and boxes, negotiated the rental and managed the move with all the aplomb of the manager who ran the Goff estates.

She still sometimes wondered where she belonged, however, because even now she wasn't always sure that she belonged to the 19th. She had made a point, however, of visiting the wives of all the men in Colby's squadron, something that wasn't always easy because they sometimes seemed to consider it condescension and many of them lived in grisly lodgings about the town. But there were always children to make a common denominator, though she was terrified of the rough-rider sergeant's wife, an enormous woman who was said to have belaboured fleeing Turkish soldiers at Balaclava and had fired a rifle against the Mutineers in India when the 19th's camp had been attacked on the way to Lucknow. As it happened, it was this very thing which enabled her to break the ice, because Augusta's grandmother had done the same thing against the Indians in New Mexico.

She had also made a point of meeting the wives of the officers, though this wasn't so easy as they were more scattered. Brosy's Grace was always there, however, as well as Claude Cosgro's Georgina, ever anxious, it seemed, to cast doubts on Colby's fidelity, and his younger brother's new wife, the same age as Augusta, and the daughter of a viscount.

She already knew more about the army than she realised: why the Scots Greys were called the Birdcatchers, why the 17th wore skull and crossed bones, why the Gloucester Regiment wore a cap badge both back and front, and the Royal Welsh a black flash under their collar and down their back. She learned to recognise the men of Colby's squadron and not fall over when the recruiting sergeant, bedizened with a sash of office and hung with red, white and blue streamers like a prize-winning horse at a May Day parade, threw her a quivering salute; and fled whenever she could to Grace la Dell who managed to make her laugh and reassure her.

Her anger at Colby's departure was quite overcome by

her joy at his return. 'Women are such frauds,' she admitted. 'They make such a show of being capable and strong, but it only requires a man to put his arms round them to make them go all soft and dependent. How long might I expect you to remain at home this time?' she asked.

Colby shrugged. 'The 19th are due for overseas,' he admitted. 'And Wolseley's promised we shall go.'

'Who's Wolseley to say?'

'The biggest man in the army at the moment. I suspect his success will go to his head, because he's as obsequious to the aristocracy as he's rude to civilians.' Colby smiled. 'There's a great deal of fighting goes on in the army, Gussie, and it's not all against the Queen's enemies. I'm to go to staff college.'

She looked startled. 'When we've just settled down here?'

He shrugged. 'Camberley's quite civilised and you get nowhere without it. The army's growing up and a career officer needs more these days than courage and the ability to conform to the contemporary concept of a gentleman.'

'Which you have,' Augusta said proudly. 'You command from personality. You're stern without harshness. Your demands are high but never more than you're willing to give yourself. You also have enthusiasm and a rigidity of principle, and I would say you're one of that small band of leaders for whom men would cheerfully go anywhere.'

He gazed at her with a mixture of pride and affection. He hadn't really known what love was when he'd married. But if love were believing in someone, if it were missing them when they weren't there, if it were what had frightened him when he'd thought in West Africa that he was going to die without seeing her again, then, by God, he loved her.

'I'm not very bright,' he said.

She was unperturbed. 'By application and hard work, you should pass through Staff College without difficulty. All I ask is that it shouldn't ruin our family life. You'll remember I planned seven children.'

He looked at her anxiously. 'Wouldn't two or three do?'

'Seven,' she said firmly. 'Then I shall be sure you'll never leave me.'

He grinned. 'Providing for seven,' he said, 'I'd never have time to.'

Staff College proved easier than Colby had expected and he could only assume that some of the men who'd been set in command of him in the past were not as bright as he'd imagined. He passed out in the top half of the list and decided to celebrate by taking his wife on a visit to the States.

They were met in Washington by Augusta's relations, among them Micah Love. His face was grave and, even as he greeted them, he produced a newspaper and laid it on the table.

'The Indians got Custer,' he said.

MASSACRE OF OUR TROOPS, the headline announced. FIVE COMPANIES KILLED. GENERAL CUSTER AND 17 COMMISSIONED OFFICERS BUTCHERED IN A BATTLE ON THE LITTLE BIG HORN.

'Seems he split his command once too often,' Love said dryly.

A job in London on Wolseley's staff followed the return to England, then, with George Laughton retired, a return to the regiment as second in command. The 19th were at Aldershot by this time and little had changed, except, thank God, Claude Cosgro had retired and got himself involved in his father's business in Leeds. Some of the glitter had gone with the reforms, Colby noticed, but there was a slicker, more businesslike look to the regiment and a great deal more professionalism. Even Cosgro's old squadron was showing some improvement without Cosgro.

By this time, Colby's son had been joined by two sisters, Helen, dark but minute, with the same elfin face as her mother, and Jane, fair and like her brother. Brosy's Grace had produced a daughter, too, which wasn't quite what Brosy had wanted but made a change after two sons. Aubrey Cosgro, now a captain in D Squadron, saluted

Colby as he arrived and gave him a grimace which was meant to be a smile, and, with Augusta and the family at Braxby, he soon found himself well in harness, burnished and polished and deeply involved with the running of the regiment.

On the whole, the men enlisting these days were better and brighter than they had been and there were far less who joined for drink. Most of them were new to the game, however, because, under the new act, most regiments had been quick to get rid of their old soldiers, but they were learning fast and the rowels of their spurs jingled well, a sure sign they were proud to be cavalrymen.

Christmas was being spent at Braxby. A squad of recruits from the depot were waiting to go south as Colby picked up the local train at York. They were awkward and uncertain and being chivvied by a sergeant like a lot of sheep, but they had a lean, tough look about them, too. It was surprising how the army could take half-developed boys from the slums and make them into men in a matter of months.

He settled himself in the corner of a first-class carriage and opened his newspaper. It was beginning, he decided, to look as though trouble was brewing in South Africa. Zulu-Boer disputes over the possession of lands on the Transvaal border were erupting into murders and it was becoming clear that before long something would have to be done about the growing power of the Zulu king, Cetze-wayo.

The house appeared to be empty when he arrived. It had been built by his father after Waterloo, a place of no great beauty but one which he held in esteem for the warmth and happiness he associated with it. The drive to the front door crunched under the wheels of the cab he'd hired and as he stepped down, he noticed that the cedar tree in the middle of the lawn looked as though it needed attention. But, with the aid of a farm manager and Tyas Ackroyd, who could speak from the experience of generations, Augusta was making a good job of running the house, the Home Farm and a family, to say nothing of the multitude of charities

262

which claimed her attention.

As he stood, staring round him, taking in the old stone and the wide windows that let in the sun when it appeared, and the draughts when it didn't, he heard footsteps and turned to see Augusta appear round the corner in riding habit, leading a pony on which his son was seated, his legs kicking at its fat flanks. Immediately, she dropped the reins and the pony came to a stop, refusing to budge despite the flailing feet on its sides, as she flung herself into Colby's arms.

'When did you arrive?'

Colby indicated his bag. 'This minute. A visit to the depot. It gives me until New Year at home.'

Christmas proved a great success. Harriet and her family turned up on Christmas Eve and there was a shoot on Boxing Day, while the whole tribe of them went out with the Braxby Hounds the day after. The weather was bitterly cold after a wet week when the rain had come down like long spikes of glass and, with the pack moving across the fields in a rippling stream, the horses skidded and slid, crashing through the hedges, for a run of six miles. The Braxby hounds were never good-lookers but they knew their job and were lean and fast; as they flowed down the hills in hot pursuit, the horses after them at a flat gallop, the bare trees smelled of fungus and damp earth among the smell of horse-sweat and leather, and the cold air was like ice crystals to the cheeks.

It was exciting, invigorating and edged with danger, and Augusta, mounted on a big high-stepping grey like a tomtit on a side of beef, her cheeks pink, her hair coming down, so enjoyed herself she invited everyone – while they were still purple-faced and panting on steaming horses with pumping sides – for a house party over the New Year.

She couldn't believe Colby's warning that it would be a disaster, but Uncle George Goff, she discovered, was known for his coarseness and, like Uncle Hedley, drank like a fish. Uncle Edward talked of nothing but how he nearly went to war in 1845 but didn't quite, and Uncle Thomas, who had been in the 4th Light Bobs, spent all his time explaining how he just missed Balaclava because he happened to have retired. She also discovered she had invited two cousins who were considered to be beyond the pale because one of them had dared to join an infantry regiment and one had even 'gone foreign' and moved to Norfolk.

As dinner finished and Augusta shooed the females out, Colby passed the port and offered cigars.

'See this new man in South Africa, Shepstone, is getting everybody's back up,' Uncle Edward observed, poking at the end of his cigar as if he expected to find gold inside it. 'Annexing the Transvaal didn't help anybody.'

'This Zulu chap –' Cousin Hedley filled his glass and passed the bottle ' – Cet – whatever he's called – he only rules from month to month. No firm policy. It'll lead to fighting.'

'Doesn't like Shepstone, I heard,' Uncle George said. 'Wants to blood his warriors. Washing the spears, *The Times* called it.'

'Good old Thunderer,' one of the cousins murmured.

'Tribal custom,' George said. 'Have to kill somebody or they don't go to heaven – or something. Or is that the Moslems? What's the latest from the Cape?'

'Dunno. Usual fog in the press. Can't make head nor tail of it. Tension's building up over the whole of Southern Africa. We shall have to go in there and sort things out before long, you see.'

Colby studied them with amused eyes. None of them had ever moved far from home and their attitudes were narrow and parochial. But they were right. The advancing Boers were pushing back the black Africans and there was a clear resentment that they were intruding on tribal domains. There had been yet another Kaffir War, the Secretary of State for the Colonies had resigned, and the commander-in-chief in South Africa had been sacked. The whole business was in the melting pot.

'They should send Wolseley,' George said. 'Our only general.'

Colby shook his head. 'Wolseley won't get himself mixed

up in this,' he pointed out. 'After Ashanti, he'll want to stay in London in case anything worth while crops up.'

When everyone had gone to bed, Augusta kicked off her shoes and stretched in front of the fire with Colby's arm round her.

'You were right,' she admitted. 'It *was* a disaster.'

The following day brought a telegram, ordering Colby to report to Whitehall. Reading it slowly, he looked up to find Augusta watching him from the stairs and began to whistle 'The Yorkshire Jockey' in a busy dedicated way that didn't delude her for a moment.

'A summons from the master?' she asked.

'Something of the sort,' Colby said. 'Shouldn't take long. I'll get the train from York and be back the day after tomorrow.'

She watched him go, desolate and bewildered. When Colby was near her she felt secure, but away from his side she was more lost than she ever let him see.

The weather in London seemed, if anything, to be worse than the weather in Yorkshire. Showers of rain and sleet beat across Whitehall as Colby was shown into an ante-room and told to wait. He had no idea what was wanted of him, but he had an uneasy suspicion that it was another staff job when he was just enjoying being back in the family atmosphere of the regiment. Eventually a porter conducted him along a corridor to a room which carried a map of South Africa on its walls. There were several other officers present and it soon became obvious that they had been summoned as the leading subordinates for a new expedition of some sort.

'Who's running the show?' Colby asked.

'Thesiger. Son of Lord Chelmsford. Rifle Brigade and Guards. Light on action and heavy with staff duties.'

'What's it all about?'

'South Africa, I suppose. He's the new C-in-C.'

Evelyn Wood arrived shortly afterwards, followed by Redvers Buller, and it was Colby's impression that Thesiger had been landed with a lot of men he hadn't asked for –

good men on the whole but devotees of Wolseley who had probably been wished on him. Thesiger himself was a tall lanky man with handsome intelligent features hidden by the thick bush of a spade beard. His personality seemed reserved and, after Wolseley's fire, he seemed colourless. His speech was clear and to the point, however.

'I'm not over-excited at the prospect of a sputtering native war at the Cape being thrust into my lap,' he admitted. 'That sort of thing's never likely to arouse enthusiasm in the breast of a British general because too many have broken their teeth on the problem.'

When Colby returned, Augusta greeted the news with unfeigned dismay.

'South Africa?' she said. 'But that's thousands of miles away. What happens to me?'

Colby looked at her. He was aware of the thoughts racing through her brain and was wary.

'Same as happens to most soldiers' wives, I suppose,' he said.

She was silent and he watched her, worried, conscious of a crisis in their marriage.

'It's only four years since you came back from the Gold Coast,' she pointed out. 'I want to be by your side.'

He frowned. 'I can't refuse,' he pointed out. 'Officers who turn down jobs don't get asked again.'

'I'm not asking you to turn it down.'

'Then what the devil *are* you asking?'

Her face changed and she grinned at him. 'They tell me the climate at the Cape is perfect,' she said. 'I'm asking you to take me with you.'

3

There was only one way for Augusta to accompany Colby
– on a trooper heading for India via the Cape.

She was still a little dazed by what she'd done as Brosy's
Grace came to see her off.

'You pregnant again?' Grace asked, studying her expression.

'No. Why?'

Grace laughed. 'Always seems to occur at the first
mention of goin' overseas,' she said. 'I'm glad you're not.
Pleased to be off?'

'I think so.' Suddenly Augusta wasn't sure.

The conditions on the trooper proved to be appalling,
though for the women of the other ranks they were an
inferno. The washing facilities were dreadful, the sanitation worse, and into the remarkably little privacy Augusta
possessed permeated the stench of ammonia from the
horses. She had a bunk so narrow it seemed like a coffin
and under the mattress were all the clothes she would need
on the voyage. All the rest went into the trunk, and whenever they dressed for dinner, Colby in his mess kit, she in
frills and furbelows, they had to do it separately because
there wasn't room for both of them.

During the second week one of the other rank children
died and, as the coffin was hammered together outside her
door, she had to descend into the inferno of the men's
quarters to comfort the weeping mother. As they passed
the Equator, the smell of horses and what Colby called the
'bouquet d'hommes' grew stronger, but at least there were
high blue skies, flying fish and stars as big as florins, and

the delight of watching small naked black boys diving for pennies when they put into port. Arriving in Cape Town with the whole family in a reasonable state of health, Augusta considered herself lucky.

Colby departed at once to join Thesiger's command at East London. Thesiger made his views on tactics clear at once at his staff conference. 'European troops aren't much good against mosquito-hordes of Bantus,' he said. 'They disappear too easily into the landscape and clear-cut victories will be out of the question.'

There were a few sidelong glances. Evelyn Wood's pale pop eyes were expressionless.

'I shall therefore use roving columns,' Thesiger went on. 'A single column would never drive the Kaffirs into a corner. They'd just retire before us and sweep round to attack our flanks and rear.' He looked at Wood, Buller, Colby and the others who had been members of the Wolseley Ring, and made a mild dig at the reformers. 'I'm also aware that, thanks to the recent changes, the men I'm getting are chiefly new recruits. Apart from the 24th, they appear to have been scraped together and most of them have less than four months' service, have never fired a musketry course and have not even finished recruits' drill.'

The army moved north immediately. The Korie Bush, where Colby found himself, was rough hilly country on the slopes leading to the high plateau of Africa and, covered with extensive patches of shrub, was difficult to operate in. The Gcamena tribesmen were armed only with assegais and a variety of ancient firearms which were as much a danger to themselves as to the men searching them out. But in the thick scrub visibility was limited to a few feet, and the business of driving them out to attack them with artillery as they ran for the next patch of scrub was infuriating work, largely profitless and not very dangerous, but never the job for unseasoned soldiers.

Buller, commanding the Frontier Light Horse, a body of volunteers raised at King William's Town, was just to the north, a strange man with a terrible temper, tremendous enthusiasm, a courage verging on the insane and a curious ability to inspire his men. Tall, strong and wiry, he enjoyed his comfort and carried cases of wine with him on patrol. Evelyn Wood, in command of another column, was his complete antithesis, a short mournful man with a tendency to catch whatever ailment came within a mile of him. He had won the Victoria Cross in the Crimea with the Navy, but, far from being a committed sailor, had eventually transferred to the cavalry, and, no more committed to the cavalry than the Navy, had then exchanged into the infantry. His gift for hard work was legendary.

In command of a unit known as the North Cape Horse, Colby found himself having to adapt to the methods of a group of colonials noted for their independence and not given to taking orders. Inevitably known like the 19th as Goff's Gamecocks, they wore brown corduroy uniforms with red stripes down their breeches and a red puggaree round a slouch hat. They were an unmilitary-looking lot made even more unmilitary by having accepted anybody who could ride and shoot and bring his own horse. Some of them wore no other uniform than a strip of red cloth attached to any headgear they happened to be wearing, whether it were a slouch hat, a top hat, a solar topee, or a forage cap scrounged from a member of the Imperial forces. They were excellent horsemen, however, and excellent shots, and seemed more than content to have Colby to tell them what to do, if only because he knew something about tactics while they relied entirely on their instincts as hunters. They were used for scouting, for covering the activities of the Regulars, or for rounding up the Gcamenas as they were flushed out of their patches of scrub. At this work they were considerably better than the half-company of Imperial troops he had, most of whom were raw recruits.

It wasn't difficult to lose all count of time and Colby rarely had the chance to think of Augusta and the children, established at Cape Town with Tyas Ackroyd and his wife, Annie, to look after them. Cape Town was beautiful, the climate was perfect, the house they had rented was large and safe, and there were beaches within reach to which Ackroyd could drive them in the hired carriage. Nevertheless, it seemed odd to be going to war with his wife and children somewhere in the background.

The fighting, in fact, spluttered and sparkled like a damp squib, with the Gcamena chief, Gendili, believed to be hidden in the bush at Kammansinga, an area of low flat-topped hills which had become the boundary between the Bantus pushing south and the advancing fringe of the Boer civilisation pushing north. With his column, Colby also had four brass seven-pounder muzzle-loaders commanded by a lieutenant of Royal Artillery and a few native soldiers who wore rags or even loin cloths and carried ancient Snider breechloaders, assegais or merely knobkerries. Fortunately, his North Cape Horse were experienced settlers who were skilled enough with rifles to be capable of drilling the eye out of a springbok without damaging the rest of the meat.

'Gendili rides a white horse,' Colby told them. 'It's a sign of his status. But he's deformed, so, if you find an animal with the saddle propped up on one side, then Gendili's near somewhere.'

As the Imperial troops were brought into line facing the patch of bush, he could see they were nervous. They were very young and their training had taught them to fight in line under the steadying hand of their officers. This new kind of fighting was unsettling work and they were uncertain, while their captain, a hesitant man called Edwards, was not the officer to help them much.

As he reported to Colby that all was ready, Colby gestured. 'Very well,' he said. 'Off you go.'

As the soldiers in their high-peaked sun helmets began to move forward, their red coats made a splash of colour against the tawny veldt. In front of them their officers walked slowly, sword in one hand, revolver in the other. The fact that they chose to carry both showed their anxiety, and the men behind them were not hurrying.

The seven-pounders were standing in the open on either side of the bush, their barrels trained on the land between the far edge of the bush and the next patch. Behind each pair of guns waited a squadron of North Cape Horse, drab in their brown and red, waiting for the dash forward when the Gcamenas broke cover.

The sun was hot as the young soldiers entered the bush and were lost to sight. Colby knew exactly what they were thinking. In there, friends and comrades disappeared, and a man found himself alone in tangled vegetation through which he could barely make his way, while behind every bush there was the likelihood of a Gcamena with an assegai waiting to rip open his belly or blow off his head with an ancient weapon as likely as not loaded with old nails. There was an even chance, in fact, that the first he would know of his presence was when he trod on him, and the soldiers were understandably nervous.

Glancing at his watch, he saw that two hours had passed. It seemed to be taking a long time to flush out Gendili and, behind him, the mounted men were growing restless. There were one or two horses with thrush, one or two windsuckers you could hear half a mile away, and several weavers which couldn't gallop straight enough to stay in a five-acre field, but their riders knew them and they were an enthusiastic lot itching to do something.

The sun was high now and it was bakingly hot, and he could see shimmers of heat rising from the barrels of the little seven-pounders. Cantering slowly to the group on the opposite side of the scrub, he still saw nothing and as the time went on he began to grow worried. Surely to God Gendili and his men weren't clever enough to swallow up a whole half-company of Imperial troops! He was just turning to speak to the officer in command of the guns when a single shot rang out, echoing among the folds of the hills behind them.

'Here we go!'

There was a sudden flurry of activity in the bush in front and he saw red coats moving, but, instead of advancing deeper into the bush, the soldiers seemed to be heading back. One of them, his sun helmet lost, emerged without his rifle, holding his hands to his face, the blood running between his fingers. As he staggered about, half-blinded by buckshot, the entire half-company burst out, all apparently trying to help him to safety.

Kicking at his horse's flanks, Colby arrived in a fury. 'Get that man to the rear!' he roared. '*Two* of you! Not the whole damned half-company! Mr Edwards, get your men in a line!'

As the wounded man was helped away, the soldiers formed an uncertain line. They kept glancing back at the bush, eyeing it uneasily.

'Do you call that a line?' Colby snapped. 'Mr Edwards, tell your sergeants to make them look like soldiers! And then I'll have you and your officers here. I want to talk to you.'

As the soldiers were bawled into better order, he glared furiously at the group of officers.

'God damn it,' he snarled. 'You're fighting uneducated, badly-armed savages. What are you hesitating about? The only way to do the job is to show some sort of drive. You will go in again and this time I will lead. I shall expect you to remain close behind me.'

As the officers glanced uneasily at each other and went back to their men, Colby moved to his horsemen and informed them what was happening.

'Half an hour from now,' he announced, 'you can expect Gendili and his men to appear at the other side.'

Turning his horse, he took up a position in front of the line of soldiers. 'Let it be known,' he said, 'that I shall punish any man who drops back unless he has a very good excuse.'

There was no question of hesitation this time. As they pushed through the scrub, there were shouts, and black faces popped up to stare at them, then the Gcamenas turned and began to run. 'Now!' Colby yelled, and the line swept forward, caught by their own enthusiasm.

Only in front of Colby was there any attempt at resistance. A tall twisted black man with a leopard skin round his waist and the headring of a Zulu stood up and levelled an ancient musket. As the battered weapon exploded, Colby's hat flew off and he felt the sting of a wound in his neck, then he hit the man over the head with Micah Love's great gun. As he collapsed, Colby instructed two of the men following him to disarm him and drag him clear.

'Alive,' he pointed out. 'It looks like Gendili.'

As the Gcamenas bolted like woodcock down the wind, from the far side of the bush, the seven-pounders loosed off a few shells. They did no harm but kicked up a lot of dust and smoke and scattered a last attempt to stand and fire, then the North Cape Horse swept down. The casualties on both sides were remarkably light: one Cape Horse poked across the ribs with an assegai, one of the Imperials shot in the face and Colby bleeding from a deep wound on the neck caused by a bent nail fired from Gendili's rusty muzzle-loader.

'That's the second time I've been wounded by a bloody bent nail,' he said bitterly.

With Gendili's little revolt ended, Colby found himself in a rented house in East London, enjoying the warm dry weather and the free and easy life of the colony. Ackroyd had arrived posthaste by sea to look after him until Augusta and Annie Ackroyd could muster the trunks and join them. The only drawback was the number of women who were taking an interest in the wounded.

The owner of the house next door was the widow of a sugar planter called Le Roux who had clearly taken a fancy to Colby and kept appearing with fruit and sweetmeats and made a point in the evening of opening her windows and singing to the piano. She looked remarkably like Georgina Cosgro, her face too plump, her mouth too soft and cherry-like, and she took to reading to him as he stretched out painfully in a cane chair. It was Ackroyd who sorted her out, appearing with a bottle and spoon and announcing to Colby that it was time for his medicine.

'What bloody medicine?' Colby snapped. 'I'm not taking medicine.'

'This is the one for your 'ysteria, sir.'

'What hysteria?'

Ackroyd smiled. 'Your family 'ave always suffered from it, sir,' he said. 'You know they 'ave. The number of times

273

I've 'ad to tie the general down when 'e was foamin' at the mouth! You know it runs in the family. It was the disease 'e picked up in India, wasn't it? You know what them Indian women are like – '

As Mrs le Roux vanished, Colby stared up indignantly.

'That was you at your brilliant best, Tyas,' he said sarcastically.

'Well, you told me to keep the women off you,' Ackroyd said calmly. 'And you often told me when we was boys that if you wanted to clear a railway carriage all you 'ad to do was cough and spit an' pretend to 'ave consumption.' Ackroyd sniffed. 'Besides, Mrs G will be 'ere soon, and you'd 'ave looked fine entertainin' that one when she walked in the door, wouldn't you?'

By the time Augusta appeared, she had gained a great deal of experience and was beginning to see what being an army wife was really like. The children were already used to travelling by steam-train, ox-waggon, horse-drawn cart, carriage or even on horseback, and she had become an expert at packing clothes, goods and treasures.

By this time the whole army was back in East London and Thesiger was reporting the end of the war to White-hall, but trusting there would be no objection if he retained his staff because there would probably be more work for them before long.

'Against Cetzewayo,' Colby explained as Augusta bent over him to dress the wound on his neck. 'Thesiger's just preparing for every eventuality.'

Augusta frowned. 'Will *you* have to go?'

'If it comes to trouble.'

'And do *they* shoot rusty nails, too? Because this one has turned bad. I expect you used a filthy handkerchief to dab at it. You ought to apply for sick leave in England.'

Turning to disagree, Colby got a dab of antiseptic in his eye, and as he jerked his head away, rubbing at the tears with a grubby handkerchief, Augusta stared at it scornfully.

'I thought so,' she said. 'You'll probably get mange now and go blind. What's *wrong* with applying for leave? The war's over.'

'Evelyn Wood's been in the saddle all day for weeks,' Colby said. 'With a temperature, swellings in his groins and armpits, and his skin peeling off. *He* hasn't applied for leave.'

She studied him angrily. 'Why do they have to go and fight another war when they've only just finished this one?'

'Scarcity of land.'

'In Africa, for God's sake?'

'Grazing land. Well-water and grassy flatlands. They're essential to both black and white. The Boers are after Zululand, but the Zulus have had their herds ravaged by lung sickness and the tsetse fly, so they're after the borderlands of the Transvaal.'

'Can't they live in peace?'

He shrugged. 'It was hoped so when we annexed the Transvaal, but the Zulus are an independent nation with a standing army of forty thousand, run by a king who's only a savage and willing to have a go at anybody. All the same, the political people have backed them over the disputed territory for fifteen years and the boundary commission says it belongs to them, so that should quieten things down.'

'I think there *will* be a war.'

Colby lifted his head warily. Augusta had her own ways of coming to conclusions. He could never fathom how she arrived at them but she usually came up with the right answers, even if for the wrong reasons. 'Why?'

'I saw Aubrey Cosgro's wife, Hetty, in Cape Town. She had a house near Wynberg.'

'Why's she here?'

'Because Aubrey's here, too! That surprises you, doesn't it?'

It did. 'Go on. I'm sure there's more.'

'He's come to join Thesiger's army.'

'*Aubrey Cosgro?*' Colby gave a neigh of laughter, and she frowned.

'It signifies something, all the same,' she said. 'She told me his father's money and her father's title had got him

Wolseley's ear and he was hoping for a staff appointment. She also let it drop that George Morrow was out here, too.'

She looked at him, remembering the vituperation she'd had to endure after the Ashanti War. He didn't disappoint her.

'What's that bloody idiot expecting?' he growled. There were still twinges where the Ashanti's bent nail had entered his back.

'He's to form a column. Hetty Cosgro said that when Thesiger went up to Natal, he found its defences in a terrible state.'

He frowned. 'They are,' he admitted. 'If it does come to a go, the only defence is an invasion of Zululand and he's applied for more troops and regular cavalry.'

She studied him carefully, her face troubled, her mind full of unexpected fears. 'I still think you ought to apply for leave in England,' she said. 'I have a feeling. And I think you men all believe that with your smart uniforms and your guns and training, this war's going to be easy. I have a feeling it isn't.'

He studied her curiously. 'What makes you think that?'

'I don't know. Maybe it's because, coming from the States, I see the wood without seeing the trees. We fought Indians, and I remember what they did to Custer. It seems to me it's going to be pretty hard to pin down people as mobile as the Zulus.'

He stared at her with amusement. 'Where did you do your staff training?' he grinned. 'That's what Thesiger thinks, too. The only way to do it is by having several columns all starting from different places.'

'To stop the Zulus slipping into Natal?'

Colby's smile died. 'No. To insure they'll attack one of them.'

'And then what?'

'They'll be smashed by superior fire power.'

'Suppose they aren't? Suppose everybody's rifle jams? Micah once said that at Antietam they fired so long they ended up with guns that wouldn't work.'

'Gussie, it won't take that much firing to destroy

savages.'

'I expect that's what Custer said, too' Augusta gazed at him anxiously, close to tears. 'I've met a few of those people you rely on. They're not all as good as you.'

He frowned. 'No,' he agreed. 'They're not. Morrow's an ass for a start. Pulleine's inclined to be too careful. Durnford's too hot-headed. Hamilton-Browne's a boor. Some of the volunteer units don't much like discipline either and the Boers are insisting that if it comes to war we'll need to concentrate on distant scouting to locate the Zulu impis at all.'

'I expect that'll be you. They'll push you out miles ahead of the army so you can get yourself killed.' She stamped on his foot deliberately to show her anger.

Colby quietly took the cotton wool and the antiseptic from her and put them down, then he put his arms round her. 'Shoving your off hind down on my toe don't prove anything,' he chided gently. 'The war hasn't even started yet and the frock coats are bound to come down on the side of the Zulus over the boundary, because they don't like the Boers any more than they do the Kaffirs.'

Despite everybody's insistence that the Zulus didn't want trouble and had no intention of harming Natal, clearly nobody was taking any chances and the army was put on a war footing just in case.

As it began to move north, Augusta watched the local newspaper with worried eyes. Considering that everyone felt there was going to be no war, it seemed to her that they were all taking a lot of pains to be ready for one.

'If there *is* a war,' she asked. 'Can I go to Durban?'

'What on earth for?'

Colby looked at her in surprise and she felt an unkind desire to brain him. In his absorption in the movements of the army, he was showing no interest in her worries; and she was furious, because she knew he could be a help if he tried. It seemed to raise a barrier between them so that the things she wished to say had to be left unsaid and she had to content herself with snapping at him.

'Is it so odd that I should wish to be close to my husband?' she said sharply. 'Durban's only a hundred and fifty miles from the army. East London's five hundred. I'm thinking of my family. I like 'em all together – you included.'

He gave her a quick unexpected grin. 'Make sure you're not letting those maternal instincts of yours come between you and common sense,' he said. 'Stop worrying.'

She stared at him indignantly, aware in the nervous mood that held her of a strong desire to kick him. 'I *feel* like worrying,' she said. 'I'm scared.'

'What of?'

She shook her head in a distressed way, as if trying to jolt her thoughts into some sort of order from the disorder they were in. In her unhappiness, the one fear that always lay at the back of her mind came to the surface.

'I don't know. Perhaps it's because I feel I shall never be part of the regiment. Perhaps it's because I'm American and don't see it the same way everybody else does.'

He tried to understand her but, brought up in the regiment as he had been, he found it impossible. As he kissed her, her arms went round him.

'Please! Let me go to Durban!'

'All right,' he said. 'I see no reason why not. Headquarters'll be at Pietermaritzburg or somewhere like that, so Durban won't be far away and I might get down to see you.'

The threat of war didn't die down and it began to seem even that a few of the government officials like Theophilus Shepstone and Bartle Frere were actually eager to have a fight to bump up their own reputations. Towards the end of the year Colby received orders to take the North Cape Horse to the northern corner of Natal.

As he vanished, Augusta flung herself into the business of packing and within three days her family plus the Ackroyds were on a ship heading for Durban. It wasn't hard to find a house to rent, because the town was growing fast and, while there was an influx of officers' wives and families, there was also an exodus of people who preferred not to be around if the Zulus invaded.

They found a house on the road to Verulam and were waiting there when Colby arrived at Port Natal. The children greeted him with delight and Augusta flung herself into his arms.

'What's all this for?' he demanded.

'Well, there *is* going to be a war, isn't there?'

He had to admit that it looked like it. 'But there's nothing to worry about,' he went on. 'They're a savage nation and we've defeated savages time and time again: India. Burma. China. The Maoris. The Abyssinians. The Ashantis. The Afghans. Why not this time?'

She lifted her face to him and he saw the unease in it. She seemed in a state of near-panic. She felt cold and stiff and twice her age because she knew he was fibbing shamelessly to bolster up her morale. For a moment she felt like weeping but she was too afraid for tears. 'I had a dream before I left Cape Town,' she said. 'I had it again last night. I dreamed you were shot. Then I saw a man holding up his arm and there was a spear sticking in his side. It came out near his throat. Colby, *could* you be shot?'

'What with?' Colby laughed. 'They've only got cheap trade flintlocks. Birmingham gas-pipes we call them.'

'You were shot by a gas-pipe gun on the Gold Coast. You were shot by a gas-pipe gun at Kammansinga. And this time you're not facing a few scattered tribesmen. You're facing a whole nation. Besides –'

'Besides what?'

She turned her face from him. Suddenly she was sagging with weariness, shadowy hollows under her eyes. 'Nothing,' she said.

'Are you still afraid?'

'Yes.'

'What about?'

'You'd be surprised.' She drew a deep breath and managed a half-hearted grin at him. 'It was nothing. It was silly, I guess. It doesn't matter.' She turned her face away again, her expression obscured. 'Where would the fighting be, Colby?'

'We'd have to burn the royal kraal and capture Cetzewayo. No other kind of defeat would be recognised by the Zulus. But we'll have over sixteen thousand men in four or five separate columns. They reckon the Zulu army's no more than twenty thousand.'

'If you have four or five separate columns, it means there'd be no more than about three thousand men to each, doesn't it?' In her worry her eyes seemed enormous. 'What happens if the whole Zulu army drops on them one at a time?'

It was quite a point. He couldn't find an answer and was careful to dodge the question. 'Perhaps there won't be a war, after all,' he said.

4

Despite the Boundary Commission's view, however, as Colby had suspected, the political authorities were intent on fighting. When the boundary award was read out, the Zulus were satisfied because their claims were largely upheld and they were actually preparing to depart to their kraals when they were summoned back and told that their army must be disbanded and their military system broken up. It was clear at once that the ultimatum was the death knell of Zulu independence and that they would resist it.

Colby vanished into the blue a week later, after a hasty visit to Durban to say goodbye to his family. After growing used to Augusta's courage, he was worried to find her still in a tearful mood and he could only assume she was tired or that the enervating heat of sub-tropical Durban was too much for her.

It was a strange army he rode with. There was not a single troop of Imperial cavalry – chiefly, he suspected, because the army in England, designed for Continental warfare, was ill adapted for native wars – and there seemed a proliferation of volunteers raised by the colonials and consisting for the most part of small outfits with grandiose names, little training and precarious discipline which might well collapse in an emergency. The native troops mostly still carried only assegais and wore nothing but their tribal dress, and they could barely form a straight line, had horses that were gun-shy and NCOs who for the most part were on horseback for the first time. Ulundi, where Cetzewayo ruled, was only seventy-five miles away across the Tugela River which bordered the colony, and a well-mounted man could ride there in a day at a pinch, but with the British government as usual willing to accept an inefficiently-conducted campaign but never an expensive one, they were stuck with ox-drawn transport with which they would take all of a month and perhaps longer.

As the units moved to their assigned positions, orders came for Colby to take the North Cape Horse to Balte Spruit in the north-west corner of the colony and on the edge of the disputed tribal land, where Evelyn Wood had established a camp from which he could lead into Zululand. As he rode out of Pietermaritzburg, the 24th Foot were also marching out for Helpmakaar, their colours flying, their band playing 'I'm Leaving Thee In Sorrow, Annie', which he'd last heard at the Burtle House in Virginia as he'd ridden off to Yellow Tavern with Micah Love's regiment. Volunteer cavalry and Boer burgher units were jogging along in front of him, dressed for the most part in anything that took their fancy. Astern were native cavalry and native infantry, their uniforms varying from an old jacket and trousers to a leopard skin and a couple of ostrich feathers. Batteries of little seven-pounders and the heavier guns of the 5th Artillery Brigade bounced and rattled behind their teams.

Where the road turned north-east towards the border, he was surprised to see Ackroyd waiting for him. He rode a roman-nosed grey and sat in the saddle with the erectness of a cavalry-trained rider, so that it wasn't hard to imagine him, despite his thickening middle, still wearing the green regimentals and flat-topped schapka of the 19th.

'What the hell are you doing here?' Colby asked. 'Something wrong with my wife?'

Ackroyd grinned. 'Not on your life, sir,' he said. 'But she's got my missis to look after 'er, to say nothin' of 'alf a dozen Kaffirs. There's also the wife of Captain Moss, of the 9th, 'oo's with the Central Column, on one side of 'er, and on the other the wife of a naval commander from *Colossus*, what's operatin' from Durban docks. Under the circumstances, I could 'ardly let you go off to war on your own, could I?'

Colby stared at him for a moment, frowning, then as he spurred his horse past without speaking, Ackroyd quietly tagged on behind.

Rorke's Drift was full of troops gathering for the advance, and Thesiger – Lord Chelmsford since the death of his father – had commandeered the old mission station with its little stone church and thatched houses as a base. The artillery came in and they formed camp on the ground below, a rash of hospital waggons, field bakeries, veterinary units and engineers, setting up their lines on the grassy slopes below the Oskarberg.

Resting the night at the Drift, the North Cape Horse rode on the next day to Bemba's Kop where Wood had moved. He was suffering from a headache and a fever and greeted Colby gloomily.

'Nice to see you, Coll,' he said, though his tone of voice implied that Colby was just one more worry. 'We've been asked to make a demonstration up here to hold down the northern tribes. I'm going to use Buller's people to scout ahead and move north-east to the Umfalozi.'

The countryside was largely rolling plainland and was swarming with independent Zulu impis. Wood had his eye on a chain of hills across the route to Ulundi which were said to contain more Zulus, and as they moved towards the river late in January they became aware at once of large forces of black warriors in the vicinity of a stone kraal. Immediately, the atmosphere changed. Wood was an expert native fighter and he moved warily because the area could hide the enemy as securely as forests or mountains. A faint roll of ground was deceptive, and a whole impi could hide itself at a distance of a few hundred yards in a place that seemed at first glance as flat as a plate.

While the North Cape Horse flanked the position, Wood scrambled at dawn up on to the hills. By early afternoon, he was back and in a hurry.

'There are four thousand of 'em drilling on the slopes of Hlobane,' he said.

The presence of the Zulus appeared to worry him and

when Buller brought in prisoners that evening, his anxiety increased.

'Cetzewayo's main impi left Ulundi on the 17th,' Buller reported. 'They mustered at Nodwengu and bivouacked on the White Umfalozi.'

'Lord Chelmsford knows all that,' Wood said. 'I informed him some time ago. What else do they say?'

'They're heading for Isipezi Hill and ought to come down across Chelmsford's route from the north-east about the 23rd.'

'How many of them are there?'

Buller shrugged. 'Hard to say. They count with their fingers. Twelve regiments, I think. Around twenty-four thousand.'

'It's already the 21st. Lord Chelmsford ought to know.' Wood looked at Colby. 'Didn't you once ride over a hundred miles at ten miles an hour?'

'Two hundred and seventy-one kilometres in thirty-one hours forty minutes, to be exact,' Colby corrected. 'But it was a prepared ride. We had oats, bran and beans at regular stops. And a picked horse.'

'Think you could ride forty-odd in twenty-four hours with a knock-kneed Natal frontier pony?'

Colby smiled. 'Just about.'

'Then it had better be you who goes. I don't want to chance this with a native rider. Inform Chelmsford that Cetzewayo's main impi's on its way towards him. You heard the numbers. Tell him we'll continue to converge on Ulundi and make demonstrations to draw 'em off wherever we can.'

Colby decided to take Ackroyd with him. He had helped set up the ride in France and was a good horse-master. If anything happened to Colby he could be expected to get through himself.

'Unless something happens to you *both*,' Wood pointed out dryly.

Ackroyd's attitude was that of a man who had long suspected that the army had so far failed to use its most experienced and useful member.

'No trouble at all, sir,' he said. 'I'll arrange bran, oats, fodder and ammunition, and I'll pick the best two nags in the outfit. We might be glad of 'em.'

Riding almost due south, they skirted the mountains, following the boundary of the disputed territory. Crossing the White Umfalozi, they found the land empty except for a few stragglers from dissident border tribes who didn't support Cetzewayo, heading towards Utrecht. The land was rich and rolling, with small knuckly heights sticking out of the plain. The night was moonless but with the first light the mist cleared and the day became dull and heavily overcast, with an ominous sultry heat. Resting at regular intervals, watering their horses wherever possible, allowing them a little grazing and feeding them the oats and bran separately, they reached Rorke's Drift at dawn the following day.

The mist which had been present on the higher ground had changed to fog and drizzling rain, and the place seemed deserted except for a grumbling detachment of the 24th, who had been left behind to garrison the buildings. Smith-Dorrien, a lanky, lantern-jawed subaltern of the 95th, whom Colby had met in Durban, was eating breakfast as they arrived.

'Chelmsford's on his way already, sir,' he said. 'He's expecting an attack.'

'He's *expecting* it?' Colby's eyebrows rose. 'That's what I've come to tell him.'

Smith-Dorrien was busy over his plate. 'Well, he got Wood's message that the Zulu army had left Ulundi and the Natal Native Contingent went out yesterday with the Mounted Police, the Carbineers, the Mounted Rifles and the Buffalo Guard. They sent back to say they keep bumping into Zulus and that they thought they were somewhere in the vicinity. They were due to scout the Isipezi Hill area and I was sent down here to send up Durnford's Irregulars. They've been gone some time. Chelmsford turned the column over to Pulleine and marched southeast towards Ulundi with reinforcements for the Native Contingent. He's taken the 2nd/24th, four guns and some native troops. If the Zulus find him, Pulleine can easily re-inforce him. Or the other way about if Pulleine's attacked.'

'Where's Pulleine now?'

'Place called Isandhlwana. Good spot. Water and wood in the valleys and a kopje at their backs for safety. South-east of Isipezi Hill.'

'That's the direction Wood expects the main impi to come from. Are they fortified?'

Smith-Dorrien shrugged. 'Turning every stop into a fortified camp would halt the whole army, sir. Everybody's quietly forgetting the regulations. There can't be much to worry about with the better part of two Imperial battalions around.'

'Except that everybody's looking towards the south-east and they're coming from the north-east.'

Smith-Dorrien swallowed his coffee and rose to his feet. 'Perhaps I'd better be getting back,' he said. 'If I were you, sir, I'd go south from here and cut across country. Go along the river bank until you come to a gap in the hills and cross there. If you head due east after that you'll hit the road about where Chelmsford ought to be. Look out for Zulus in the dongas.'

There were no spare horses and Ackroyd's mount was beginning to founder, so Colby sent him back to Wood and turned his mare's head south. The river followed a twisting course between high land south of the mission station until it reached wet lowlands where, crossing by a drift, he set the horse at the slopes opposite, climbing until he reached a level plain. A strange-shaped kopje lay in the distance to his left and round its base he could see the white specks of Pulleine's tents, with Isipezi Hill beyond on the skyline.

In view of Smith-Dorrien's warning that there were Zulus in some of the dongas, he rode easily, reserving the mare's fading strength for a sudden spurt if necessary, and held Micah Love's murderous LeMatt in his right hand ready. By the time he had been riding for an hour, he was beginning to grow a little worried. The land seemed immense and extraordinarily quiet. There were no birds and not a scrap of game about and, wondering if this were a sign that the Zulus were around, he remembered Micah Love's comment fifteen years before about Indian fighting. 'The silence was the worst,' he had said. 'You'd be waitin' with your heart thumpin' and your breath caught in your throat, then suddenly they'd be all round you, shootin' and cuttin' and stabbin'.'

The mare was beginning to falter now but there was no sign of Chelmsford's group, which was surely big enough to be seen, and he wondered if he'd gone too far west. Tired himself by this time, he decided to swing north towards the road.

The day was hot despite the cloud cover, and a sticky heat seemed to rise out of the baking plain. Reaching the road by an outcrop of rocks, he paused for a moment, studying the empty land, then swung west in the direction of the camp. The mare had been ridden hard for the whole of the previous day and night with little rest and had already carried his weight that morning for several hours. But she was an army mount and knew that army camps meant food and rest and, as her pace quickened, Colby looked up to see the scattering of white tents not far away and the curious shape of the kopje.

The tents seemed busier than normal, with red-coated figures moving among them like disturbed ants. For a second he wondered if they'd had news of Cetzewayo's main impi, then with a shock it dawned on him that the figures had black faces and that instead of Martini-Henrys they carried assegais. They were Zulu warriors – the realisation came with a gasp of incredulity – thousands of them, braying in triumph and carrying bloodied spears! Discarding their head rings and feathers, they had clapped white British sun helmets on their woolly skulls and dragged on the scarlet coats of British soldiers!

Wrenching the mare to a standstill, Colby stared ahead, his eyes almost starting from his head, totally disbelieving. The enormity of what must have happened was slow in his tired state to reach him, but when it did it struck him like a physical blow. Only a complete disaster could have allowed Zulus to be in a British camp wearing British clothes! But he found it impossible to believe such a thing had occurred and sat the trembling mare for several minutes, trying to make his tired brain accept the fact.

He was even on the point of moving slowly forward for a better look, convinced he was suffering from hallucinations, when a black face appeared alongside. As the Zulu lifted his arm to thrust with the long-bladed assegai, he came to life abruptly, shocked into action. Lifting the LeMatt, he pulled the trigger and the heavy bullet hit the Zulu in the throat, knocking him backwards, a great spurt of blood coming from his jugular. Then Colby saw other Zulus running between the rocks towards him and realised that hundreds of bodies, red-coated or in skin loin cloths, were spread everywhere through the tents.

Still unable to grasp what had happened, he dragged at the reins. The mare, eager for food, fought against him, getting her hind legs under her and stiffening her neck to iron. Savagely, he wrenched her head round and kicked wildly at her flanks until she broke into an unwilling trot away from the camp. An assegai stirred the dust in front of him and, glancing back, he realised he was closer to death at that moment than he'd ever been. Cruelly, he lashed the mare with the slack of the reins, the sound like the beating of a carpet, and as she jogged unwillingly away, he noticed a cluster of white men lying in a heap on the edge of a dip, stark pale shapes sprawled in puddles of blood among a mass of entrails. Every one of them had had his jacket and trousers opened and his body slashed from chest to groin.

Still he couldn't believe what he saw, but then the mare faltered and he heard the running Zulus give a yell of anticipation. His heart stopped as the mare stumbled to her knees, exhausted, and, jumping from the saddle as she went down, he dragged at her frantically, knowing perfectly well that he could never escape on foot. The black figures behind him were yelling in triumph and, cursing, sweating and terrified, he got the mare to her feet and trotting after him. As she recovered a little, he mounted her again, his mind numb with shock. The base camp had fallen! The main Zulu impi had somehow come down on it when it was unprepared – it could only have been when it was unprepared! – and had slaughtered every man!

A shout lifted his head as a group of Natal Kaffirs popped up out of a donga, their weapons at the ready. He was gasping out his news to a white NCO, when a man with an Irish accent appeared at a run.

'I know, I know,' he panted. 'I've been watching. Lord save us, there wasn't a bloody thing I could do *but* watch. They came pouring over the lip of the escarpment like black treacle slithering over the edge of a plate – thousands of 'em. All we could do was sent a message on to his Bloody Holiness and wait.'

'Where's Chelmsford now?'

'About five miles further on.' The Irishman gestured towards the east.

A horse was found and, mounting it, swaying with fatigue, Colby set off along the dusty track.

Chelmsford was still reconnoitring south-east and clearly didn't believe Colby's news. 'Be more explicit,' he snapped. 'How many Zulus were there?'

Did the bloody man expect him to go back and count them, Colby wondered irritatedly. Fatigue was enveloping him and his temper, never the most placid, was rising when Chelmsford spoke again.

'It's inconceivable that the entire force has been wiped out,' he said. 'Surely a part of it's managed to fall back on Rorke's Drift!'

Colby had his doubts and he reckoned Chelmsford's position was perilous. His, too! He'd seen Cetzewayo's Zulus at close quarters and what he'd seen he hadn't much liked, and he found himself wishing to God Chelmsford would do something.

Even as his thoughts raced through his brain, Chelmsford came to life. An aide went pounding off to bring his column back, then, while Colby snatched something to eat at the side of the road, the native infantry was formed into line with mounted infantry on their flanks and began to move westwards. When Colby caught them up, Chelmsford had halted again and sent the mounted infantry forward to reconnoitre. They were just reporting back, wild-eyed and scared: thousands of Zulus were still at Isandhlwana, they said, swarming across the plain, burning the tents, looting, and dragging away their dead and wounded. As they waited, nerves like bow strings, Chelmsford's main column appeared with the guns. Through his weariness, Colby recognised Aubrey Cosgro with the staff as the men and horses, exhausted after marching all day, limped and stumbled to a halt.

Chelmsford told them what had happened and to Colby the cheer that came in reply sounded as if it was given to bolster up their spirits. Then, with the guns in the centre and the Imperial infantry on either side, they began to move back. The heavy overcast had disappeared now and as the sun went down they could see the tall spire of the kopje silhouetted against a golden sky. By the time they had reached within a mile of the camp, however, the light had gone and all they could see was the stark outline of the mountain, with waggons standing in groups and a few figures moving over the edge of the plateau to the north, which they assumed were the last of the Zulu impi retreating.

All round them were dead men and, as they drew nearer the camp, the groups grew bigger and more widespread.

'Christ,' Cosgro muttered uneasily, and somewhere in the darkness a man was intoning the Lord's Prayer.

'– Thy Kingdom Come
Thy will be done . . .'

Stupefied with tiredness, Colby was jerked awake as the guns barked. The fuses could be seen in the sky against the dark mountain before they burst in white flashes near the crest.

'Shrapnel,' somebody said in the shadows. 'That ought to shift 'em.' There was a pause. 'They had guns in the camp. Why in Christ's name didn't they use 'em?'

They were aware now of thousands of expended cartridges in the grass about their feet, but there was no sound from the tents as three companies of infantry, with fixed bayonets moved off into the darkness. Waiting was eerie. For all they knew, there were thousands of black shapes watching them.

Weariness was catching up on Colby and he found he kept nodding off to sleep in the saddle. As they moved forward after the infantry, the scared native contingent began to hesitate and Cosgro grabbed their induna by his headring and pulled out his pistol.

'You get those black bastards moving!' he snarled. 'Or I'll blow your blasted brains out!'

A volley in the darkness ahead shattered the silence and there was the sound of cheering.

'They've retaken the camp!'

Night had come completely when they stopped to bivouac. As they sank down someone let out a yelp, and, as a light appeared, they saw they were surrounded by scores of slaughtered oxen and horses, lying in lumpish groups. Human remains lay among them, and the exhausted men began to drag them out of the way so they could wait for daylight.

Now they had arrived, Colby had recovered. Somewhere on the slope, he could hear someone singing, an African song, full of half notes and meandering phrases that went nowhere and ended in the air.

'Zulu,' someone said. 'Bugger's been looting the brandy.'

The song went on through the darkness, a drunken babble in the silence. The thought that they were surrounded by hundreds of corpses was unnerving and one or two men, with brothers in the camp, tried to slip off, only to be brought back at once. Certain they were surrounded by the main impi, they were all convinced they would never see daylight.

The voice that had been intoning the Lord's Prayer had changed to the Twenty-Third Psalm '– Though I walk through the Valley of the Shadow of Death I fear no evil –'

The bugger's lucky, Colby thought. *I* do.

But the psalm continued and the high-pitched drunken

African voice on the slope went on. As fatigue caught up with them, men began to sink down, indifferent.

Half way through the night, Colby started awake. The stars were glowing above his head as only African stars could. Nearby, an officer was handing out rations to his men and, as he heard European voices, he remembered he was on the site of a disaster of unbelievable proportions. Far from conquering Cetzewayo, Chelmsford appeared, within eleven days of starting, to have lost his whole army.

When he woke at dawn, he was aware of the smell of death, and turning, he saw the body of a white man with his stomach slit open, lying in the pile of his own entrails. Jumping to his feet, terrified, he was thankful to see other men moving about. A party of them had been into the camp but it was deserted except for corpses. Cosgro had been with them and had found his spare horses dead on the picket rope, their groom lying between them, his dog skewered to the ground by an assegai. Pale and shaken, he was wiping vomit from his tunic.

'Every bloody man,' he was saying in a shaking voice. 'There wasn't one left alive! Not one! There must be hundreds of them, both black and white!'

As the sky paled, they were fallen in again, and, turning towards the west, Colby saw smoke hanging in the sky.

'There was fighting at Rorke's Drift,' Cosgro said. 'They must have swept straight on after destroying this place. Chelmsford's expecting to find another disaster there.'

He was clearly beside himself with terror. 'We ought to be moving back,' he said. 'We must be running short of food by now.'

'We can always eat each other,' Colby growled. 'Starting with you.'

As Cosgro turned away, his eyes full of hatred and fear, Colby's heart went cold. Busy with bitter thoughts about the politicals who had started the war, he decided it would be God help the colonists if the Zulus slipped past. There was little in the way of military strength at Helpmakaar and, if they could wipe out a camp as strong as Isandhlwana there was nothing to stop them heading for Pietermaritzburg as well.

Thank God, he thought, that Gussie and the children were in Durban.

5

But they weren't.

The feeling in Augusta's bones that something dreadful was imminent had set her chafing. The terrifying dream had come again, disturbing and upsetting and, hearing of an officer's wife in Pietermaritzburg whose husband had been sent to the Cape with a broken leg after his horse had fallen on him, she snatched at the opportunity and obtained the house she was evacuating. After all, she thought, she was almost in Durban. Pietermaritzburg was only fifty-six miles to the north-west.

It was an attractive town with streets wide enough to accept the eighteen-oxen voortrekker spans and, built on a sloping plain at an altitude of over two thousand feet, was noted for its healthy climate. Unlike many South African towns, it had even been in existence for forty years; British troops had been garrisoned there for a long time and, though it had been denuded for the march into Zululand, there were still a few of them around.

Despite the corrugated houses, which were stifling in the midday heat, the place was not unpleasant to live in, with its flowering trees, exotic birds and the splendour of the skies at dawn or sunset. There was plenty of entertaining and the black servants were silent, efficient and affectionate, despite their disconcerting habit of serving meals with their foreheads plastered with round coloured labels which Augusta identified as coming off her cotton reels. There were gardens, and the surrounding countryside was full of superb lakes, streams and waterfalls where picnics could be taken. And, unlike England, it was possible to arrange them well ahead and know the weather would be fine. Already the children had settled down happily, and with Annie Ackroyd an excellent housekeeper, it seemed safe enough, with the Zulus almost a hundred miles to the north, two bad drifts at the Tugela and Mooi Rivers to stop any invading force, and the track dotted with troop detachments all the way back as they moved up to Helmakaar.

Aubrey Cosgro's wife turned up unexpectedly shortly after they had settled in, a silly little creature who matched her husband for lack of sense. She had almost caused a riot in the ship in which she had come out by insisting that she should have the best cabin because her child, being in line for a title, was more important than the other children. She was a sad woman, too, because she clearly didn't trust her husband to behave himself when she wasn't by his side, but, because she was lonely and missed England and because she was another army wife, Augusta cultivated her, feeling it might help to heal the rift between Colby and the Cosgro family.

She had just been on a picnic with her in the carriage to the Karkloof Falls and as she descended and started to unload the children, she saw Annie Ackroyd standing on the stoep with one of the black servants. Her face was pale and she looked worried. It was obvious at once that something had happened, but Augusta gave no sign until she had sent the carriage on its way and taken the children indoors.

'What is it, Annie?' she asked quietly. 'Has something happened?'

Annie Ackroyd looked worried. 'I don't know, Ma'am, to be sure. But Tom Asimano here came in an hour ago to say that horsemen arrived from Rorke's Drift last night. He heard that Colonel Durnford's native column's been defeated.'

A cold hand clutched at Augusta's heart. 'Where did he hear this?' she asked, forcing her voice to be steady.

'He says from one of the native servants at Sir Bartle Frere's house. He said the column had been cut to ribbons and Colonel Durnford killed.'

Augusta drew a deep breath. 'If it's as bad as it sounds, I think we ought to be prepared to make a hurried move back to the coast.'

Annie's eyes widened. 'Surely, Ma'am, the Zulus won't come here.'

Augusta was still struggling with her voice, her mind full of her dream. 'I don't know, Annie,' she said. 'But if they've destroyed Colonel Durnford's column, there must be a large force of them near the Tugela and it might easily get behind the other columns and invade Natal.'

For the rest of that evening, they moved quietly round the house, placing things handy. Augusta had had enough experience of war in her adolescence to know what to do. Above all, she told herself, she mustn't panic. Panic spread. There must be no reason for anyone else in the house to be frightened.

The rumours persisted and the following morning as they went outside for the first time she was aware of groups of people standing in the street talking under the jacaranda and gum trees and by the spiky leaves of the aloe hedges. There was a strange atmosphere of suspense and even of dread. Nobody was showing it yet but it was there and, as the hours dragged by, the shadow of a disaster brooded over them all.

During the morning, Hetty Cosgro arrived. She was close to tears.

'No news is good news,' Augusta told her inadequately. 'We've just got to go on waiting. It'll probably all turn out to be a mistake. Some native runner who's got the wrong end of the stick.'

But then Annie, returning in the carriage from shopping, said crowds were waiting at the Raadzaal for information and that quite definitely it had been heard that there had been a battle and something had gone terribly wrong. Nobody was saying anything yet, but snippets of news were leaking out and it seemed there had been a major disaster, though nobody knew yet where it had occurred or what exactly had happened.

'I think, Annie,' Augusta said quietly, 'that we had

better pack a few things. We must be prepared to go quickly.'

'Won't the Major expect you to be here, Ma'am?'

'The Major,' Augusta said firmly, 'will expect me to make sure his children are safe. Just prepare a suitcase or two, then make sure the horses are in the carriage and that Tom Asimano is handy to drive us.'

Annie gave her a scared look and Augusta knew exactly what she was thinking. With all the best horses taken by the army, what were left weren't very good. The two they'd hired with the carriage were galled at girth and neck and had a habit of jibbing or rearing like squealing unicorns, and their favourite pastime was to bolt downhill then suddenly sit on their haunches as if they hoped the harness would break and the carriage crash over them and end their lives. They had never once attempted to pull without attempting to commit suicide and there had been occasions when the only way to move them was for Tom Asimano to reeve a rope under their fetlocks and haul on it while Augusta beat them about the ears with the whip.

'I know, Annie,' she said. 'Tom Asimano might bolt. But in that case I'll do the driving.'

The town was unnaturally quiet all day in the sultry heat. Men were moving on horseback to and from the centre, trying to find out what had happened, and there were carriages waiting in the wide square near the Raadzaal. That evening the first real news was brought in by deserting Kaffirs who had cut across country instead of following the road, and were fleshed out by a trooper of the Natal Mounted Police who had ridden into town to give the alarm. Finally, two British officers, one from the 24th and one from the 3rd, arrived. All the way behind them towards the frontier everybody was busy laagering for their defence, and settlers in the tiny dorps were barricading and provisioning their houses.

The wildest rumours were hurrying about: the whole British and Colonial army had been wiped out and there was nothing between the Zulus and the coast. Dundee,

Helpmakaar and Weenen had fallen and the Zulu army was heading for Greytown which was only fifty miles away. Pearson's column was besieged in Eshowe and Wood's column had been forced into the Orange Free State. Rorke's Drift was surrounded and in flames, and Chelmsford had been butchered with all his men. The two officers who had galloped in to alert the authorities to the danger were suddenly seen as deserters.

By evening the reaction had reached talk of lynching, and Hetty Cosgro, quite certain that she was a widow, was arranging to return to Durban, when a newspaperman who had been with the army appeared. The disaster, it seemed, had occurred at a place called Isandhlwana and out of a force of eighteen hundred black and white soldiers only a handful had escaped. Six full companies of the 2nd/24th had died without a single survivor and of the Europeans who had officered native units, most were dead. The appearance of the men who had ridden in with the news suddenly took on a different aspect. In a disaster of this proportion, there must have been a general sauve qui peut and the only intelligent thing for any survivor to do was get away from the scene as fast as he could.

The newspaperman, an ex-officer himself, brought official confirmation in the form of letters from Chelmsford. Rorke's drift, it seemed, was safe, but only after a tremendous fight, and so was Helpmakaar, but the casualty list he brought was far from complete and seemed impossibly long.

The town was shocked. Terrified but still calm, Augusta continued with her packing. Several times, people appeared, asking to buy the horses and carriage which stood outside the door and she became so concerned that someone would steal them, she and Annie led them round the house and tethered them, still in the shafts, to the back stoep where they couldn't be seen.

In every mind was the thought of a vast Zulu impi heading towards them, and the measures for the defence of the town were so energetic everybody came to the conclusion that the Zulus were already on their way. A garrison order was issued that soldiers must always be armed, because an officer had been murdered on the east of the town by a half-witted Kaffir, and the following morning an aide appeared on the stoep to inform Augusta that the house was to be barricaded.

'We're laying out a laager,' he explained. 'It will cover several of the town's streets. Your house, I fear, lies on the perimeter. I advise you to leave for Durban at once.'

Augusta's temper flared. 'Don't be stupid,' she snapped. 'My husband's with Lord Chelmsford. I shan't move until I know either that he's safe or that he'll never be returning.'

By Sunday, everyone was numb with fear. The Maritzburg Rifles, a volunteer infantry unit, had been mustered, but since there were only just over seventy of them, every male capable of carrying a rifle was also being armed, and families were being ordered to set aside bedding and rations for the wounded and to be prepared for an attack if they heard three guns fired from the fort. Normal life had come to a standstill, and the exuberance that had existed on the invasion of Zululand had given way to panic. After violently underestimating the Zulus, it appeared to Augusta – who had heard such stories before about the Sioux and the Cheyennes – that they were now heavily overestimating them.

Colby was still with Chelmsford as a member of his staff as he rode into Pietermaritzburg. The Commander-in-Chief was tired and discouraged. His invasion had come to an end within eleven days of starting, two of his columns were still cut off out in the blue, and the very safety of the colony itself now seemed in doubt. All he could do was regroup his forces to protect Natal until reinforcements came.

'And they'll *have* to come,' he said. 'I can't even begin to plan the next phase until I learn what they are and when they'll arrive.'

Considering that his command had suffered a disastrous defeat and that he was assailed by intolerable pressures, his mind seemed to be working clearly. A man of colourless personality, he nevertheless impressed Colby with his method, tenacity and moral strength, and he was alarmed by the mood of the town.

'I think we need to calm the place down,' he said. 'There isn't a Zulu on this side of the Tugela. You'd better let me have a report on what's being done, Colby, because I see no point in terrifying every woman in Natal.'

It was late when Colby rode out, accompanied by a young officer from the Pietermaritzburg garrison who was so inexperienced he wasn't at all sure what was expected of him. Here and there a head poked through a loophole cut in the shuttered houses, but the sight of an officer in uniform was too much for most people and they began to crowd into the street. Had they heard of Gregorius Retief? Did they know who was safe from the Natal Mounted Infantry? How about the Edendale Contingent? Colby answered the questions carefully, cautious not to give hope yet at the same time not to encourage despair, and was just about to mount again when he heard his name called. As he turned, he saw a figure running through the dusk towards him. To his amazement it was Augusta. She was in a state of near-panic, made worse by her efforts to control it, and the dream she had seen had grown over the last days to monstrous proportions. Normally a realist unafraid to look a fact in the face, a future without Colby had been too terrible to contemplate.

'Jesus Christ in the Mountains!' he said angrily as she clung to him. 'What are *you* doing here?'

'I was afraid.'

'You'd have had less to be afraid of in Durban,' he snapped. He was tired and his temper was close to the surface. Then he saw the agony in her face, the relief, the strain, and the tears in her eyes, and he put his arms round her.

'I wanted to be near you,' she was saying. 'I was afraid something was going to happen.'

'Something did,' he said harshly. 'By God, it did!'

As her knees gave way, she sat down abruptly on the edge of the stoep, her handkerchief balled in her fist and damp from the tears of relief. Then she drew a deep breath and got control of herself. 'I kept dreaming,' she said in a shaking voice. 'I had you stone dead and the children orphans. I had you lying stark and white in the moonlight with a spear through you. There've been terrible stories of what the Zulus do and I couldn't even think of it. What happened, Colby?'

'Some bloody fool must have gone off his head,' Colby said. 'Half the force had been taken out of camp to meet the Zulus. There was no reason for a defeat and Chelmsford's baffled because he overlooked nothing. He ignored none of the warnings that were sent him.'

Her misery was subsiding rapidly. 'What'll happen now?'

Colby drew a deep breath. 'They'll auction off the effects of the dead and Chelmsford will ask for reinforcements.'

'Will he get them?'

'I expect so. He knows the government's bloody meanness and he's going to ask only for three infantry battalions, two cavalry regiments and enough artillery and engineers to make possible what he intends. Personally, I think he's erring on the side of understanding. I'd have made no bloody bones about it. I'd have demanded that the people at home dig into their pockets. If they want an empire, they shouldn't expect to get it on the cheap.' He shrugged. 'Perhaps that's why Chelmsford's a general and I'm only a brevet lieutenant-colonel.'

Augusta's fingers were working in his. 'What about us?' she asked. 'What happens now?'

'I'm to return to the North Cape Horse,' Colby said. 'And you, Madame, are going to Durban where you'll be safe.'

She turned to face him, her face pink, her eyes dangerously bright.

'No, Coll,' she said, her vehemence startling him. 'I'm staying here.'

'You could be in danger if the Zulus come.'

'Where I came from, people were constantly in danger from savages. Along the frontier in Arkansas and Oregon they still are. I'm staying here. I'm scared.'

She didn't look scared. At that moment, with her eyes flashing and her small jaw set, she looked ready to take on Colby, Chelmsford, the Army Council, the authorities in Natal and the Government at home.

His face slipped into a smile, and in her anxiety, she immediately snapped at him. 'Be serious!'

His jocularity died. 'I'm always serious when I look at you, Gussie, and see you're worried.' His face was grave again. 'You're the nicest thing that ever happened to me.'

She was startled by the confession, because it was so unlike him to let her know, but her heart swelled with pride at the knowledge.

'You were afraid last time,' he reminded her quietly. 'And I rode through half the Zulu army without a scratch.'

She had a feeling that there ought to be arguments to counter what he pointed out but for the life of her she couldn't think of any. She was only aware of a numbness and fear that refused to go away.

'You might not again,' she said. 'Besides –'

His expression changed. He reached forward quickly and took her by the arms, pulling her round to face him. 'Besides *what*?' he demanded sharply. 'You said "Besides –" last time. Besides *what*?'

She gazed at him, her eyes full of tears, then her face grew pink and her temper flared again. 'Because I'm having another baby,' she said.

The grip on her arms loosened and he straightened up. 'Good God!' he said. '*Another*?'

'The way we go at it, it's not all that surprising.'

'But you were having one when I left for the Gold Coast!'

'And I'm having one now you're leaving for Zululand.'

'Do you want it?'

'Of course I want it.'

He stared at her, bewildered by the intensity of her emotions. 'Then why are we worrying?' he asked.

'I'm not worrying about the damn baby,' she stormed. 'I'm worrying about you! Or at least about your children! Suppose you're killed? There'll be four of them without a father!'

6

By the time they started thinking of moving into Zululand once more, Augusta was already ungainly with the coming child and was finding the heat in Pietermaritzburg trying.

The shock of Isandhlwana was finally beginning to wear off and as the panic died so the grief died a little too. But Colby was rarely with her because the army had been demoralised and he spent most of his time moving about the country reorganising, reshuffling and recruiting. Before they could even consider crossing the Tugela again, they had to wait for the five infantry battalions and three cavalry regiments which were due to arrive from England. 'We've got more Imperial reinforcements than the number we started with,' he announced on one of his rare visits home. 'They've decided there should be two regiments of lancers because they're more effective in the long grass, and one of them's to be the 19th, so with luck I ought to be back with the regiment before long.'

Perspiring, uncomfortable, and faintly worried by the thought that the arrival of the regiment meant nothing to her, Augusta listened to her husband's thoughts unhappily. The idea that he would be leaving again before long depressed her, the dream she had had terrified her and always at the back of her mind was a heavy feeling that she would never understand what the regiment meant to those who belonged to it. Yet, when Colby's hopes of returning to it were dashed by a note from Chelmsford informing him that, like Wood, Buller and a few others, he was too experienced to be wasted on regimental duties, she rushed to console him, trying desperately to make him feel it mattered to her when actually she had been praying that he'd remain on the staff and not sent forward to the fighting.

'Perhaps it's only for a time,' she said, clinging to him on the stoep as he prepared to leave.

It seemed most unlikely. 'You'll be in command of the North Cape Horse,' Chelmsford told him when he reported, 'and will join a new column assembling at Potgeiter's Drift. You'll be second in command to George Morrow.'

The name dropped into the conversation with the sullenness of a signal gun, and Chelmsford's expression changed as he saw Colby's frown. 'He did well in Burma,' he pointed out. 'He's been sent out at the request of General Wolseley, who also asked that you should be available to assist him with your knowledge of Zulu methods.'

'I'd prefer to be with Wood, sir,' Colby said stiffly.

'Doubtless you would,' Chelmsford said dryly. 'But "England's Only General" has made the request and it would be difficult to ignore it.'

'Can't I persuade – ?'

'No, sir, you can't!' Chelmsford snapped. 'I already have too much on my mind. Pearson has to be rescued from Eshowe, Wood's still far from safe, and Wolseley's itching to get out here to snatch any kudos that's going.' Chelmsford sounded bitter, and concluded his instructions unsmilingly. 'You'll join Morrow's column at the end of the week.'

As Colby rode north, every man of his party leading a spare horse for Wood's hard-pressed men, he was in a sour mood. England's Only General would have done better, he thought, to keep his nose out of Colby's business. Wolseley's damned Ring was in danger of taking over the army.

Wood was pleased to receive his remounts but was curiously unforthcoming about the activities of the column further north, as if he, too, had had occasion to doubt Morrow's ability. Potgeiter's Drift was heavy with the acrid odour of horses when Colby arrived and he didn't like the look of it from the start. There was a shortage of outposts and Morrow seemed to think they had nothing to fear from the Zulus. He greeted Colby cheerfully, clearly with no thought in his mind that he had ever let him down.

'I wanted Buller,' he said. 'But Wood insists on hanging on to him, so I asked for you.'

Colby said nothing. It was nice, he thought, to be informed he was second-best.

Morrow was friendly enough but full of sage and patronising comments which sounded strange from a man who had just arrived. He clearly didn't like Irregulars.

'We have to pull this column together,' he said. 'They're nothing but rank amateurs. Look at this wretched site they chose. The drainage's abysmal and the ground's fouled already. Nothing on earth seems to make these wretched Kaffirs and Boers use latrines.'

His head was full of plans and he spoke quickly, his hand running over his maps. 'I intend to smite the Zulus,' he went on. 'Hip and thigh. Pearson's still high and dry at Eshowe, but Wood wants to leave Kambula and I'm intrigued by the idea of getting some of the semi-autonomous chiefs to defect to us. I think we might do it with the right men. I have a Boer called Deyer who hopes to win them round and there's a chief called Mbini whose people are at a place called Tshethoslane whom he hopes to see. I want you to see he gets safely back.'

'When does he go?'

'Oh, he's gone,' Morrow said cheerfully. 'Two days ago. You'd better be off.'

Colby vanished to his command in a fuming temper. Morrow seemed to think going out to meet the Zulus required no more preparation than going out to meet a girl in Hyde Park.

The North Cape Horse and Burger, the Boer who was second-in-command, were pleased to see him back, clearly happy to have a strong figure in control, though Ackroyd's face was graver than normal.

'You'll never guess 'oo 'e's got on 'is staff?' he said.

'Not Aubrey Cosgro?'

'And very much in favour, too, sir,' Ackroyd said.

'Where is he now?'

'He went out with half a dozen men with messages for

this Deyer feller. They're expecting to bring Mbini in.'

'Well, I've news for you, Tyas,' Colby said with grim amusement. '*We're* going out to escort them.'

Morrow was in a pompous mood as he gave Colby his orders. 'I want to destroy these people,' he said sternly. 'They're nothing but gadflies bothering us. I've heard Wood's been joined by Buller now, so that ought to keep the tribes down there busy, and I've also heard the Transvaal Boers are gathering on the High Veldt. We have nothing to fear, therefore, and I'll be following you with the rest of the column just in case Mbini doesn't come in. If Deyer isn't successful it'll be up to us to see he puts his words more forcefully.'

Riding out from Potgeiter's Drift, late in the afternoon, Colby felt he'd been in the saddle forever, most of the time soaked by rain.

The grass was growing fast on the bare plains and was already tall enough to conceal war parties of Zulus so that it was a nervous business moving out into the blue. The Natalians were in no doubts about what would happen if they relaxed their vigilance, however, and for safety, Colby doubled his sentries and placed a ring of outposts well outside the camp at night.

On the third day, they spotted black figures in the distance and, as they rode forward, hoping to intercept them, a whole cloud of warriors rose from the long grass. They were clearly a scouting party and, while they did no damage and bolted with the loss of one man shot, Colby was doubly alert. The following morning he saw smoke in the distance and soon afterwards a group of horsemen galloping towards them. They were coming at a pace that suggested panic, their excited horses almost out of control.

'Cosgro!' Colby bellowed. 'What in the name of Jesus Christ and all His pink angels is going on?'

Aubrey Cosgro struggled with his straining horse, holding it with difficulty as it wheeled and circled.

'Get hold of that damned animal!' Colby roared. 'What do you think you are, a flat-footed bloody infantryman?'

Cosgro's face was white and strained. He pointed back-wards, gasping.

'The whole Zulu impi's back there,' he said.

'To hell with the Zulu impi! Where's Deyer?'

We were too late! They'd already got him. That's what the smoke is. They're burning his waggons.'

'Didn't you make any attempt to rescue him?'

'There was no chance! It had started before we arrived. I lost three men as it was. I'd better go on and inform Morrow!'

'Contain yourself, dammit!' Colby's voice rose again. 'I want to know where the buggers are.'

'They're on Tshethoslane.' Cosgro gained control of himself and pointed to a hill rising from the flat veldt in a blue flat-topped peak. 'I'd better go on.'

Colby stared at him for a moment then waved him away in disgust. Cosgro didn't need any telling, but set spurs to his horse and disappeared with his escort behind them.

There was no sense in trying to find what was left of Deyer's party in the fading twilight, so Colby turned his column towards a small hill called Umbogitwini to his left. Heights meant safety, and up there, he could defend himself until Morrow arrived, and he wouldn't miss the first signs of the Zulu impi.

At first light, still shivering and trying to bring life back to his cramped and frozen limbs, he stared over the lightening plain. The veldt was changing from violet to apricot and would soon become a mass of blues and greens and duns as the light grew stronger. He could see little patches of monkey thorn and a few trees but no sign of the Zulus. The column of smoke was still rising in the distance, but the plain seemed empty. Then he saw a cloud of birds – guinea fowl he supposed – rise from the grass, and then a flicker of white like sunshine on a stream. It indicated buck running and he knew it meant the presence of Zulus.

Calling for his horse, he told Ackroyd to collect fifty men and, leaving the camp in the command of Burger, began to head towards the smoke. As they drew nearer, with scouts out in front, behind and on each flank, watching the grass for Zulu war parties, he saw a group of vultures flap awkwardly into the sky. A few more lolloped off out of sight, too gorged to fly.

There were five waggons close to a donga, all charred and burning. Deyer had made an effort to laager, but he had been overwhelmed. There was no sign of the Zulus beyond an abandoned shield and one or two assegais, and Deyer lay on his back alongside one of the waggons. He was naked, his body slit from groin to chest. Another man leaned against an anthill, also naked, his belly ripped open and swarming with ants, a spear through his body under his arm. He was skewered like a joint of meat and Colby thought immediately of Augusta's dream.

His insides twisted with nausea, he slipped his foot from the stirrup and slid to the ground belly-to in cavalry style. The waggons had been looted and an empty gin bottle lay by one of the wheels. Clothing was scattered about and there were pools of blood everywhere. Deyer's party seemed to have been massacred without a single survivor.

Collecting the bodies, they dug a hole and tumbled them in. The vultures had been at them and the sun had completed the destruction. It was an unpleasant and difficult job and Colby kept a mounted party well strung out and circling the camp in case the Zulus had not all disappeared.

They were on edge and nervous as they began to move slowly back to Umbogitwini. As they reached the hill, a horseman appeared, trailing a cloud of dust.

'The column's coming,' he yelled. 'You can see it from up there!'

Morrow's face was grim as he appeared. Cosgro was with him, white-faced and nervous-looking but clearly a great deal happier with the full strength of the column round him.

'I've just buried Deyer,' Colby said.

Morrow's mouth tightened. 'I think you must have been a little late in reaching him, don't you?' he said.

Colby's jaw set. It was Ashanti all over again, with Morrow trying to shuffle off responsibility by shoving the blame on somebody else.

'Where are the Zulus now?' Morrow demanded.

'They're on Tshethoslane. Two thousand of them, at least.'

Morrow laughed. 'There can't be that many. They couldn't get that many on top. I'm going to remove them.'

'The sides of Tshethoslane are almost unscaleable,' Colby warned.

Morrow gave his narrow little smile. 'Cosgro reconnoitred the place three days ago,' he said. 'Before you arrived. We marked two routes to the top. The eastern end lifts to a plateau where the Zulus keep cattle under a few herdsmen.'

'I suspect there are more than a few herdsmen,' Colby said.

Morrow dismissed the warning as if it came from someone nervous and inexperienced. 'Very well,' he said. 'Then we'll make it a two-pronged attack. You'll take your people up by the eastern route after dark and chase them down in the morning as soon as it's light enough to see. I'll be waiting at the western end. Cosgro will show you the way.'

He seemed to be assuming a great deal. 'What about the grassland to the east?' Colby asked. 'How do we know there aren't more Zulus there?'

'It's been reconnoitred,' Morrow said irritatedly. 'Cosgro covered it.'

'Suppose we fail to gain the summit unopposed?'

'You have weapons. Any more questions?'

Morrow's icy contempt made Colby boil with fury. The bloody half-wit persisted in treating the business as if it were an afternoon ride from Aldershot.

'I feel I must protest, sir,' he growled. 'It seems to me we shall be in danger of being caught on the hill. I feel it could be a highly dangerous situation.'

'It's not the business of a second-in-command to question his superior's orders.' Morrow's eyes glittered. 'I will note your protest, nevertheless. It will go in my report and we'll leave Lord Chelmsford to decide who's right. For the moment, sir, do as you're told. You'll take the Boers and one of the rocket tubes, the Natal Horse, the Mixed Irregulars and the Natal Kaffir Irregulars. It should be enough to drive them off. After that, *I'll* deal with them.'

As the column camped in the shadow of Umbogitwini, Colby noticed that Morrow failed to place look-outs on the slopes. On his own responsibility, he sent men to the top and, as an extra precaution, placed sentries wide of his encampment. There was no question of informing Morrow of what had been done. He was sulking at the questioning of his orders and was not available.

During the night there was the sort of downpour that changed the dongas from dustpans to swirling rivers and the camp was awake early next morning, damp and shivering with cold. As they moved out, Colby separated his command into four troops and they rode in column of half-sections. There were around four hundred men but, apart from his own North Cape Horse, Colby had grave doubts about their ability. Morrow's column wasn't the same as Wood's.

They stopped in the early afternoon to rest the animals and eat and soon afterwards were skirting the slopes of Tshethoselane – known to everybody by this time as Shithouse Lane. Smoke was rising from the top but, though scattered musket fire was directed at them, there was no other sign of life.

A deserted kraal was torn down to make fires to boil their coffee and, distrusting Morrow's information, Colby allowed his men time to eat, then, as soon as it was dark, ordered the camp to be moved and the fires to be built up and left blazing. Cosgro arrived soon afterwards – with a strong escort, Colby noticed, and in a clear state of funk. He brought Morrow's final orders.

'They've changed,' he announced. 'He's decided to circle the plain and wait at the bottom, after all, to ambush them as they run from your trap.'

'A fine time to tell me all this,' Colby growled. 'And they won't wait to be trapped. They don't use horses. They can get down slopes we can't get down.'

'The colonel also suggested we should leave our mounts with horse-holders and go up on foot.'

Colby leaned from the saddle closer to Cosgro. 'Would you?' he asked.

Cosgro looked nervous. 'I'd prefer to have a horse,' he said.

Colby grinned. 'After Isandhlwana,' he said, 'so would I.'

As the moon vanished they started up the slopes. Cosgro looked unhappy and Colby took a delight in watching him. Morrow had thought up a shocker for them that would hardly be to Cosgro's fastidious tastes.

As the path grew steeper, they dismounted and began to lead the horses and there was a lot of muttering behind as the animals slipped and struggled, and strings of Afrikaner curses as the route petered out into a narrow trail skirting the edge of a sheer drop, much of it washed away by the previous night's rainwater streaming from the plateau.

Burger appeared alongside Colby, almost spitting with rage. 'Three horses have gone over the side,' he snarled. 'Who chose this verdomde route?'

As they reached the summit, sporadic firing broke out and several men were hit and one of them killed. The plateau proved to be more of a pasturage than they'd been led to expect, with thick bushes that blocked the view across the plain, and, sending Ackroyd ahead with three Transvaalers to reconnoitre, Colby was startled as they came hurrying back to announce that the plateau was full of Zulus.

'It can't be!' Cosgro bleated.

'It *is*,' Ackroyd said with grim satisfaction. 'What's more, as far as I can see, the buggers are already slipping down the slope and getting round be'ind us.'

'They can't harm us much if we keep together,' Colby said. 'Let's have the Cape Horse dismounted along the ridge and the Irregulars forward to watch the Zulus. They'll probably bolt when they realise Morrow's waiting for them.'

For more than an hour they waited for signs of Morrow's arrival below and, when nothing happened, Colby decided to move towards the western edge of the plateau to cover the route down. He had gone only a few yards in the darkness when a burst of firing behind him made him whip round in the saddle, and a message came forward that Zulus were in contact with the tail of the column.

The light was increasing as he started back, but almost at once he heard yelling and was surrounded by running men. 'They're all round us,' someone shouted in his face through the darkness. 'Hundreds of 'em!'

The firing behind them had increased and there seemed to be more coming from the plain; Morrow had either found the Zulus or the Zulus had found Morrow.

Moving among the panicking men, Colby lashed out with fists and boots and riding crop until they stopped yelling and settled back to firing on the sniping Zulus who were now edging up the path they'd used. Then, as the light increased further, beyond the puffs of smoke that marked where they were, he saw the plain come into view. About three miles away several columns of Zulus were heading towards them and, snatching up his glasses, he could see yelling black faces, assegais beating against shields, and feathers blowing in the speed of their advance. The situation had changed in a second. There were enough warriors in the plain to overwhelm them and anybody caught on Tshethoslane was going to be trapped.

The columns were already opening out into the Zulu battle formation of a head with horns, the tips spreading out to flank the kopje. The massed warriors, their black skins glistening, their red and white shields flickering in the increasing light, had moved to north and south of the hill and there would clearly be no escape for anyone unless they moved fast. Then, down on the plain, he saw Morrow's troops in confusion among the scrub. He had foolishly broken up his column and his men were scattered in groups about the bush, the most distant of them already pounding westwards in terror before the advancing Zulus.

'God damn Morrow,' he snarled. 'He's humbugged me again!'

*   *   *

The plateau terminated at the western end in a steep narrow path, muddy and dangerous after the rain. It descended in a series of switchback drops to the plain and was flanked by enormous rocks that lay in a ragged fringe choked by shrubs and vines. Everywhere else, the sides of the hill fell away in sheer precipices.

'Is this what you call a route down?' Colby snapped at Cosgro. 'We're riding horses, not mountain goats!' He called Burger, his second-in-command to him. There was nothing they could expect from Morrow. Having got them into a terrifying situation, he was in no position to help.

'Let's have the Kaffirs away,' he said. 'They have no horses and can make their own way down.' Swinging round to Ackroyd, he jerked a hand to the west. 'You go with 'em, Tyas!'

'I'm stayin' with you,' Ackroyd insisted.

'I'm damned if you are! There are women and children in Pietermaritzburg who'll need you if anything happens to me.'

Ackroyd gazed at him for a second then he turned to the edge of the plateau. Without hesitating, he led his horse over and began the terrifying descent of the muddy path.

As the Kaffirs moved off the western rim, the Cape Horse began to pull back, still in good order. Mounting their horses, they began to ride across the top of the kopje towards the path. But, though they held their formation, the ill-trained units from Morrow's column were already drifting after them, firing as they went at the Zulus who were sniping from behind the rocks. Reaching for his horse as the last of his men hurried past, Colby found himself surrounded by black figures. As they appeared in front of him, he fired at them and saw one of them fall, but not before a razor-sharp assegai had opened his arm. As he cantered towards the western lip of the plateau, more Zulus came pouring over the edge in a disorganised bunch, and digging in his spurs, he gave the horse its head and headed for a gap in their line.

The shooting had broken the Kaffir contingent into a disorganised mob and they were sliding down the slippery path to the plain and scattering in all directions. The left horn of the Zulu impi was already almost round the hill and warriors were appearing from the folds and crevices of the ground to attack, while those who had circled the upper plateau were filtering down the baboon trails and working their way along the slopes to join in the butchery.

With the entire command packed into the end of the plateau, intermingled with bellowing Zulu cattle, it was becoming impossible to move. The frightened Kaffirs prevented an orderly retreat, but braver men were setting their horses at the path and going down in ones and twos. As he reached the edge, Colby saw a horse slip and roll over the edge, carrying three others and their riders with it.

A descent with horses seemed impossible, yet without a horse they were going to certain death on the plain, and more men urged their mounts at the slope, driven on by constant showers of bullets. Turning to form a rearguard, Colby was knocked flying by a group of bellowing terrified cattle and rolled over the edge of the plateau to a small ridge below. Bruised and dazed, he scrambled to his feet to see Cosgro pushing his way through the press of men. He was using his fists to fight his way clear and Colby turned from the line he was forming to hold back the Zulus, to knock him flying with a tremendous clout at the side of the head.

'Stand still and face up the slope!' he roared.

'It's too late!' Cosgro yelled.

'Where's your bloody horse?'

Cosgros face was strained as he pointed.

'You'd better get it!' Colby snapped. 'Unless you can run faster than the Zulus. Nobody's going to get away without one.'

Cosgro turned away, but, after two or three steps, Colby saw him swing aside and vanish into the press of men again. Then, noticing a small party of the rearguard trapped against a pile of rocks, he gathered a few men about him and led a rush up the slope to enable them to break free. Another stand held the Zulus for a few more vital minutes, then they swept forward again, stabbing and

314

slashing at the horses, and the fight began to disintegrate into a rout as men and animals slithered down the path, dislodging dirt and boulders as they went. Then, as the carcass of a horse rolled down, sweeping aside everything in its path, the Zulus swept after it and the rearguard melted away.

The impi on the plain had swept round the kopje now and as the last of his men broke free, Colby looked around to see if there were any more. He had managed to get away most of his command, though isolated men were still picking their way down and he stormed backwards and forwards across the slope, a revolver in one hand, a sabre in the other, to allow them to reach the grassland. Most of the Boers were already moving away but there were still a few struggling to find mounts. More horses than men had been lost and a few of the riders had swept up dismounted soldiers behind them.

His own horse lost as he had been knocked down the slope, Colby grabbed a big grey as it came past, but it had been wounded in the side and he was just wondering how long it would stay on its feet when rocks, dislodged by the Zulus, came rolling down and he was swept aside by a rush of men running to escape them and rolled the rest of the way down to the plain. As he scrambled to his feet, he saw the grey above him on its back and thrashing about in a crevice.

As a riderless horse came past, he swung to the saddle. Running men were being stabbed and he heard their yells of fear as they tried to hide in the grass. Among them was Cosgro, and Burger stopped to pick him up. Cosgro was limping and the Afrikaner dismounted to help him, but before he could swing up behind, Cosgro kicked at the horse's flanks and it leapt away, sending Burger sprawling.

Spurring his horse, Colby raced across the front of the Zulu line under a shower of assegais. The Afrikaner had scrambled to his feet and was facing them, working the bolt of his rifle, his face bleak.

'Get up! Get aboard!' Colby yelled.

'By Christ, man!' Burger yelled as he swung up behind

Colby. 'If I ever meet that verdomde skellum – !'

As they galloped away, another riderless horse crossed their path. Turning over the one he was riding to the Boer and pushing up a running man behind him, Colby began to round up more men and horses and send them westwards, riding double towards Umbogitwini. Then, livid with rage, he turned to look for Morrow. But he could see nothing and the crackle of musketry in the distance began to grow weaker and finally died altogether.

Most of his men were safely away when he set off after them, riding slowly because his horse was limping badly and the saddle was slipping. Dismounting, he carefully straightened it and tightened the girth. The animal was clearly in pain, its stride hesitant, but it was enough to dodge the groups of warriors dotting the plain and, collecting a few Kaffir Irregulars and men on limping horses, he organised them into a unit able to defend itself. As he saw the base camp appear in front, a horseman caught up with him from behind with the news that Morrow was dead.

As they stumbled in, it occurred to Colby that he had ridden forty miles or more every day for the last week and hadn't slept or laid down for forty-eight hours. Reaching the first of the waggons, the stumbling horse he rode crashed to the ground, blowing bloody froth from its nostrils. Someone shot it for him and he staggered the rest of the way stiff-legged to collect more men and horses before setting out again to find what was left of Morrow's command.

As he returned a second time, Ackroyd was waiting for him. He wore a bandage round his head but he managed a shaky grin.

'Where's Cosgro?' Colby snarled.

'Gone off to Chelmsford to let 'im know what 'appened?' Ackroyd said.

'Who sent him?'

Ackroyd pulled a face. 'I think 'e sent 'isself, sir.'

The disaster was complete. Morrow and most of his command had been lost. From Colby's half-column alone seven officers and fifty-one men had been killed and several others wounded. The Kaffirs had been wiped out, the rocket tube and its carriage lost, the Natal Irregulars decimated and the North Cape Horse crippled.

The night was cold and quiet. Most of them were hungry and cold and many had lost all their belongings. A few horses and a few unexpected survivors stumbled in. No one was in any doubt who was to blame, and the battered column was mutinous, the Colonials swearing they'd never be commanded again by an Imperial officer.

Sitting gloomily in his tent, staring at the map, wondering in a depressed mood whether to stay where he was or head rearwards, Colby's mind was made up for him when a rider appeared, bringing a message from Brosy la Dell.

'*Colonel thrown from horse. Leg broken. You are senior officer. Goff's Gamecocks need a Goff to take command once more.*'

He drew a deep breath of satisfaction. It was every soldier's ambition to command his own regiment and the message left him in no doubt about what to do. There was no one capable of taking command of what was left of Morrow's column if he disappeared and the only sensible thing to do was take it back to Potgeiter's Drift and turn it over to Wood.

As he rose to give the orders that would get it under way, Ackroyd appeared. His face was grim.

'Now what?'

'One of Deyer's men came in, sir.'

Colby whirled. 'What the hell do you mean? Deyer's men were all butchered.'

'Not this one, sir. 'E's got a slit in his leg as long as your arm but 'e managed to dive into the donga and get away. 'E was out there for three days. 'E saw the fight at Shithouse Lane and came in on a riderless horse 'e caught.'

Colby was frowning. 'How the hell – ?' he began. Then he stopped. 'Cosgro said they were all dead.'

'Yes, sir. But this chap says they were all alive and fighting when 'e bolted. Three of his men had dismounted and he didn't even stop to give 'em orders. 'E 'opped it as soon as the Zulus appeared.'

Colby glared at Ackroyd with red-rimmed eyes. 'You'd

better be sure of what you're saying, Tyas,' he snarled.

Ackroyd pulled a face. 'I know what I'm saying, sir. I know what it means, too. 'E was shoutin' it around the camp, so I put 'im under a guard so nobody could talk to 'im. I thought you'd want to see 'im first.'

7

The 19th Lancers were in poor shape when Colby took over at Greytown. After a month below decks in the transports, the horses were as thin as whippets. They were refusing to touch the grass, while the two hundred pounds of man and accoutrements plus saddle and equipment they were being asked to carry was proving too much for them. They had staring coats and a tucked-up look, and could cover only ten miles in twenty-four hours, with a rest every third day and ASC detachments to carry fodder. The men, unused to field conditions, were in an angry mood: Despite the edict issued by Chelmsford against pipe clay, Canning had tried to keep them up to peacetime standards and they were finding life difficult in the heat.

'We'll wean the horses to local grazing,' Colby decided at once as he and Brosy la Dell sat with the adjutant and the squadron officers in the little office that had been set up in the back room of the only hotel Greytown could boast. 'And we'll cut equipment to the bone. From now on, officers will be limited to forty pounds packed in a single valise. They will abandon their hammocks, washstands and india-rubber mattresses.'

'They're not going to like it,' Brosy murmured.

'Then they'll have to learn to lump it,' Colby snapped. 'The Zulus move fast and we have to do the same. There've already been too many disasters and it seems to me that there's something wrong with the army. It needs to pull its socks up and realise it exists for fighting, not going on picnics.'

'Halts,' he continued. 'The habit of dismounting to rest

the horses will be constantly practised. Whenever there's time to justify the "Sit easy", there's time to dismount. When reforming ranks after remounting, the horses will stand square. In action there will be complete control at all times otherwise we'll arrive where we're going in small groups, and then there'll be no more impact than of a single troop arriving in good order. Our safest bet is the weight of the horses and the Zulus are quick to take advantage of loose riders.'

He glanced at the notes he'd made. 'On the march: laagering and entrenching will always be undertaken. The men won't like that, because British cavalry's always taken the view that it's above such mundane things. In America they learned to look after themselves and not just sit in their saddles waiting for someone else to do it for 'em. There'll be a stand-to at dusk and two hours before dawn when we operate on our own; otherwise, according to what Lord Chelmsford orders. I expect there to be a lot of alarms and excursions but we'll learn to deal with 'em.'

'Officers' mess?' the adjutant asked.

'There won't be one. Officers will mess by companies and I expect they'll soon learn to live off chunks of stringy slaughter beef like everybody else. It's better simmered than parboiled, incidentally. They'll breakfast off the remains of their suppers. They won't like that either, but it'll do them no harm. There'll be no hard liquor for the men.'

'And the officers?' the adjutant asked.

'God help anybody I find with it when his men can't have it. Any man found drunk will be in trouble, and so will his officer. A sharp eye will also be kept on equipment. Otherwise it'll disappear. The Kaffirs run off horses and transport after dark if they get a chance. Even Lord Chelmsford lost his horse and found it in the camp of a mounted volunteer unit. We shall not lose *our* horses. One last thing: this is a bad country for disease. We shall take the greatest care with sanitation. Regimental police will make sure that any Kaffirs we employ will not perform their ablutions within the camp. Horse lines will be moved regularly. Manure will be buried. Latrine pits will be regularly filled and changed. And when we camp alongside a river, water will not be drawn downstream of our own or anybody else's horse lines.'

As they rose the officers disappeared in a thoughtful silence. At the door Brosy turned and smiled his lazy, good-natured smile.

'I think it's going to be hell,' he said.

Within a week orders came to join the main column at Landman's Drift and units began to move up to the Buffalo River from all over Northern Natal.

Chelmsford's new regiments, fresh from England, were finding South Africa hard going. Most of them had been scraped up from the depots and were largely new recruits, weighed down with needless impedimenta. Though they were carried to Pietermaritzburg by train, their first marches were almost too much for them, and the precautions attending the nightly laagering were backbreaking and seemingly endless.

With them had come a horde of newspapermen and foreign observers, who had finally noticed that the sputtering native war in South Africa was bigger than they'd thought and had arrived to see what was happening. Almost the first of them Colby met was von Hartmann.

'You following me about?' he snapped.

'No.' Von Hartmann was cheerful and friendly. 'I'm following *war* about. It's my job. I think you have quite a problem here.'

'It'll be sorted out,' Colby growled.

'Oh, I've no doubt,' the Prussian said condescendingly. 'In time. Of course, you have some splendid men here. The Boers, for instance. They would make excellent German allies.'

With the newspapermen and observers came Napoleon Eugène Louis Jean Joseph Bonaparte, the son of Napoleon III and the Prince Imperial of France, whom Colby had last seen in Metz as a small frightened boy with his sick father as they had taken their leave of the Army of the

Rhine. He was now almost more British than the British themselves, though he was noticeably cool to von Hartmann, and his views on Waterloo conflicted with the British version. He had opted for the artillery and, bored and impulsive, had insisted on joining the British reinforcements.

When they reached Helpmakaar a few of the sick who had been left behind in Pietermaritzburg caught up with them. With them was Cosgro, bumptious and self-satisfied.

'What are you doing here?' Colby snapped.

Cosgro gestured. 'Morrow's column was disbanded,' he said. 'I've been returned to the regiment.'

Colby stared hostilely at him. He was sick of the Cosgros and he was determined this time to have done with the lot of them. 'Well, I don't want you,' he said. 'Get out of my sight!'

As Brosy's jaw dropped and Cosgro flushed, Colby went on. 'I don't want you with me because I couldn't trust you as far as I could throw you. I saw you at Tshethoselane and I know what happened when Deyer's column was attacked. I think the best thing you can do is resign your commission before you're cashiered.'

Cosgro's face went white. 'You wouldn't dare!'

'I most certainly would dare,' Colby said coldly. 'Lord Chelmsford already has a report of what happened at Tshethoselane and he will support me. When Moriarity was overwhelmed at Myers' Drift, Harward, who was in charge at the other side of the river, left his command to a sergeant and rode for help. *He* was court martialled.'

'And acquitted,' Cosgro pointed out triumphantly.

'The proceedings have gone to Sir Garnet Wolseley for review. He won't reverse the verdict, but I know what he'll say about it: "No officer with a party of soldiers engaged against the enemy should abandon them – *under any pretext whatsoever*." That's what Wolseley will feel and he'll make sure it's read at the head of every regiment in the service. What Harward did, you did twice. There's no place for you in this regiment. I suspect even there's no place for you in

322

the army. You'd be wiser to go home. I'll give you five minutes to leave the camp.'

Cosgro left the camp that night and they heard later he had resigned his commission on the grounds of ill health and set off for Durban to pick up a ship.

It was obvious within twenty-four hours that the story had gone round the camp. Colby guessed that the sergeant clerk had been listening at the door, but he didn't consider that it mattered. Nevertheless, it left everyone wary and anxious not to get into trouble. Immediately, especially following the first punishments, there was a marked improvement in bearing, health and behaviour. The 19th began to look like a regiment on active service. The complaints from the officers never rose above a murmur and in no time at all they began to find they were better soldiers and proud to be able to do what other regiments could not do. Transport officers who said something couldn't be done were treated to a blistering tongue-lashing that made them change their minds at full speed. Quartermasters who were difficult received a searing dressing down. An unsavoury surgeon, an obstructive quartermaster and a stout and lazy officer from C Squadron were whisked away to other jobs or regiments, the loudest grumblers in the ranks were punished or promoted according to their characters, whiners were threatened, and soldiers who got into fights with men of other regiments were in trouble unless they managed to emerge the winners.

'Do you know,' Brosy said, his lazy smile puzzled, 'it works. We're all in step and cantering on the right rein – all bright-eyed and bushy-tailed again.'

The regiment was among the first to move over the new pontoon bridge into Zululand. There was a telegraph running back to Pietermaritzburg now and the orders that came on it were to move towards Rorke's Drift. The following day they were twelve miles into Zululand and passing the field of Isandhlwana.

Joined by other cavalry, a battery of guns, infantry and a force of mounted volunteers, the lancers moved through the wrecked camp, the nine-foot spears dipping and rising as they searched for corpses. Grain spilled from the looted waggons had sprouted to conceal the remains, but a few were identified by their clothes.

As the bodies were collected and placed in shallow graves, dismounted men moved through the camp looking for personal belongings or trinkets the Zulus had missed. Most of them kept one eye over their shoulder because what had happened was still a nightmare and they were all in terror of it happening again. As evening came, they drove away those of the waggons that would still move with led horses between the shafts. Reaching the river, still oppressed by the tragedy, they were cheered by the arrival of mail from home.

There was a whole batch of letters from Augusta. She was uncomfortable, lonely and unhappy and there was such a sense of desperation about them Colby could think of nothing else but her misery. He was just trying to force her image from his mind when news came in that some fool had managed to get the Prince Imperial stabbed to death by a party of Zulus, and that the government at home, badgered incessantly about the slow progress of the war, had finally sent out their 'only general.' Wolseley, with a clique of Ringers, was on his way, and it suddenly seemed important that the war should be finished before he could arrive and claim credit for it.

It was quite clear that Chelmsford had no wish to be superseded, and the Prince Imperial's body was no sooner despatched for home than the army began to move across a mimosa-covered slope cut by ravines, to drop into a deep valley through which a river meandered. Columns of smoke filled the air and it didn't surprise Colby to bump into Buller watching his men fighting dismounted, from the top of a large antheap.

'Hello, Coll,' he said cheerfully, his big frame tense. 'I hope you've taught those dressed-up dummies of yours how we fight out here.'

As he spoke, a crackling fire started and the Zulus ahead disappeared into the bush. Immediately, return fire came from among bunches of aloes, then as a flanking volley came from a mealie patch, Buller's men began to fall back and a vast impi began to swarm down the slopes and through the brush to the river.

Splashing across the stream as the volunteers retired, it was obvious that the officer commanding the cavalry was itching to have a go. The 1st Dragoon Guards moved right and left and the 17th Lancers trotted backwards and forwards through the mealies looking for someone to spear, while the 19th moved up in support. But it was bad country for cavalry and, as the Zulus vanished to cover, a troop of the 17th was dismounted to return the fire. They were too close, however, and an officer and several men fell. As they extricated themselves with the bodies of the dead and wounded across the saddles of led horses, Colby galloped the 19th across their rear to a line of aloes.

'Dismount! Tell off your horseholders! Keep them moving! Don't bunch!'

As the Zulus swarmed down, they were stopped dead with a crashing volley. As the cavalry retired, the 19th were always between them and the rest of the force, and by the time they returned to the river there was a new feeling in the regiment that they had discovered how to fight. Their little action had been neat and well-executed and not a man had been lost or a horse hurt.

The following day the army was on the move again, the whole ungainly, unwieldly lot of them, almost a thousand waggons dragging through the muddy drifts, the vanguard waiting all the time for the rest to catch up. It was well-known now that Wolseley was on his way, and among those men who had been in Zululand from the beginning a curious loyalty had sprung up for the hard-pressed Chelmsford. The sincere hope was that the thing would be done with before Wolseley could interfere.

Pushing ahead determinedly, regiments and brigades leap-frogging over each other to keep up the pace, the army still moved only at a mere five or six miles a day. A month later, however, they could see Ulundi, the Zulus' capital, plainly visible across the White Umfalozi, with the Indian

Ocean glittering in the distance to the east. Three days later they were moving across a cactus-covered plain within striking distance of the royal kraal and, with news arriving that Wolseley was at Pietermaritzburg, everybody was praying that he'd fall off his horse or have a fit that would delay him just long enough for them to finish the job before he arrived.

Judging by the prisoners they took, the Zulu urge for war had subsided rapidly. Startled by the unexpected early victories of his impis, Cetzewayo was now trying to mediate. Messages had been received but they were vague and could give no guarantees, though one or two of the minor chiefs, clearly growing concerned, were coming in with their followers. At the end of the week, a message arrived to say that Ziwedi, a chief with a kraal near the river, wished to surrender but daren't because of the proximity of the main Zulu army, and the 19th were sent out to escort him in with his wives and children and all his tribe.

Establishing a small fort in a group of abandoned buildings on top of a hill which had once been a mission station, Colby left Brosy in command. The fort was within reach of the main army and could pass on signals by heliograph, but the expedition was risky and from time to time they saw groups of Zulus, some of them still wearing red coats taken from Isandhlwana or Myers' Drift.

Ziwedi's people were holed out in caves and it was after dark before they reached the area. As they bivouacked, the guides spread out and all through the night old men, women and children hurried in. At first light, news came that an impi was approaching and that stragglers were being speared.

As they returned to the fort, the exhausted children were riding behind troopers muttering darkly about 'bloody black vermin' but surreptitiously slipping them portions of their rations. Colby arrived with half a dozen clinging to his jacket. His own children had often ridden with him in the same way, and it made him think of Augusta.

As they drew nearer, a rider burst from the fort, lashing at his mount. 'Sir! They're trying to flash a message!'

Handing over his small passengers, Colby spurred

forward, Brosy was waiting for him, frowning.

'They've been trying to contact us all day,' he said. 'But there's too much cloud and we can't get the message.'

As the last of Ziwedi's people straggled in, followed by a line of lancers watching their rear, Colby was called to the heliograph once more.

'It's a private message, sir,' the sergeant pointed out. 'It's addressed to you and it says "Personal". It said "Mrs. Goff is –"'

'Is *what*?'

'Then the clouds came back again, sir,'

Furious, worried, aware of Augusta's uncertainties, Colby went to watch the Ziwedi's people arrive. The fittest were already pushing west towards the main army when the sun came out again and the sergeant at the heliograph shouted.

He was taking down the last of the message as Colby reached him and he handed over his slip of paper with a grin.

'"Mrs Goff is well and delivered of a son,"' he said. 'Congratulations, sir.'

Late in June, the army moved into the valley of the White Umfalozi – without tents or kits and with rations for only ten days. That there were Zulus about was obvious. Groups were seen from time to time and the watering parties heading for the river were constantly fired on.

Splashing through the stream, Colby led the 19th forward in an attempt to goad them into attacking, splitting up his men in the hope that they would draw the black hordes down on them. The game went on again the next day, this time with Buller leading the mounted force. On this occasion, however, the Zulus were waiting in the long grass and only the fact that Buller was an old hand and suspected a trap enabled him to extricate his force with few losses. That evening, they learned the army was to move on Ulundi the following day. As the orders went out, a messenger arrived from Wolseley instructing Chelmsford to retire and complaining about the way the campaign was being handled. There was a great deal of hilarity as the message was relayed through the camp.

The moon rose on the army sleeping in the open in a rising mist. It was cold and there was a continuous wailing and shouting from across the river. The Natal Kaffirs knew exactly what was going on and, as they announced that the men Buller had lost that morning had been turned over to the Zulu women, soldiers who had been chaffing a few moments before became silent, because they knew what it meant; with the battle impending, in every mind was the memory of Isandhlwana and the knowledge that even against savages things could go wrong.

The 19th supplied the outlying pickets, watching nervously through the hours of darkness and not returning to the camp until first light. The place had already come to life and a few of the Colonials were holding a prayer meeting to prepare themselves for the coming battle. As Colby hobbled stiffly among his men, von Hartmann offered him a hundred guineas there would be no battle.

As the cavalry formed up with the Frontier Light Horse, the leaden-hued lance-points catching the light, Colby waited in brooding immobility, tapping his saddle-bow with impatience and watched warily by his officers. Finally moving out across the drift to cover the crossing, they watched regiment after regiment splash through the water and labour up the slope on the other side, blocks of scarlet and blue topped with the white of their sun helmets. As they came together again, they formed a huge hollow square with the Gatlings and the guns in position at the corners.

'Keep your dressing.'

'Move back B Company.'

'*Mister* Hutchinson, will you, for God's sake, watch what you're doing!'

The shouts rang out in the still air as they took their places. The native contingent was placed in the centre, surrounded by waggons and carts laden with tools, medical supplies and ammunition. The cavalry rode ahead and on the flanks, pushing through the long grass to flush out any groups of Zulus that were in hiding. It was a large force, powerful and well-drilled, but they were all aware that if anything went wrong and a side of the square collapsed there were enough Zulus to overwhelm them. Company officers, their taut faces concealing their thoughts, moved along the lines, watching the dressing and keeping the lines closed up as the square moved forward. They needed nothing now but the Zulus.

As they edged ponderously across the Mahlabatini plain, the bandsmen were playing regimental marches. The plain was bare and the few kraals they passed were empty. Then a shout rang out and all eyes followed the pointing finger. In the distance they could see Zulus on the hills in groups that grew bigger all the time as they began to swarm down the slopes and vanish into the hollows. As they began to find the bodies of the men killed during Buller's near-ambush the previous day, over on the right a large kraal was burning, the smoke held low by the breeze and rolling among the mimosa and euphorbia trees. Gradually they edged nearer to Ulundi and began to climb a gentle slope. Then, as the mounted men scrambled out of the river-bed, they saw the plain ahead come to life.

A Zulu regiment had risen silently out of the grass and, one after the other, more appeared on either side, parting the tall grass to display their shields and plumes. More appeared on the heights and began to join them until the plain was ringed by groups of black figures.

Alongside Colby, Von Hartmann was watching through binoculars. 'There will be a battle after all,' he said. 'How many do you reckon there are?'

'Over ten thousand. Over fifteen even. Less than thirty. Say twenty.'

'Shall we prevail?'

Colby paused. Everybody at Isandhlwana had thought they would win. 'We'll prevail,' he said quietly. 'These aren't the Zulus of the early days. They've lost too many, and the old men aren't eager any longer.'

The square had been halted with the rear and sides turned outwards, ready for an attack from any quarter.

Every man was watching the Zulus who were moving forward slowly, the regiments marked by their distinctively-coloured shields. As they broke into a sprawling semi-circle running from east through north to west, cutting off the track to the river and forcing the mounted men back towards the square, another huge mass of warriors appeared behind the burning kraal on the right, waiting to close the circle when needed.

'Here they come!'

The black masses were moving forward more quickly now, one or two of the regiments breaking into a trot. Others joined them until the whole circle of black figures was approaching at a flat run. A humming had started, a low noise like a vast beehive, ominous and menacing, above it the rattle of spears on the cowhide shields and the swish of grass as thousands of warriors pushed through it.

'Load!'

The weapons clattered as every man checked his rifle. Buller's horsemen were falling back slowly, allowing the Zulus to come dangerously close before firing their carbines and wheeling to reload.

'What are those madmen up to?' von Hartmann asked.

'They're trying to goad them into a charge,' Colby said. 'Once they start, the whole lot'll come.'

There was a roar and a swish as a rocket battery on the corner of the square came into action. The rockets soared too high, trailing smoke, sparks and flame, and the crews adjusted screw settings, studied the wind a little and tried a new elevation. As the second salvo shot away, the Zulus paused, then there was a howl as they came forward in a rush.

As they surged forward, the mounted men wheeled and cantered for the square, always just ahead of the moving Zulus.

'Close ranks! Move up there! Shoulder to shoulder!'

'Fix bayonets!'

Steel glittered in the sunshine and, as the guns were brought forward, the horsemen found themselves riding along the front of the square.

'Open up, God damn you!' a furious officer yelled.

Nobody was willing to take chances, until Chelmsford appeared. The line was reformed quickly, nervously, with almost too much haste, because the Zulus were close now. Behind them in the carts, the ammunition boxes had opened. There was to be no repetition of Isandhlwana where men had run out of cartridges because they had not been opened in time. Drummer boys stood ready with helmets and haversacks ready for the first call. Behind them, quartermasters waited by the open boxes.

The Zulus had steadied, almost as if dressing their line. They were watched in silence. The shouted orders had died away. The sides of the square, four-deep, waited quietly, the men with their ammunition pouches open, jockeying a little to get a clear field of fire. Behind them, Colby watched Chelmsford calmly waiting on his horse. This time the thing had to come off to prove that his planning had not been wrong at Isandhlwana, and that the disaster had resulted from faulty handling by the men in command there.

Though the grass had been trampled flat for a hundred yards all round, beyond it the undergrowth still hid the bulk of the advancing Zulus. Then the artillery opened with a crash. Horses snatched at bridles in the hands of troopers, and one or two whinnied with fear. Puffs of dirty white smoke, splashed with red, appeared on the edge of the grass, jabbed at by the puzzled Zulus with their assegais. As they emerged, the orders rang out and the rifles came up.

'Fire!'

The crash of hundreds of rifles was cut across by the tearing sound of the Gatlings carving a bloody path through the massed black bodies. Regiment after regiment appeared but as the red-coated soldiers fired, the volleys crashing out one after the other in quick time, whole rows of Zulus went down. Waving plumes paused and sagged to the ground, the following waves trampling over the writhing bodies. But through the smoke more black figures appeared, eyes gleaming, mouths open, teeth like white cages.

'Himmelherrgott!' von Hartmann breathed. 'They don't lack courage!'

The steady rolling roar of firing surged louder. The Zulus couldn't reach nearer than thirty yards from the square, and lay in piles over which the following waves struggled to climb, only to crash in midstride themselves under the next volley. The square was full of smoke and echoing with the hammering of the firing. Native troops cowered in terror under the waggons, their officers trying to kick them to their feet. Some of the Volunteer horsemen were yelling encouragement and one or two were even standing on their saddles to see better or to add their shots to the battle. A few of the horsemen had been hit and wounded during Buller's retreat and, as the Zulus started firing from the grass, men in the line fell out and were carried by bandsmen to the dressing station where the regimental surgeons worked.

'Close up, there! Close up! Keep the line closed!'

One of the horses near Colby squealed in pain and started to plunge wildly.

'Slap cold water and a compress on the hole,' he heard the sergeant shout. 'Or shoot the poor bugger and put him out of his misery.'

Just in front of where they waited a large pit had been dug and the chaplain was reading a never-ending burial service as men were lifted from bloodstained stretchers and laid inside it. Chelmsford was moving slowly round the square, followed by his staff, stopping occasionally to encourage.

'Faster there, 13th, please! Mr Harding, take your Gatling to the opposite corner!'

As the weapon was pulled out, the officer's leg buckled under him, pumping blood. He was dragged aside and the gun clattered across the square. The impassive Buller, his big frame relaxed, sat motionless on his horse, watching, a cigarette in his mouth.

Nowhere had the square been broken or even reached, but now they saw the last reserve of the Zulu army waiting near the burning kraal rise to its feet. Led by a man on a horse, they formed a long line and at a shout surged forward. The guns blasted a gap in their line at once, bringing down the running warriors in screaming heaps. Only for a few moments more was the momentum sustained, and the Zulus seemed just about to break into the square when a final volley shattered the charge.

The last line of warriors crashed down almost at the feet of the redcoats and the wounded began to crawl back down the slopes, dragging themselves through the grass. One defiant man, his leg smashed by a bullet, raised his arm and the flung assegai struck a corporal in the square full in the chest. As he fell back, an officer shot the Zulu in the head. Desperate, frustrated warriors danced and yelled on the fringe of the grass, circling for an opening, but there seemed little spirit left now, as if they had all along sensed there was no hope of victory.

Chelmsford turned in the saddle to face the cavalry. Taking off his helmet, he waved in the direction of the retreating reserve.

'Now, I think,' he said. 'Go at them! 94th, 21st, move aside. Let the horsemen out.'

'Mount!'

There were the usual scufflings as unruly horses barged and shoved, and a four-year-old started a crabwise retreat from the end of the line, pursued by a sergeant swearing at the rider. As they moved forward, heads tossing, curb chains clinking, the infantry made a gap, and they moved out in columns of fours, with the mounted Volunteers behind them.

Passing round the square, the 17th cantered to the top of the slope. Moving the other way, Colby formed up the 19th above the donga. There was still a crackle of firing from the Zulus and a man fell from his saddle with a crash, then a horse thumped to the ground, lifted its head and let it fall back with a thud as it began to thrash with its forelegs. As its rider struggled free, two more men, hit by flying bullets, backed their horses out of line.

Colby turned in the saddle. 'Form troops! Form squadron! Walk – march!'

As they moved into line abreast, the trumpeter sounded the Trot. The fluttering red and green pennons caught the sun and the lines straightened.

'Extend!'

As they began to open out, the men began to bump up and down in the saddles. The 17th were already thundering into a charge as the 19th moved away from their own side of the square, and the firing died down as everybody stopped to watch. One of the 17th fell from his horse, hit by a spent bullet, and an officer reeled in the saddle, struck in the face. Moving aside to let the pounding horses pass, he dabbed at his features with a handkerchief before spurring after his men.

It was so easy, it was almost sickening. Without breaking formation, the cavalrymen crashed through the retreating Zulus, spitting the fleeing warriors on the points of the spears, then, with an outward flick of the wrist, clearing the point for it to swing up and forward again for the next victim. Then, just in front, an unexpected dip appeared and Colby roared for a halt. As the trumpet sounded, the forward movement stopped just in time. Several hundred warriors concealed in the grass rose, and as they poured in an erratic volley, Colby saw two men go down. The riderless mounts careered along the edge of the dip but the rest of the regiment was moving warily into the grass in a series of disconnected fights. The Zulus were standing their ground, grabbing at lances and stabbing at the horses' bellies, and by now, most of the riders had discarded their awkward nine-foot weapons and were using their sabres, slashing, cutting and thrusting at the running figures.

Moving ahead with his men, Colby saw a new line of rifles appear and saw the flash and smoke as they fired. Something struck him in the shoulder, almost wrenching him from the saddle, and the riding whip, which was all he was carrying, dropped from his hand. As he swayed, Cornet Lord Ellesmere thudded up to him.

'You all right, sir?'

'Yes, yes.'

Turning, Colby was about to call out to Brosy to take over when he saw his horse go down. As it crashed to the ground, Brosy dropped his sword and, as he scrambled to his feet, stooping to pick it up, a black figure rose from the grass alongside him, thrusting viciously with an assegai. The point entered Brosy's body under his outstretched arm and reappeared from his neck just below his jaw.

His eyes wide with horror and fear, Brosy swung round, looking for his assailant. Unable to help with his useless arm, Colby could only kick frantically at his horse's flanks, but young Ellesmere had launched himself forward at the same time and his sabre carved into the Zulu's neck at the very moment that the shoulder of Colby's horse caught him and sent him head over heels under Ellesmere's mount. As the animal pecked, recovered and swung round, its eyes wild, Ellesmere dragged on the reins.

Twisted in the saddle with his own wound, Colby saw that Brosy had sunk to his knees, his fingers fumbling weakly at the assegai protruding near his throat. As Ellesmere slipped to the ground, Colby drew rein alongside, and Ellesmere's head lifted, a look of agony on his face.

'Oh, God, sir,' he said, 'what can we do?'

8

Pietermaritzburg held its breath. News had arrived that the Zulus had finally been defeated.

Anxious about Colby, Augusta was among the crowd waiting outside Government House. The people around her had the same strained look on their faces she had seen after Isandhlwana, but news was at a premium and the guards had been doubled to prevent anyone invading the governor's residence.

There was nothing to learn and she returned to the rented house, aware of Annie Ackroyd watching her every expression and change of tone. Now that the war was over and they would be going home, she realised she had become strangely attached to the ugly little stone and corrugated-iron building. When they left it, no one would remember they had ever been there, and that fact more than any other indicated to her how true the army wives' saying was – that they were so often on the move home was nowhere. Somehow it helped her to understand the mystique surrounding the 19th that she had so often failed to grasp.

Two days later a grave blond man appeared outside the house on a lathered horse asking for her.

'Colonel Graf von Hartmann, Madame,' he introduced himself. 'I have just left your husband's side.'

He had ridden alone across country as soon as the battle had finished, bringing only a few personal letters for relatives.

'I came to inform you about your husband,' he said. 'I have known him a long time – ever since the war in your country, Madame. He is a man I highly respect and I have sad news for you. He was hurt by a stray bullet in the last moments of the battle. I felt you would wish to be prepared.'

As he disappeared, she stared after him, bewildered. Colby had never mentioned von Hartmann and she wondered for a moment if he were tormenting her with some outrageous lie. Then, as panic caught her, she turned and, crying for Annie Ackroyd, began to search out linen for use as bandages.

Some days later, in an agony of apprehension, she heard that the 19th were escorting a convoy of wounded to the Coast and she wondered if they had been chosen because Colby was incapable of commanding. But they could learn nothing beyond that Wolseley had finally reached the army and his favourites were taking over, only to find that things were much more difficult than they had expected. The old hands were all going home.

'Wood's been in the field for eight months,' she was informed, 'and he's on the verge of a nervous breakdown. Buller can barely walk for saddle sores. Pearson's sick. Colby Goff was brought down at Ulundi.'

Brought down! Did it indicate he had been mortally wounded? There seemed so much meaning behind those two simple words.

Von Hartmann reappeared and offered to ride to meet the approaching convoy to find out more for her. She was touched by his concern and his clear regard for her husband.

'I am a Prussian, Madame,' he told her. 'One day he and I may well find ourselves on the opposite sides of the battle lines, but there is always such a thing as honour.'

Two days later they heard the convoy was expected within a few hours, and late in the afternoon someone ran past to say they had seen lancers in the distance.

As they ran into the road, they saw the tall spears among the trees and then the waggons carrying the wounded, and as her terror rushed to her throat, choking her, she felt she was as near to fainting as she would ever be and had to grasp Annie's hand to steady the whirling world.

It had been a murderous journey. There had been a hundred miles of trackless country with the waggons, moving at a snail's pace, totally devoid of springs; and when the officer next to Colby, who had been shot through both thighs, started to bleed, they had had to stop to amputate one of his legs. Fortunately, Ackroyd had turned up, appearing in the 19th's lines and resisting all attempts to send him away.

'How bad is it?' Colby asked as he untied the bandages.

'Not so good, that's a fact.' Ackroyd managed a twisted grin. 'But not so bad either. What 'appened?'

Colby tried to tell him. The shock of Brosy's death remained. The agony on his face as he had been rushed to the surgeon, the startled realisation that he was already a dead man, had been clear in his eyes and in the strangled cry that had escaped his lips. There was nothing they could do, and when the assegai had been removed the blood that had gushed out had carried away his life. As he thought about it, Colby found tears prickling his eyes. Brosy had been alongside him all through his life. He had been to the same school and with him at Balaclava, had even brought him home from America. Why did it have to be kind, good-hearted Brosy, he wondered, and he remembered something von Hartmann had said at Mars-la-Tour – 'It is always the tallest poppies that are picked.'

Feeling miserably that he had failed his friend, he told himself again and again that death was a chance they all took and he couldn't have done more than he had. What in God's name will I tell Grace, he wondered.

Four days later, as they jolted south, the officer with the amputated leg died. They buried him at Landman's Drift and a surgeon who looked and smelled like a vet wrenched off the bandages from Colby's wound, cleaned it and strapped the arm to his chest. The prospect of another hundred miles in a waggon was more than he could bear.

'For God's sake, Tyas,' he said to Ackroyd. 'Find me some old nag that won't throw me and shove me in a saddle.'

Seated on an old horse that looked like a hat-rack and made a noise in its throat like a German band, and stiff as a tinker with brandy to kill the pain, he was at the head of his men as they appeared outside Pietermaritzburg. Von Hartmann had turned up again, concerned and behaving as if he were Moses and had seen the tablets on the mountain.

'I think I was wrong at Mars-la-Tour,' he said. 'Ulundi will justify the existence of cavalry for a few more years.'

He told Colby that Augusta had been informed of his wound and Colby couldn't make up his mind whether to be grateful or regard it as bloody interference. His shoulder was hurting and he was still depressed by Brosy's death. Try as he might, he couldn't push from his mind the image of him on his knees by the river, the shaft of the assegai sticking out under his arm, the long blade protruding from his neck, the agony and fear in his eyes with the knowledge of death, and the soundless scream that was coming from his lips.

As the 19th appeared, Augusta, numb with apprehension, kept moving from one foot to the other in her nervous agitation. Her marriage had long since passed through that state when her emotions were a confusion of despair, delight, obsession and adoration, and she had entered a calmer period when she asked nothing more of life than to have her husband alongside her and her children growing up around her.

Then suddenly she saw Ackroyd, dressed in the cord of the Cape Light Horse, cantering past, and both she and Annie screamed and started to wave frantically. As he slid from the saddle he was smiling, and Augusta's heart, which had been thudding inside her chest, calmed. Ackroyd smiling could mean only one thing.

'My husband, Tyas,' she managed.

''E's all right, Ma'am. Bit uncomfortable because 'e got 'it. You'll see 'im in a minute.'

She was aware of tears of relief in her eyes. 'What about all the others?'

Ackroyd's face changed. 'Lost one or two, Ma'am. Sergeant 'Arding, for one. You'll remember 'im. I doubt if you'll know the others. And – and –' he paused '– Mr la Dell, Ma'am.'

'What happened to him, Tyas?'

''E's dead, Ma'am.'

'Oh, no! Poor Grace! How?'

'Assegai, Ma'am.'

Then she knew that her dream had been broken. It hadn't been Colby at all, as she had expected, but Grace's Brosy.

As she moved back to the edge of the road, she saw the 19th appear beyond the trees, smudges of rifle-green and red. They looked shabbier than when she'd last seen them but were well in charge of themselves. Then she saw Colby. He was riding in front, accompanied by his trumpeter and his orderly. His right arm was strapped to his chest and he was riding a staid raw-boned horse that he wouldn't normally have been seen dead on, but despite everything he looked remarkably fit.

As he passed her, Colby saluted gravely, and he saw the other officers also acknowledge her: Radliffe. Johnson. Morby-Smith. Young Ellesmere – so brown now there was no sign of his acne. And, as he saw her hands go to her throat, he knew she had realised they were saluting her, not because she was the colonel's wife but because she was one of them.

All round him people were cheering and hats were tumbling in salute. Then he saw Augusta's face and shining eyes and saw that she was laughing, too – and crying and cheering all at the same time – and he had a feeling that at last she had realised why it was that old soldiers always came back whenever they could, wearing their medals, to be part of the regiment. The mystique had touched her as it had touched them, and for the first time she could see what lay behind the reverence for the regimental souvenirs; why the adoption and dedication of the regimental chapel in Ripon Cathedral was so important; why the faded colours that hung under the arches at York were embossed with names like Talavera, Salamanca, Vittoria, Waterloo and Bala-clava; why Trumpeter Sparks' instrument hung in a glass case in the hall of the officers' mess at the depot where everybody could see it.

The blunt, unclever British soldier, whether he were a private or a field marshal, lived, fought, married, begat children and finally retired under an extraordinary influence as powerful and binding as the medieval church. It wasn't the Queen they fought for. It wasn't the army even. It was the regiment.

There was no longer any question of where she belonged. She belonged with the regiment.

Wherever it was.

COTTON'S WAR

John Harris

If it hadn't been for the shopkeeper in Heraklion, Cotton might never have been involved . . .

In the spring of 1941 the Nazis were storming their way through Greece. The *Loukia* was crucial to the British cause and the Greek resistance – and her cargo even more so. When the *Loukia* is wrecked in enemy territory, the British gathered together a handful of 'volunteers' for a dangerous mission of retrieval: two RASC men, some sailors, one German-speaking airman and Mihale Andoni Cotonou – otherwise known as Corporal Cotton of the Marines.

A superb story of action and character, *Cotton's War* is one of John Harris's most exciting war novels.

£1·10

COVENANT WITH DEATH

John Harris

More than five hundred thousand men fell at the Battle of the Somme before the terrible conflict finally withered and died in the winter mud. Five hundred thousand men, and the Germans lost another five hundred thousand. A million men altogether. A dead generation. This is the story of one voluntary city battalion from its inception in 1914 to its destruction on 1 July 1916.

'True and terrible' *Observer*

'The blood and guts, the nightmare stink of cordite . . . appalling realism' *Daily Telegraph*

£1·95

ARMY OF SHADOWS

John Harris

France – Winter 1944. The long-awaited liberation is at hand.

The bombing mission had gone well. The crew of the Lancaster bomber began to relax. Then the Messerschmitt came out of the darkness, its guns blazing.

Of the nine-man crew only Neville and Urquhart survived, parachuting into the heart of occupied France. Now, for both of them, the testing time had begun: a time of peril as the fliers joined forces with the Army of Shadows – the men of the French Resistance – and entered a deadly game of cat and mouse with a ruthless and desperate enemy.

'John Harris writes about war as few men can. . . . With gathering speed, the story moves to a thundering climax – and a cracking good read it makes' *Daily Mail*

90p

THE YEAR OF THE FRENCH

Thomas Flanagan

In 1798 the French landed in County Mayo to lead the Irish rebels against the English. It was the year of the French.

Out of a half-forgotten, legendary episode in Irish history comes one of the most extraordinary novels of our time.

'A most impressive, important and timely novel' *Mary Renault*

'If this book doesn't get read and esteemed then there is something dreadfully wrong with our literary world' *C. P. Snow, Financial Times*

'Magnificent in its scope and comprehension' *Robert Fisk, The Times*

£1.95

THE GULAG RATS

K. N. Kostov

He was known as 'the colonel'. Once he had been an honoured hero, a beloved general – but then came Stalin's purges and he had been imprisoned, humiliated, stripped of all dignity. But that had been in the 1930s.

Now it is 1944, and he is needed again. Needed to lead a battalion of criminals, pimps, murderers, thieves and perverts. Needed to keep them together as they sweep over Russia's border, heading west, killing, burning, raping, ravaging – destroying everything that gets in their way. He is the proud, lonely officer known as 'the colonel', and they are the gulag rats.

£1.10

BESTSELLERS FROM ARROW

All these books are available from your bookshop or newsagent or you can order them direct. Just tick the titles you want and complete the form below.

THE GRAVE OF TRUTH	Evelyn Anthony	£1.25
BRUACH BLEND	Lillian Beckwith	95p
THE HISTORY MAN	Malcolm Bradbury	£1.25
A LITTLE ZIT ON THE SIDE	Jasper Carrott	£1.00
SOUTHERN CROSS	Terry Coleman	£1.75
DEATH OF A POLITICIAN	Richard Condon	£1.50
HERO	Leslie Deane	£1.75
TRAVELS WITH FORTUNE	Christine Dodwell	£1.50
INSCRUTABLE CHARLIE MUFFIN	Brian Freemantle	£1.25
9th ARROW BOOK OF CROSSWORDS	Frank Henchard	75p
THE LOW CALORIE MENU BOOK	Joyce Hughes	90p
THE PALMISTRY OF LOVE	David Brandon-Jones	£1.50
DEATH DREAMS	William Katz	£1.25
PASSAGE TO MUTINY	Alexander Kent	£1.25
HEARTSOUNDS	Martha Weinman Lear	£1.50
SAVAGE SURRENDER	Natasha Peters	£1.60
STRIKE FROM THE SEA	Douglas Reeman	90p
INCIDENT ON ATH	E. C. Tubb	£1.15
STAND BY YOUR MAN	Tammy Wynette	£1.75
DEATH ON ACCOUNT	Margaret Yorke	£1.00

Postage _____

Total _____

ARROW BOOKS, BOOKSERVICE BY POST, PO BOX 29, DOUGLAS, ISLE OF MAN, BRITISH ISLES

Please enclose a cheque or postal order made out to Arrow Books Limited for the amount due including 10p per book for postage and packing for orders within the UK and 12p for overseas orders.

Please print clearly

NAME ....

ADDRESS...

....

Whilst every effort is made to keep prices down and to keep popular books in print, Arrow Books cannot guarantee that prices will be the same as those advertised here or that the books will be available.